Letters To Pilgrim

Vickie,
Thank you for your
moral support. I
hope you enjoy the
book.

Herb LePore

To order additional copies, please contact us.
BookSurge, LLC
www.booksurge.com
1-866-308-6235
orders@booksurge.com

Letters
To Pilgrim

Herbert P. LePore

2006

Letters To Pilgrim

ACKNOWLEDGEMENTS

Though I have written this book, I owe much to many. I am in arrears emotionally and spiritually to friends who encouraged me to venture into a hitherto unknown realm in order to write about a little girl who tragically died because others never looked past their self-absorption and sinful ways to affirm her right to live. Simultaneously, I have been touched by the Lord to honor Pilgrim with the missive about hers' and my time together as father and daughter.

I appreciate the experience of having undergone the Rachel's Vineyards abortion healing service in Joliet, Illinois, the last weekend of April 2004. I acknowledge the support, love, and partnering that the staff and retreat participants gave one another that emotionally searing weekend. I affirm the placing of all the names of the participants' unborn babies in the Book of Life that weekend—for that I am eternally grateful.

I extend my warmest regards and thanks to Professor Sarah McDowell of Augustana College for her expert editing of the text, and for her timely and sensitive suggestions regarding the book. She is a wonderful friend, confidant, and academician. My most sincere gratitude and admiration is extended to Catherine T. Coyle, Ph.D., University of Wisconsin, Madison, for her reading of my manuscript, coupled with her incisive comments and suggestions, and for her friendship. Her seminal work, *Men and Abortion: A Path to Healing* was a source of inspiration. It must be read. I also offer my sincere thanks and best wishes to Kerri Lawrence and Carol Martin of the National Memorial for the Unborn in Chattanooga, Tennessee, both of who exhorted me to memorialize Pilgrim with a plaque.

Sara J. Beck, *therapist extraordinaire*, is acknowledged for her uncanny ability to listen and direct my thoughts and emotions in such a way as to help me understand my pain, grief, love, and anger regarding Pilgrim's death. Sarah is a gem of a human being and a true Christian.

To my dear friend and "soul mate" of sorts, Marianne Cannon, thanks for having been the first person to read a draft of my manuscript, and to have deftly offered suggestions and support of my efforts. I cannot thank you enough. I also thank Mark Tosi for his wonderful sketch for the book cover.

Finally, I acknowledge the love, patience and support of our Heavenly Father as I struggled to write this tendentious book. Without Him, I could not have written this story.

As an addendum, I gladly and enthusiastically acknowledge my daughter Pilgrim. She is what this missive is all about.

Herbert P. LePore

Lovingly dedicated to my daughter Pilgrim
Who will always be with me.

INTRODUCTION

I am writing a series of letters to a daughter I never had. I am not composing this manuscript because I am either politically liberal or conservative. Instead, I am telling this story forty-one years after my child's death, because now is the time to do it, and I am the father that she never knew. The story deals with a daughter who never lived in this world. Had she lived, she would be in her early forties, possibly with children, and maybe even grandchildren. My daughter has never known life because she was aborted in the late summer of 1963. I have, however, given her the name Pilgrim because though she has died a horrible death, she still warrants a birth name. Her name is a beautiful one. Moreover, I believe it is in the Book of Life.

The name Pilgrim denotes someone who takes a difficult journey to find a better place, and in the case of Pilgrim, it was to find her way to Heaven. Pilgrim's time in her mother's body was very brief, violent, and cut short by abortion. Pilgrim, however, has been redeemed by being taken to Heaven where she resides with countless other unborn children in the bosom of the Lord. As millions of other fathers of aborted children, I grieve because I never had the chance to anticipate Pilgrim's birth or to see her born. I was not able to gaze into my daughter's face and see the mystery of life, or to hold her in my arms. I did not joyously bring Pilgrim home from the hospital; thus, I have been denied ever holding her. I never felt her head against my chest. She never instinctively clutched my finger. I never heard my little daughter's first laugh, nor wiped her very first tears from her eyes, or saw her first smile. Pilgrim never had her first tooth, or took her first step as she tumbled gleefully into my arms.

She and I never walked hand in hand on the beach and stopped as she cautiously watched the ebbing tide while clutching my hand. Pilgrim never met her family or relatives. I did not have the opportunity to take her to her first recital or see Pilgrim in her first play. Pilgrim never played sports; therefore, I could not cheer for her, as any admiring father would do. Pilgrim had no loving mother to be at her school events and to discuss with her all facets of life. Nor did Pilgrim have any siblings with whom she could fight, play, and share her things. Pilgrim's mother and I were not be able to watch her from the screen door as she and her date got into his car to go to their first prom. As Pilgrim's parents, we never sat at the kitchen table over cups of coffee talking as we waited for our daughter to come home from the prom. Our daughter never had that "special" boyfriend to show off to her parents. I never drove Pilgrim to college nor helped move her many boxes into her dorm room, while she chatted incessantly with her new roommate.

I was denied the wonderful opportunity to give Pilgrim away in marriage to a young man with whom I would forever have to share her love. Pilgrim and I never had the first dance at her wedding. Finally, Pilgrim never gave her mother and I our first grandchild who we would have spoiled rotten.

Pilgrim was not the result of a chance sexual encounter nor was she the consequence of a rape or sexual assault. Her presence in her mother's womb did not warrant a medical danger either to her mother or to herself. Pilgrim was only guilty of the fact that several people believed her to be an inconvenience or an impediment and, therefore, not worthy to come to term. Simply put, my daughter's life underwent degradation—from life to death. Pilgrim's only crime was that two immature, arrogant, thoughtless, angry, and careless young adults conceived her in Southern California in 1963—they being her mother and I. Her mother's name was "Willow." She and I were willing participants in the beginning of the sexual revolution that was pervasive on the West Coast in the 1960s, and then later throughout much of the United States.

As millions of other young people in the 1960s, Willow and I believed we had answers to everything, only to tragically find out that we had no answers whatsoever. The two of us did not only come into our relationship with the conventional baggage of immaturity and a lack of healthy experiences, but also with emotional garbage that precluded the likelihood of anything good happening between two immature adults. Willow and I were not wired for success. Moreover, we defaulted in the area of mutual respect and likeability. We were adults who, with the abortion of our unborn child, have had to live with the grief and pain of the abortion—even years later. Willow and I eventually married others, acquired further education, and monetary and professional success at the cost of having deprived our daughter of her life. Yet, Pilgrim was our first child, and no matter how many other children we brought into this world by our respective spouses, we memorialize Pilgrim everyday—whether we want to or not. Willow and I, for a very brief time, were Pilgrim's earthly parents and in turn, she was our first child. She, however, is immutably with us—her two parents—though we, her mother and father are thousands of miles apart, and years and experiences removed from one another. Whether or not we acknowledge our parentage of her, Willow and I are irrevocably tied together by our conception of Pilgrim. I daresay we both realize that—even four decades later.

The inextricable link between my daughter and me has influenced me to do the following: I am going to be writing to my daughter, and about her, because she is worthy of being written about. I will tell her story and her impact upon my subsequent life, had she lived, because what happened to her illustrates the tragic shock that abortion has upon lives—even years later.

Pilgrim's mother aborted her during a decade when abortions were illegal throughout most of the country, and medically dangerous. People did not discuss abortion during the decade of the 1960s. Other than me, Pilgrim had no advocates. Nevertheless, I am writing about my daughter because the Lord gave her life—while she was in her mother's womb. No matter what, Pilgrim warrants being memorialized. The letters I will be writing illustrate my love for her.

I must, however, revert to the 1960s. If a woman lived in Southern California during the 1960s, and wanted an abortion, it meant either going to Mexico or to a local doctor who clandestinely performed abortions. In either instance, there was a strong possibility of infection or other related complications to the mother that, if not attended to right away could lead to death or paralysis.

No doubt, the risk of medical complications and possible death to the mother during an abortion in the 1960s was worth the danger to women undertaking such a procedure. However, to this day, for a woman to arbitrarily risk her physical and emotional health in order to destroy an unborn child illustrates somewhat desperate behavior. Unfortunately, though, abortion has become the, "weapon of choice" in the dispelling of unwanted and unplanned pregnancies—particularly after *Roe v. Wade 1973*.

I believe that many women have come to expect that abortion will mitigate the legal, social, economic, cultural, and emotional problems, associated with either keeping a baby or putting it up for adoption. Either choice is difficult. Though not a woman, I can well imagine the dilemma of an unwanted pregnancy. The woman often sees the issue as simply being one of her life versus the life of an unwanted baby. In essence, which life should prevail? There is the conundrum of the legal(*Roe v. Wade*) component versus the moral—("That shall not kill") factor.

Sadly, it is not that simple. Many women, ironically, who abort, eventually believe that the killing of an innocent baby is wrong. However, they are caught up in a desperate move—that being abortion—because they believe they have no other viable choice. A baby simply becomes a figurative millstone around the neck of a woman not willing to be a mother. Women try not to moralize about their decision; however, abortion, within time, often becomes a great psychological burden, with which they live.

However, generally speaking, abortion is considered wrong, with the exception of a health danger to the mother or rape. Pilgrim's death was not predicated on either of these two aberrant events. There is, of course, the definitive issue of responsibility and maturity of men and women necessary in sexual relationships to prevent unwanted or unplanned pregnancies. Yet, young adults—including Willow and I—had no emotional maturity regarding our sexuality and its implications on others.

In 1963 when Willow and I were dating, the birth control pill was not on the market. Contraception was primarily by condom and/or diaphragm. Brave souls, such as Willow and I, stared pregnancy in the face every time we had sex by using the "rhythm method or no method." These procedures worked for a while, and then we obviously tested fate too often and lost the role of the dice, so to speak. Willow and I were not sexual novices when we began dating one another. Therefore, we should have been aware of the consequences—but we chose not to heed them—until it was too late.

Pilgrim died in 1963 because one of her parents made the choice that she not live. The other parent futilely pleaded that Pilgrim not be killed. Alas, Pilgrim died. Having alluded to the two previous sentences, I must say that those people responsible for my daughter's death were not hardened, vile monsters, worthy of study by criminologists, psychologists or sociologists, but otherwise, apparently rational and compassionate people. Yet, their actions and motives regarding Pilgrim's death were worthy of sharp criticism. However, since 1973, with *Roe v. Wade*, every day in the

United States, women legally abort untold numbers of babies possibly for reasons such as conflicts over priorities, pressure by others to abort, dismemberment of marriages and relationships, and rape—which in actuality constitutes a very small percentage of abortion. Women, who plan to either keep their unborn children, or to abort them, make definitive, but often difficult "choices" that they live with their entire lives. As I mentioned in a previous paragraph, those who abort unborn children tend to eventually come to the realization that they have taken the life of a defenseless, innocent baby. Tragically, however, the law does not, nor did it protect aborted babies such as Pilgrim. Paradoxically, hardened rapists and murderers have the right of "due process" and the opportunity for appeal—regarding their prison sentences and their lives. These criminals usually have their lives spared and spend them in prison. Aborted babies have no such legal rights. Pilgrim had no such rights. Nor were there any legal advocates to defend her in a court of law. Since 1973, however, women are legally the ultimate arbiters regarding the lives of their unborn children. I think I understand the difficulty that often beset women who have to make painful choices regarding abortion.

However, at the same time I am still against abortion as a definitive course of action. Moreover, I feel sadness for women who have difficult decisions concerning the issue of abortion. They possibly feel they are "damned if they do, and damned if they don't."

Unfortunately, however, the judicial system, and society in general, have forgotten that in most circumstances, there is another party to the abortion issue. The other player in the abortion scenario, to which little reference is made, is the father of an aborted baby. Society exhibits little tolerance toward the fathers of unborn children. It tends to consider such fathers as pariahs, meddlers, sexist, irresponsible, and insignificant—therefore, not worthy of any consideration—such as whether their child should be allowed to come to term. Our culture simply labels these men so broadly because most people do not see men as being a significant part of the abortion equation. Nevertheless, men are an integral part of the abortion scenario.

A large percentage of men are responsible and supportive of their pregnant partners. However, when it comes time to a decision for an abortion by the mother, the woman certainly has to make the final decision whether she will abort or keep the baby. That is her legal right. Having said that, it is puzzling, though, that society and the legal system have not allowed men to have any forums to express their feelings concerning what happens to their unborn children. These men, after all have had a significant role in the creation of their unborn babies; society, however, pays little attention to them. Unfortunately, men of unborn or aborted babies have no advocates. Fathers of aborted babies are therefore believed to be of no consequence. Only now is the plight of the father of aborted babies being written about.

Sadly, most people do not understand that no one escapes the effects of an abortion—be it the father or the mother or family members. In a large majority (thought to be about ninety percent), the mother—eventually—undergoes emotional suffering associated with an abortion. This malady is known as Post Abortion Stress Syndrome (PASS). Its symptoms are depression, blame, anger, grief, guilt, remorse, alcoholism, suicidal thoughts, anxiety, and denial. These symptoms are attempts to repress the abortion, and everything associated with it. (*Post Abortion Stress Syndrome* information can be found by getting on the internet). However, the father of the aborted baby often suffers the identical symptoms and problems—particularly if he did not want his child aborted. I refer to PASS because I have lived with these feelings for a long time. I hope by now, the reader knows that I did not want my daughter Pilgrim aborted. I perceive that morally speaking, abortion is nothing more than the murder and cruel abandonment of an innocent unborn baby. Our daughter's mother knew that; her parents knew that; and I knew that.

A woman psychologist who deals with abortion therapy told me that PASS often comes upon either the mother or the father of the aborted baby when least expected. She stated that many women and men believe that they have risen above the abortion issue and associated memories, only to discover that PASS strikes them with great and sometimes debilitating impact. The psychologist commented on the fact that older women are coming in for treatment after years of attempting to repress the memories of their abortions, or, trying to place the blame on others—such as the father of their child.

The therapist further remarked that parents of an aborted baby deal with abortion every day—subtly or otherwise—and the imagery of an abortion is with the mother and father for a lifetime. Tragically, though, in the United States, life is not as sacred as it once was, thus abortion has become an integral part of our society—and a killing machine of sorts.

An example of this is that Pilgrim's mother and I have taken it for granted that *our* lives are uniquely important; yet, we unfortunately did not embrace that same feeling for Pilgrim's life. The following question warrants being asked: what if someone arbitrarily thought that Pilgrim's mother's life and my life were insignificant, and that we no longer warranted living, and in spite of our pleas to be spared, our lives were taken? What would happen is that in all likelihood, our legal system would unalterably issue the verdict that we had been murdered, and justice would be meted out to the perpetrators. The American legal system, however, did not come to the aid of our daughter—nor would it. Instead, what happened was that three adults eventually believed it within their purview to be God, judge, jury, and executioner; thus, little Pilgrim died. These adults believed that they could, and did, in fact, get away with murder. Many people though would without hesitation, have said that Pilgrim had every right to be born and to live.

As I introduce my letters to my unborn daughter beginning with the next segment, I want briefly to relate one important reason I am writing to and about Pilgrim. In late April and early May 2004, I attended the Rachel's Vineyard Abortion Healing Retreat in Joliet, Illinois. I was uncertain as to whether or not it would be of help to me. However, I knew I needed to heal. The retreat went from Friday evening to Sunday afternoon. It involved people from as young as 25 to as old as 68 (my age then). Also included in the retreat were a Catholic priest, a psychologist and the staff. So as not to betray confidences, no references will be made regarding names or information about the retreat participants.

The weekend was quite intensive. It included group discussions, individual introductions and comments about what caused the abortions. The priest and the psychologist assisted the participants to deal with the loss of their child, the attendant grief, denial, anger, bewilderment, shame and guilt. We were reminded that there was an obvious disconnect with the baby, since, prior to the retreat, there was not a body to bury nor had there likely previously been a funeral service.

All of us at the retreat learned that we were dealing with death from a new perspective—that of a non-existent physical baby. I can tell the reader that from the beginning to the end of the retreat, all of us were on an emotional roller coaster. I knew that I was in a state of turmoil. For one thing, other people were going to learn about Pilgrim; in turn, I would become knowledgeable about their babies. Thus, all of us would be bearing our souls. Initially, I was somewhat defensive about being vulnerable. I felt exposed in that I was one of only two men at the retreat. I thought that possibly the women participants would look upon me in either a condescending or contemptible manner. After all, I had gotten a woman pregnant, which conceivably began the whole ball of wax regarding the eventuation of the abortion of my daughter. Actually, the women were very kind and sensitive to both my male colleague and me.

Nevertheless, I was apprehensive. I was going to have to relive the horror of everything associated with the loss of Pilgrim. Frankly, I was not ready to do that. However, I realized that the regurgitation of emotions relative to the abortion—no matter how deeply buried in my psyche—was necessary if I was to heal. Sure enough, though, I had a difficult time purging the emotions and events associated with Pilgrim being aborted. However, all of the participants had the same difficulty. Though each of us was encumbered with a plethora of negative emotions, we were able to provide emotional and spiritual support to one another. The psychologist and the priest also provided us immeasurable help in facing our pain.

On Saturday evening, of that weekend, each of the parents of aborted babies was given a beautiful, stuffed doll that represented the child we lost by abortion. The staff instructed us to take our dolls with us wherever we went. We were told to also give our dolls names that we might have given our babies had they lived—or names that bonded us to the memories of our aborted babies. As I mentioned earlier, I already had named my daughter Pilgrim. Later that evening, the staff asked the participants to take their dolls into the main chapel. We were to write a letter to our doll—who represented the aborted child—saying whatever we wanted to it. Pilgrim was next to me in the pew while I wrote my letter to her.

Everyone had difficult time writing because we were all sobbing. Between bouts of weeping, I wrote Pilgrim a long letter, in which I told her how much I missed her, and how sorry I was for what happened to cause the abortion. I told her I loved her so very much and that she would always be my first child. I briefly told Pilgrim about her younger brother Mark, now an adult. I asked her forgiveness for both of her parents. I said to my daughter, that both Willow and I loved her, and that she was always with us. I finally finished the letter and was emotionally drained. I then tottered off to bed with Pilgrim in my arms—as I would have held her had she been a live infant. I put Pilgrim in the adjoining bed, tucked her in, slept somewhat fitfully throughout the night, and once or twice got up and actually checked on her!

On Sunday morning, after breakfast—the roughest part of the retreat—we went into the chapel with our dolls. One young woman had actually put a face on her doll, with an eye shadow marker. Each parent took his or her doll to the alter, where they read their letters aloud to their unborn children. It took us forever to get through our letters. We were unabashedly sobbing for so many reasons. After we all got through reading our letters, we took our dolls one-by-one and placed them in a lovely soft down basket that signified their returning back to Heaven and to the bosom of the Lord. I had a difficult time putting Pilgrim in the basket; however, I gave her a final hug and kiss and put her in the basket. Then, one by one, we each lit a candle for our child and told it that we loved it and said goodbye to our child. I had not cried as long and hard as I did that Sunday morning—since Pilgrim's actual death forty-one years earlier. However, I was glad I wept copious tears. I only wish Willow could have been at that retreat.

We were all given certificates on which were the names of each of our children. Each certificate said that each name was recorded in the church and in Heaven. I felt so good when I got my certificate and read it. The retreat ended and we then said goodbye to each other and went our separate ways.

The above retreat was wonderful. I felt Pilgrim's presence, and I am certain that the other participants sensed the aura of their unborn babies. I feel somewhat comfortable about Pilgrim's mother Willow now—though I have to deal with the abortion in subsequent letters. She is no longer my nemesis.

For whatever reason(s) Willow aborted Pilgrim, I, however, have had to face with anger, shock and grief what she and her parents did. Yes, I felt bitterness, grief, and, at times, rage toward Willow and her parents and it has taken me a very long time to process my emotions to forgive them. Such feelings are normal and warranted. The psychologist told us that though we forgive someone for their part in the abortion, it is not imperative that we "free up" people from their responsibility in the abortion—no matter if it is the other parent. In fact, the adage, "Forgive everything, forget nothing" constituted the way I worked my way to eventually forgive

Willow and her parents for the loss of our daughter. By the way, political arguments over pro-life or pro-choice were of little significance in my decision to be healed of the past, as it related to the abortion of my daughter four decades ago. Regardless of politics and emotions, it was simply time to heal and forgive—but not to naively forget the selfishness and pain associated with Pilgrim's death.

Forgiveness comes slowly like the blooming of a flower. It needs to be watered and nourished. Forgiveness does not mean forgetting; indeed, there are lessons to be learned from facing the sin and heartbreak of abortion. I would never want to forget what happened to Pilgrim. The survivors of the Holocaust could not be expected to ever forget the inhumanity and terror inflicted upon them. Why should I overlook what happened to my daughter? What befell her was odious and beyond comprehension—and her mother and I have had no choice but to acknowledge our respective roles in her death. The priest and psychologist further told us that as we process or have processed our feelings, they will no longer be the burden they once were, but we were told that we have to ask the Lord for forgiveness for others and ourselves, as so stated in the New Testament. Having asked the Lord for forgiveness of others involved in an abortion, we, the parents of the unborn child, must also ask each other for forgiveness, if we are to truly be forgiven by the Lord. I know that is difficult for many reasons—some that I will shortly explain.

As I remind the reader, forgiveness is to provide mercy and pardoning of the other parent and others involved in the abortion. I have also asked the Lord's forgiveness for my role in the abortion, which also meant that I was required to openly ask our Heavenly Father to forgive Willow and her parents as he would forgive me, and, in turn, I am to forgive Willow and her parents. After all, the Lord expects us to make amends to one another. This requires that Willow and I should ask one another's forgiveness through some means or another, because not to do so is a sin of exclusion. Yet, tragically, many people involved in an abortion attempt to waive their responsibility of forgiveness by saying, "let's not open up another can of worms" regarding asking for forgiveness. Forgiveness can be done honoring anonymity. The reader should be aware that an abortion, in itself, is , "another can of worms" that has already been opened, and emits the horrible stench of cruelty and death.

Once opened, it cannot ever be closed. Thus, the rotten smell of death will always be associated with the abortion unless those people involved with the abortion can overcome the putridness of the selfish, arbitrary behavior associated with an abortion, by acknowledging their respective roles in the abortion, and asking forgiveness of one another. The Lord forgives us when we confess our sins and ask His forgiveness. Yet, we still have to deal with the consequences of our sins. Pilgrim, our Father in Heaven also expects the parents of an aborted baby to contritely and with Agape Love, to ask one other for forgiveness, and above all, ask the baby for forgiveness.

Pride is a sin, and until your mother and I admit our wrongdoing to one another, and ask forgiveness of each other, we are not letting go of our sinful nature. We may profess loudly that we are dedicated Christians, or whatever; we may also go to church every Sunday, synagogue every Saturday, or to the mosque every week; and be recognized for our public service, etc. Nevertheless, only when Willow and I put aside our pretentiousness, and ask one another for forgiveness and mercy for our respective roles regarding your death Pilgrim, are we truly worthy of being called Christians—that we profess to be. I will deal with this again later in the manuscript.

The pain and blame of abortion are extremely difficult to overcome. A therapist told me that men and women often attempt to repress an abortion, and, "put it in the past" and "go on with their lives" or pass it off as, "it was a youthful indiscretion." She said those of us who had a role in an abortion better overcome the illusion that abortions go away. Abortions do not disappear. Some parents attempt to rationalize their inability to ask forgiveness of each other because they do not want to acknowledge their part in what happened, and thus they use the above clichés to defend their ill will or false pride. The therapist said that Pilgrim's death will always be in Willow's and my psyches, and that our everyday lives are affected by it. She also said that Willow and I will always be linked together by the fact we conceived Pilgrim, and that she was and still is our first child. The therapist's comments really hit me; earlier in my life, I had fallen prey to making the same effort not to face the issue of our child being aborted. I must admit, however, that Willow and Pilgrim have at least been on my mind countless times these last forty-one years. I have periodically attempted to modulate my thoughts about the abortion, and about Willow and our daughter, to keep myself emotional on keel. The retreat I attended, however, liberated me from the past and subsequently made me realize how blessed I am to have Pilgrim as my child.

Since attending the retreat, I decided to write a book. I stated in the first paragraph of this monograph why I was writing this book. The missive is to memorialize Pilgrim and to share with the reader the lingering effects of abortion on those who have had to deal with it. I am also writing from the prospective of the father of a daughter who was aborted—and who I miss so very much. I will use pseudonyms for all the people to whom I refer. I want to respect and guard their right of anonymity.

In the monograph, I will hopefully weave both a biographical and autobiographical missive that includes Pilgrim's and my life—particularly if Pilgrim had been allowed to live. The story is not fictional, but is based upon the reality of what might have been, along with the actuality of what has taken place since Pilgrim's abortion. As my child, Pilgrim deserves to blend into my life with her spirit. Had she lived, she would have been an earthly part of my life. However, freed from the cruel death that was inflicted upon her, Pilgrim's spirit is in heaven. Yet, I will spend enough time dealing with the ignominy and sin of abortion; however, I want to write to my daughter and about her. Right now, she is in Heaven. Yet, figuratively speaking, I will ask the Lord if I might borrow Pilgrim from Heaven to take on an odyssey with me—her father—through four decades. I believe the Lord will grant me that wish. I will share my life with my daughter. In addition, I invite the reader will come with us on our journey. Pilgrim and I look forward to having you along. My letters to Pilgrim follow. Enjoy.

WILLOW

Pilgrim, I met your mother in the spring of 1963 while attending a state college in Southern California. Willow caught my attention one day as I was walking through the library. I am not certain why I was in the library, because normally any college library was an intellectual aberration as far as I was concerned. Well, no matter why I was there, I saw Willow. She was attractive. Willow was tall, somewhat big-boned, with angular, but prominent features, and long hair. When Willow smiled—which was unfortunately not often enough—it was an elfish smile. I still remember though, after four decades, that Willow had a sense of unhappiness about her. She had a vulnerability that she attempted to conceal in order not to show her pain and grief; she did this often by being distant. Yet, at times, I felt uneasy being around her, because I never knew her real feelings.

I first saw Willow as she was on her way out the door to smoke a cigarette. Our conversation was inconsequential, other than the fact I asked her if she was going to be in the library the following day, and would she meet me there. She agreed to meet on campus the next day. Willow lived in one of the cities in an adjoining county, and had the requisite family of the 1950s and 1960s, that being a set of parents and three younger siblings. Her family was of Northern European stock and lived in an upscale neighborhood. Her parents were courteous, but somewhat reserved. I perceived her father, however, to be the type of individual who was controlling. I never was completely comfortable with him. As an aside, Willow also had the proclivity to be controlling. Often, when at Willow's home, I noticed that Willow and her father had little eye contact with one another. When the two of them spoke to each other, there appeared to be a sense of annoyance between them, and their conversation with one another seemed hurried. A tenuous agenda took place between Willow and her father—and it appeared to have been of long standing. Their relationship seemed to be a strained one.

Pilgrim, your mother was an intelligent woman. I always enjoyed hearing her comments on a myriad of topics. She and I were comfortable with one another talking about subjects such as existentialism, literature, our experiences, etc. Willow majored in the humanities and was to eventually teach at a local college in Southern California. She was a woman who had definite opinions about certain things, and when she began talking about them, I usually just listened. However, Willow and I did not agree on many things—such as politics and social issues—but I knew better than to interrupt her. Besides, she was an interesting woman with whom to be.

When and Willow I began seeing one another, she would listen to what few aspirations I had regarding the future. However, I sensed Willow condescendingly encouraged me to pursue whatever dreams I might have; I believe that she really thought many of my goals were not attainable, because I did not come across as being realistic, capable, or let alone inspired to do anything significant with my life. Yet, whether or not Willow had any real confidence in me, she did much to provide the impetus necessary for me eventually achieving my goals. Whether she intended to do so or not, Willow challenged me. Within time, I would acknowledge her for inspiring me to work hard and achieve a number of wonderful goals.

When your mother and I met, we had no inkling of what a tumultuous relationship we would have. Having said that though, I still believe I might have not hesitated to venture into what became the dark abyss of pain for the two of us because I came to love your mother as I have never loved another woman! However, I will digress and get back to Willow and me.

Willow and I went to the beach on our first date. We had to use her car because I had no automobile. My means of transportation was a ten-speed bike. One might ask that if I lived in Southern California, why was I without a car? It is a very good question, and deserves a straight answer. I had no car because I could not afford one. I was a college graduate who had no focus. I had done very little with my degree and with my life. I had jobs, but I either left them or was fired. My immature aim in life was simply that I wanted to spend my life on the beach and go surfing—but I could not even afford to do that. Instead, I went to graduate school for a semester because I had just enough money to do that. I was what might be referred to as an "adolescent adult." My obvious shortcomings lent themselves to this label.

However, though I seemed to be intellectually and socially dull, and possibly emotionally challenged, as well, I was fascinated with Willow's ability to ostensibly be passionate about certain issues. For example, I was amused when Willow, during our conversation on the beach remonstrated against unemployment insurance, as a travesty of the work ethic. That issue was apparently her *bete noire*. I knew that politically speaking—particularly on that issue—we were light years apart. However, I deferentially reassured Willow that government doles were not my style—though I should have told her that I had gone to college under the Korean War GI Bill. I must say though that Willow's intractable attitudes both amused me and annoyed me. Everything was either black or white—that was until later in the summer of 1963.

Putting aside me, Willow and I had a wonderful time on the beach that day, talking and laughing about other inconsequential things, and discussing our respective lives. Willow then suggested we drive up to Hollywood to a bookstore where we spent time perusing through the books. We shared a wonderful day and evening together; we formed the basis of what I truly expected to be a superb friendship/relationship. Willow and I subsequently acquired a mutual attraction for one another that eventually elevated into an intimate involvement. We believed we were in love, and that life fully belonged to us. Initially the two of us enjoyed the ecstasy of being together, sharing one another's bodies, hearts, and minds, and touching each other's souls. Willow and I looked forward to our time together both on and off campus. I still remember that I felt a sense of joy every time when I saw Willow walking across the campus toward me—especially when she had a smile on her face. A person does not forget those things. However, having said that, I must remind myself that Willow and I were not responsible or mature about a number of things—including the use of contraceptives. Our irresponsibility had tragic consequences because they led to you being conceived and aborted. We ignored the fact that our sexual activities were not those of a mature, thoughtful couple, but instead between two reckless, selfish young adults. We were in love, but it was not a healthy love based on trust and respect. Willow was 21, I was 26, and though we both were sexually experienced, we were emotionally very thoughtless and self-absorbed. As many other young men and women during the early 1960s, Willow and I were encumbered by earlier mentioned" emotional "baggage" that we brought into our relationship.

Most of our baggage dated back into either our early or adolescent lives and had not ever been opened for perusal. Thus, Willow and I were not ever able to air out our emotional luggage, because to attempt to do so would have been painful. Therefore, we had no time for pain—let alone growth.

Pilgrim, perhaps in another time and another place, Willow and I might have made a wonderful match—likely after we had both grown up. She and I were, however, to find out very rapidly that our relationship in 1963 was as flawed, as were we. The blame for the obvious mismatch fell not only to the two of us, but also to the ever-lurking presence of issues that neither of us could overcome. A maddening example was the tendency the two of us, at times, had to attempt to either control the other person or the situation, when, in reality we were unable to control ourselves! It was but a brief period before we were metaphorically drifting with speed down the rapids of personal destruction without even being aware of what was happening. I think Pilgrim that your mother and I just never bothered to deal with the reality of disappointment and despair.   There were times though that I wished that Willow and I had worked to develop our relationship. I loved her, but never had the wherewithal to prevent her from manipulating me to the extent that I felt confusion and embarrassment. Another issue was that I was unable to be the type of man she wanted. Yet, I admired and loved Willow and was proud to be with her, and I enjoyed introducing Willow to a number of my friends, because I was impressed with her so much that I wanted to show her off. Instead of shaping my own sense of identity, for a short time, I seemingly existed vicariously through Willow. In my mind, she was a far better individual than I was—simply because I had no self-assurance. I was the quintessential codependent. Therefore, I put Willow on a pedestal, and guess what, as most people eventually have happen, Willow fell from the pedestal on which I had placed her. Wow!

I found out later in therapy that in many ways Willow was no different than me. In reality, what had actually attracted us to one another was the fact we were similar in many ways. We mirrored each other. Similarities can and often do attract as well as opposites. The reason we became one-dimensional in our relationship was that, sadly, our sexuality was the only marker we had to keep our connection intact—and even that would not be enough to prevent the disaster that eventually took place.

Nevertheless, within time, I introduced Willow to two wonderful friends of mine. They were Craig and Laura, and they were the parents of five children. Craig was a firefighter, and Laura stayed home and raised the family. I had known Craig, Laura, and their children for many years, and

I adored all of them. They were my substitute family during the years I lived in Southern California. Moreover, they cared enough about me to not hesitate to straighten me out when necessary. Craig and Laura were thus surrogate parents. I was very proud to introduce Willow to them; they immediately liked her. The fact Craig and Laura liked Willow imbued me with confidence regarding Willow's and my relationship.

However, one time when Laura and I were alone, she stated that she thought that Willow and I should go easy regarding the relationship. She made the comment that it appeared to be too intense, and that Willow seemingly was running the show—which could actually have been the case. At that time, I chose to ignore Laura's admonitions, because I was in love—thus I refused to listen to the advice of a wise woman. As I reflect on that period of my life with your mother, I know that I was in love with her—however, I doubt if she ever fully reciprocated my feelings.

Yet, Willow was actually the first woman to bring out feelings that I never had with other women. Before meeting Willow, I had been somewhat guarded with other women. After meeting Willow, I relaxed my defenses. For a time, we became soul mates and could talk and discuss anything. Therefore, for a while, we were able to transcend the murkiness of our particular environment(s), and be open and honest with one another. Unfortunately, though, it was but a short while before we began to criticize one another and attack the confidences that the other partner had shared. Guess what, Willow and I began vying in earnest for control of the relationship.

Why Willow and I suddenly began to display this emotionally aberrant behavior remains a puzzle to this day. People who purportedly love and respect each other are not supposed to fall prey to doing such things—or so I thought. Pilgrim, what simply happened was that Willow and I were not able or willing to show our vulnerability to one another. We were deathly afraid of being "real people." Both of us had family issues that made it difficult to accept others for whom they were. Willow and I had been so busy attempting to obtain one another's total approval that we had no opportunity to be ourselves. We were too busy jumping through hoops; therefore, we unfortunately had very little time, emotionally speaking, to give each other. This meant that we never had the time to develop a friendship, let alone, a healthy relationship. What we had instead was only a symbiotic connection that was obviously unhealthy. This connection played a major role in our breakup.

Yet, I certainly must look at my contributions to our relationship, or lack thereof. For starters, back in 1963, I appeared to be only marginally capable of either academic or professional skills, and I had few, if any, discernable personal attributes. I also seemingly had no direction. Another issue as I mentioned earlier, was the fact that I did not even have a car. Willow had to come over to where I lived to pick me when we went some place. Understandably, Willow became quickly annoyed with me. She chided me about my not having an automobile. Looking retrospectively, I later wondered if Willow believed having a car would have made me a more responsible person. It would have taken more than owning a vehicle to have increased my stock with Willow.

As the summer of 1963 moved along, Willow and I began distancing ourselves from our relationship. We spent some time with each other; however, we began drifting apart, eventually saw less of one another. The both of us knew that our relationship was spinning out of control. It was not long, thereafter, that our relationship would eventually crash.

I loved Willow; however, she and I were too similar, in that we had the same bad habits. Our mutual lack of honesty, tendency for self-absorption, coupled with our immaturity, precluded a healthy, loving connection. Willow and I used lying as our tangible means to deceive one another. In some ways, I probably seemed to be weak, and maybe I was weaker in personality than Willow. This possible epiphany really hurt. I had no choice but to accept it. Years later, when I worked through the pain of our past relationship and the events surrounding it, I was able to see that two immature young people, many years earlier, had embarked together upon a tragic journey—with a horrible ending.

Retrospectively, I should have put discernible and healthy boundaries on our relationship. However, I failed to do so. To compound this shortcoming, Willow and I unexplainably did not have the common sense to end the relationship—which no longer was salvageable. No matter which of the two of us would have closed the door on the relationship, the ending likely would have been traumatic and bitter for both of us. However, what eventually happened that brought about the tragic end of the relationship was the fact that Willow found out she was pregnant in the summer of 1963.

Pilgrim, I love you so very much.

Dad

PILGRIM

Darling Pilgrim, this is your story. Sadly, it is a very difficult one to write about and tell you. Even to this day, I feel depressed and overcome with emotion because I think about the events of which I will be writing. They bring back terrible memories. Moreover, for forty-one years since your death, I keep asking why you died? As I write, I want the reader to know that I am somewhat politically liberal, but am spiritually dependent on the Lord. Therefore, taking an innocent unborn baby's life transcends politics and morality. Unless it is to save the life of a mother, I have a difficult time countenancing abortion—which is the unwarranted killing of an unborn baby. It cannot really be referred to as anything else. However, you, our unborn child were murdered.

Remember that I am writing from the viewpoint of a man who was the father of a baby that was aborted. As I said earlier, you, my daughter had no advocates other than me. And tragically, I was unable to prevent you from being murdered. Perhaps, Pilgrim, as you, a heavenly spirit reads or discerns this letter, you will understand your mother's and my frailties, and the attendant anger, denial, grief, remorse and pain that your abortion brought to the two of us. Willow and I have had the rest of our lives to deal with losing you. As I write this letter, Pilgrim, I am near tears because I miss you and regret not having you as my earthly daughter. That being said, you have every right to know what happened to you and why.

I do not remember the date that Willow told me the news. However, no matter what the date was, that Sunday (Black Sunday) was a very bad day. I only know that it was a Sunday afternoon in early August 1963 when Willow came over to my place to pick me up to go to the beach. I got into her car and noticed that she had assumed a harsh, distant demeanor. In fact, Willow hardly acknowledged me. It was not long, however, when three things happened: Willow said she was pregnant; she wanted an abortion; and she did not want to see me anymore! Willow had obviously given some thought to what she said. There was unbridled anger in her voice when she told me what she wanted. I made no comment because I was so surprised. I am certain that I would have been better able to handle her remarks had she been willing to discuss one issue at a time. When Willow quick-pitched her comments, I had no time to address them. What followed were the moments of silence punctuated by both of us looking askance at one another as we drove toward the beach.

Yes, I should have realized the possibility of a pregnancy—now obviously no longer a possibility—but instead a reality. While Willow was driving, I finally recovered enough to begin asking questions. I asked her if she was certain she was pregnant; how long had she been pregnant; and if she had seen a doctor? I also asked Willow if there were test results. She responded to the questions by not answering them; Willow simply said that she was pregnant. She subsequently became further upset at the questions and told me it was none of my business if she had gotten any test results or if she had been to a doctor for confirmation. I would have expected any male partner involved in a pregnancy to rightfully have asked the same questions.

I attempted to convince Willow otherwise by saying that as the father of the baby, I had the right to ask such questions. Willow simply looked angrily at me and said nothing. She never divulged the dynamics concerning her pregnancy—which bothered me. Willow obviously thought I was being intrusive, and that my prying was not warranted. I attempted to convince Willow otherwise—however, to no avail. I realized later that Willow's non-committal answers were nothing more than an indication of her need to control what was happening. I perceived, however, there was something that likely was not right or that Willow was hiding something—relative to the pregnancy. That thought has entered my mind on an intermittent basis throughout the four decades since Willow's abortion. Willow appeared to be determined not to divulge anything, and she stridently did not disclose any information whatsoever. Nevertheless, the longer the two of us were together, the less civility we accorded each other. Also, remember that abortions were not legal in 1963, and, therefore, often quite dangerous to have. I am certain that both Willow and I were aware of the risks associated with abortions.

I skirted Willow's comment about her not wanting to see me any longer and continued on to her remarks about having an abortion. I evaded the above remark because Willow's comment about an abortion was far more important than worrying about whether I was being rejected. I had not given any thought to an abortion, because I believed abortion should not be a choice that we would consider. However, I had not planned for Willow to become pregnant, nor had I wanted her pregnant, yet I had to acknowledge my paternity. I never fathomed that I would be a father, nor initially did I want to be one. Yet, I believed our unborn child had every right to be born. I also believed it was my responsibility to be your father, Pilgrim. I came to terms with my role in your mother's pregnancy. However, I could not, nor would I, agree that Willow have an abortion. As expected, Willow's point of view was diametrically opposed to mine. Yet, simply put, Willow had to be the final arbiter as to whether or not you would be born or aborted. She had, however, made up her mind at that point, that she would have an abortion. At that time I believed that women had abortions only when there were no other plausible options. It was obvious that I knew little about a woman's psyche—particularly Willow's.

Abortions were in most states illegal in the 1960s, and dangerous as well. And as I mentioned earlier, there were no legal provisions allowing men to have any say regarding abortions. Only a woman could decide the fate of her unborn baby back in the 1960s, and that still is true today. No matter my opinion on abortion, or my religiosity, I accept the legal right of a woman to decide whether she chooses to have an abortion or carry the baby to term.

Nevertheless, I told Willow that as parents of an unborn child, we should think about the life of an innocent baby. She ignored my comments. Pilgrim, I kept thinking aloud that you were our baby and that we had no rationale to abort you. Willow and I, however, spent the rest of that afternoon arguing and, as might be expected, became angry and insulting toward one another. That Sunday would signal the eventual ending of our relationship. Neither of us from here on out would detour from our respective views. It seemed we were at war.

We were driving back to my apartment when Willow fired off another surprise: she wanted me to give her money for an abortion. Willow said an abortion would cost $500. I had no idea where she got the dollar amount for the abortion, but I could guess—possibly from a friend who already had an abortion. Willow was adamant in her determination have an abortion. I angrily told her that we would talk about the pregnancy another time. Emotionally we were on overload. I had enough of Willow and the pregnancy for that day—especially the part dealing with her demands for the abortion.

We got back to my apartment, and I got out of her car. I simply went into my apartment and sat down feeling numb. I had no doubt Willow was busy examining her own emotions as well. Pilgrim, in no way had I or would I minimize the fact that your mother was frightened, embarrassed, and felt alone. I felt the same way. Willow, however, never opened up to me. I had little, if any, knowledge as to what was really happening to her. It was apparent that the two of us were shutting down our avenues of communication with one another. I remember while in my apartment that evening, an event that took place earlier during the spring of 1963 came to mind. One evening. Willow and I visited a college friend of mine (Bill), his wife (Leslie), and their new baby. During the evening, my friend's wife went into the bedroom to either change and or feed the baby. I believe Willow asked if she could accompany Leslie to change the baby. Shortly thereafter, Bill and I traipsed into the bedroom, and to my amazement, Willow was ecstatically changing the baby, and later holding the baby in her arms. Having said what I have, I will leave that episode alone; after all, circumstances and people change.

The Monday after Willow told me she was pregnant, she came over and asked me to take a drive with her; so, off we went in her car heading somewhere around the Los Angeles area. I had no idea why we were going where we were. I initially thought that perhaps Willow had changed her mind and decided to have you Pilgrim. I at least hoped that was her plan. However, Willow's agenda that evening was to find her friend who could direct her to an abortionist. The friend was not home, so we drove back, saying very little, and once again, Willow let me out at my apartment, and drove away. The reason I remembered the above drive was that Willow said very little about where we were going, but there was no denying that she was attempting to arrange whatever was necessary for her to have an abortion. Simultaneously, I was preparing for a long and intense struggle with Willow trying to convince her not go through with an abortion. However, viscerally speaking, I sensed I would lose the battle and the war. I eventually lost both.

It seemed that what was best for you Pilgrim was of little importance as far as Willow was concerned. Whenever Willow and I saw one another, we spent most of our time energetically defending our respective positions about your future. It became obvious that individually we had created our own courts of law, along with the criteria for guilt and innocence as far as the pregnancy, and whether or not you should or would be aborted. Each of us had our own ideas as to what should be done regarding you darling child. While Willow opted only for an abortion, I conversely pleaded for your life. There were no plea bargains—nor would there ever be. We obviously had etched our respective verdicts in stone.

Nevertheless, Willow and I were occasionally civil enough to implement truces, whereby, we would attempt some form of dialogue with one another. These, however, were short-lived because we maintained our respective stances. The more the two of us attempted to bring clarity and possibly resolution to the abortion issue, the more apparent it became that nothing had changed. In fact, it was not long before Willow became hateful towards me. She began to put the entire blame for the pregnancy on me. All she would talk about was her determination to have an abortion, and that it was my fault that she was planning to have one.

One time I inadvertently badgered Willow about something, and in a fit of anger, she scornfully asked how certain was I that I was your father. I simply did not respond because I was embarrassed, hurt and angry—and that possibility was scary. Actually, I believed that her derisive comment was not likely true, or at least I hoped that was not the case. Willow though had me where she wanted me. The only recourse I had was to get out of your mother's space. I finally disengaged, hoping the time and space the two of us had away from each other would reduce the tensions, and that Willow still might change her mind. That would not be the case Pilgrim. The longer you were in Willow's womb, the more distressed she became, and more determined she was to abort you. Even when my older sister Anne, who lived in New York, asked Willow to stay with her and her family, and have you there, Willow declined her invitation. Anne told Willow she would guarantee that Willow would get the best pre-natal care while she stayed with her. Willow, however, said she was going to have an abortion and that was all to it. My sister later told me that she pled with Willow not to "play God" with your life, at which time Willow hung up. It was about a week later that a troubling event took place.

It was late one evening during the summer of 1963 when Willow phoned my friend Laura. Her husband Craig was at work and would not be home until the next morning. Therefore, only Laura and her children were home when Willow phoned. Willow angrily told Laura that she had a gun and that unless I gave her money for an abortion she was going to kill me then herself! The call upset Laura who had no indication, whatsoever, as to what Willow was going to do. I took that phone call as a serious source of concern—as well, I should have. Things now were getting out of hand. Laura later told me that Willow wanted her to let me know that she meant what she said and then hung up. When Laura told me about Willow's threats, I became embarrassed for Willow, yet simultaneously quite angry with her for upsetting Laura. I became concerned for Laura and her children, but Laura assured me that she would lock all the doors to their house. I was humiliated by Willow's irrational behavior—which I am certain she wanted me to be. In fact, that evening, I locked my apartment door and put a chair against it. I simply was not going to take any chances. "Crazy is as crazy does." It did not take long, however, to realize that Willow's apparent desperate behavior was anything but that: it was actually contrived so that Willow could obtain a measure of leverage against me.

Her likely objective was to have my credibility besmirched. Before this disturbing action by Willow, I never thought that the pregnancy would have actuated such apparent bitter behavior by one or the other of us. In my opinion—which stands even these many years later—Willow purposely crossed the lines of decency and propriety by the above actions. She was not desperate; she was simply determined to embarrass me. In fact, Willow made no further effort to contact me until she was certain that I would give her money to have an abortion. Willow measured her strategy and tactics well.

When Craig came home the next morning, Laura told him what happened. He was quite angry at Willow and me, and not in that order. Craig had every right to be angry. Willow had conveyed a lethal threat. Craig and Laura had no idea if she would come over to their house gun in hand, looking for me. I quickly apologized to him and told him that I would get a handle on what was going on. Craig told me not to have anything more to do with Willow because he and Laura believed that she was emotionally short-circuiting. However, I believed Willow simply implemented feigned histrionics to get her way. But, I hoped that Willow was not the type of person who would shoot herself and me as well.

I surmised that Willow's ego would not have allowed that self-destructive behavior. Nevertheless, I did fear for Willow because it was apparent that she wanted quick resolution of her pregnancy—which meant having an abortion. I remember that I worried that she might attempt to perform one on herself—which was a frightening thought.

Something or someone had likely caused Willow to make some precipitous decisions. I guessed it possibly had been her parents. The next morning, I phoned Willow at her home. When I talked with her, she was calm, and lucid, with no hint, whatsoever, of any anger. She did not threaten me or make any unusual demands of me. In fact, Willow acted if nothing had happened the previous evening. I sensed when talking to Willow on the phone, that she had ostensibly told her parents that she was pregnant. In fact, though Willow told me otherwise, I believed she had possibly told them earlier in the summer, and that they, in turn, had told her to get me to give her money to abort you Pilgrim. Anyway, I talked with Willow, and said to her that her phone call to Laura was wrong. I further commented that I had too much respect for her and her parents to ever think about doing anything to hurt or embarrass either her or them. I asked her not to phone Laura and Craig again. Willow, however, made no apologies, but only said something to the effect that she did what she believed she had to do.

I had no choice but to stop the unhealthy behavior by the two of us from going any further. The only way I believed this could be undertaken was if I simply did not see Willow, nor maintain any contact with her whatsoever—and this is what I did. I left Willow to her own designs. However, I came to the realization that she and her parents had already agreed to you being aborted. Willow's parents, in all likelihood, championed the abortion; to them it was the best course of action because it meant that they would not have to explain Willow's pregnancy to any one. Also, they and Willow could, "get on with their lives." While the above was taking place, I finally got a job.

I say this because being employed meant that if Willow planned to bring you to term, I could and would be able to pay for your delivery and care. During that first week of work, I attempted not to think of your mother. Nevertheless, I still hoped for a last minute miracle of sorts, whereby Willow would have opted to give you life. However, such would not be the case.

However, I had already obtained $500 dollars to give to your mother to pay for your abortion. I had enough of dealing with Willow. The money was hers if she wanted it. She could do with it what she believed to be necessary. I even thought that if Willow actually asked me for the money that I would simply mail it to her. In fact, Pilgrim, my sister Anne suggested I have no contact whatsoever with your mother. Anne said to just mail Willow the money, since whatever decision Willow made ultimately belonged to her and/or her parents. Even after four decades, I am perplexed as to why I did not mail the money to Willow, as opposed to my ultimate action—that being to give her money in person. I should have listened to Anne's admonition.

During the first four days at work, I did not hear from Willow—which in many ways was a relief. Frankly, I just wanted to end the sordid mess—with little if any contact with Willow. Yet, I had to face the inescapable fact that both Willow and I were responsible for you being conceived Pilgrim. However, killing you could not have been justified in any manner or under any circumstance. Willow hated me, but she likely had as much self-loathing for herself as she did hatred for me. I sensed that Willow's hatred toward me and her self-loathing would have consequences—and they did. It also became apparent that Willow's family had nothing but contempt for me—whether it was warranted or not.

The apparent abhorrence that Willow and her family had towards me was based on their determination that by having gotten Willow pregnant, I had inextricably undermined the family unit, and simultaneously, had brought about an unsettling dilemma. Subsequently, the likely consensus by Willow and her parents was that it was necessary to abort you Pilgrim in order to protect her—regardless of her part in becoming pregnant—and also to safeguard the family's reputation.

My good fortune ended though, when I received a phone call at work on a Friday afternoon from Willow. I realized there was nothing I could do but listen to her. When Willow began talking, she sounded calm, and civil; there was no emotion in her voice. However, I was wary of such overtures because I knew that all she wanted was the $500. Her forced civility was easy to discern, especially when it became difficult for her to maintain it over the telephone. Willow asked that I come over to the house that evening—in fact she insisted. I was surprised that she simply had not asked me to mail the money to her. However, Willow made no such request.

I surmised that Willow phoned me that afternoon just to get me to give her the money. What she and her parents did with it would be their decision. Yet, the money, in some ways was my attempt to buy off Willow so as not to have anything more to do with her or her parents. Pilgrim, at that time, I was even too numb to be angry with your mother for her forthcoming decision to abort you. Even four decades later, I know that Willow and her parents had a reason to have me bring the money, as opposed to sending a cashier's check. It was simple: to humiliate me in front of Willow and either one or both of her parents, thereby, hopefully negating Willow's responsibility in the abortion, and instead to embarrass me.

Craig offered me the use of his truck that Friday evening to take the money to Willow. He insisted, however, that I leave Willow's address and phone number. He said that if I was not back by a certain time, he would phone the local police or sheriff's office in the county where Willow lived. Craig said that after Willow's earlier threats, he had little confidence that everything would go smoothly over at her house. I attempted to assure him that I would be safe—though in reality—I thought I was far braver than realistic. However, I left the requisite information with him. I can still remember as I drove to Willow's house, I kept thinking that I should turn the truck around; drive back to Craig's and Laura's house; phone Willow and tell her that the "check is in the mail," and simply send a bank check to her. Looking back, I often believe that I should have done that. I realized later that evening that Willow and her father did what they could to sabotage any real semblance of civility, propriety, and compassion concerning the interaction and exchange of money between Willow and me. That money was going to be used to take your life Pilgrim, and Willow and her father wanted the 500 dollars in cash.

I finally arrived at Willow's house, and quickly noticed there were no cars in the circular driveway. Normally, there were at least one or two vehicles in the driveway. If I had only mailed the money to Willow! However, I got out of the truck and walked to the door, not being certain as to what type of reception I would receive. Frankly, per Willow's earlier threat to kill the both of us, I was actually briefly afraid that she might come to the door with a gun and begin shooting. I remember that sometime later, a psychiatrist said that a lethal threat should always be taken seriously, no matter its dynamics. Moreover, to this day, I have never forgotten Willow's lethal threat.

Had Willow, come to the door, asked me for the money, and then requested that I leave, that would have been the end of our contact. Willow, however, opened the door and asked me to come into the house.

After forty-one years, I can still clearly remember the almost bizarre feeling that nearly overwhelmed me as I walked into Willow's house. What took place was a stifling tension in the air. There was also an added sense of evil, despair, and sadness in the house. I remember so well that I actually thought I could almost reach out and touch death. The house seemed dark and cold, though it was still summertime and light outside.

I recall there was a foreboding presence in the room where Willow and I were standing. It was akin to being at Ground Zero! There was an attendant sense of helplessness! I think Willow sensed all of the above as well. However, she was devoid of any emotion, and, in fact, looked ashen. Her eye contact with me was minimal. Pilgrim, Willow obviously knew that it would not be long before you would be aborted—if you had not already been aborted. We were alone for maybe less than thirty seconds, when Willow's father walked in from an adjoining room. Now the third player of the triangle was present. The show must go on and it did! Willow's father and I muttered some inane comments to one another. Then the three of us glanced quickly at one another, as if we had to check our cue cards one more time before the "blood" money transaction between Willow and I began.

I remember glancing at Willow to see if she appeared pregnant. I was not able to tell whether she was or not. I remember Willow was wearing a long skirt and gray blouse. Actually, what I wanted to do was to simply walk over to Willow, quickly give her the money and leave. Dialogue was not necessary or desired—at least by me. Instead, I did nothing. I just waited for some signal to begin the horrific money transaction.

Finally, I made a comment as to, "Well, I guess it's time to get this over with!" I remember taking out the five 100 dollar bills and counting them as I handed them to Willow. Her eyes averted mine. She did, however, glance every so often at her father who stood impassively observing our transaction. Otherwise, Willow showed no visible feelings, but simply looked at the money being placed into her hands. Willow's father reminded me of a notary public witnessing a transaction. I thought, "What the hell is going on with him?" Fortunately, there was a minimum of emotion in the transference of the money; Willow looked relieved to have the money in her hands. Nevertheless, I noticed her eyes beginning to well up with tears. Yet, Willow was attempting to hide any emotions—and was doing a good job of it. She had never cried in front of me before, nor did she this time. There had been a time that I would have coveted Willow's tears.

In turn, Willow's father continued being expressionless. Yet, there was a hurried expectation to end the exchange of money. Willow, her father, and I were almost the personification of the biblical temple moneylenders as depicted in the New Testament. As what had taken place at the Temple in Jerusalem some 2000 years ago, there seemed to be the contemporaneous replication of a similar exchange of money for evil purposes at Willow's house that Friday evening.

Frankly, the above scenario could have been averted if Willow's father had simply met me at the front door, asked me for the $500, and then upon counting it, just told me to leave.

Most fathers would have done that. In fact, I am certain that the majority of fathers would have had enough love and respect for their daughters not to want to embarrass them. This, however, was not the case regarding your mother and her father. There was something terribly wrong going on between them. I sensed a degree of uneasiness connecting Willow and her father. I underwent a measure of anxiety and awkwardness. The three of us had no real script. Nevertheless, there apparently was enough implied or actual acquiescence though between Willow and her father that you would lose your life.

The entire situation from start to finish was surreal and evil, because an innocent unborn baby was going to die. Willow and her father, however, would eventually have to face themselves and their actions regarding your abortion—and they knew that only too well. Meanwhile, to them, I was to be the recipient of their blame and contempt. Obviously, Willow and her father looked minimally at their role in the above sordid transaction—or at Willow's place in the pregnancy equation. Their goal, Pilgrim was to simply get the money, and implement the abortion of you as rapidly as possible—if they had not done so already. Willow and her father's likely secondary objective was to dehumanize me, so as to deflect any responsibility belonging to Willow regarding the sordid mess. Their tertiary goal was to get me quickly out of their house and their lives.

I saw the despair and pain on Willow's face. Nevertheless, she still avoided my eyes. What I remember, with clarity, however, was that Willow's countenance changed from a rather blank expression to one of anger. I think her animus toward me was that as long as I was in the room with her and her father, I was a constant reminder of their plan to abort you. Pilgrim, I have no idea if either Willow or her father entertained any feelings of guilt or ambivalence toward aborting you. I doubt it.

Though her father was in the room, I hardly noticed him because I was watching Willow attempting to hide her emotions. Yet, as I earlier mentioned, I believe that Willow and her father were vindictive enough to want to embarrass me or intimidate me. Her father likely thought this was the way to protect Willow—no matter what her role in the abortion. Actually, Willow's father was probably safeguarding his own agenda—whatever that was. Though he was possibly the chief or associate architect of the eventual abortion, Willow's father seemingly wiped his hands of the abortion when I gave her the $500, while likely putting Willow on notice of her accountability in what he perceived to be a socially and emotionally indelicate situation for the family. What this likely meant was that Willow, her father, and possibly her mother as well, agreed to the abortion, because the earlier you were aborted Pilgrim, the sooner Willow's family could go on with their lives as if nothing unusual had happened.

This was probably a win-win situation for Willow and her family. In essence, darling Pilgrim, it was not about you; it was about Willow and her family. Willow and her parents chose Willow's well-being and self-worth over your life. The three of them made a loathsome, selfish, and cruel choice, as to what should happen to you.

However, no matter what happened, your mother could never disavow the bonds of blood and hormones that the Lord gave to the two of you at your conception. Willow would eventually have to confront that epiphany—and likely it would not be easy.

What Willow and her father did that evening was to sentence you to death. They knew that they were in control of what would happen to you little one. I do not think that Willow could or would today in good faith conjure up valid excuses for her and her father's behavior—though it would not have been unusual for her to initially disavow her part in your being aborted. . As an aside, Willow and her father knew they were never in any danger from me; however, after dealing with her earlier threat to shoot me, I was likely to be in more danger by going to her house than Willow could have ever been with me. I was not intimidated; however, I was humiliated and angered because of my inability to prevent your death. You were going to be murdered—if you had not been already.

Regarding the transaction, it seemed for the three of us that time could not pass quickly enough. It was obvious that we all had enough of one another. After Willow counted the money that I gave her, it was time to leave. However, before I left, I asked Willow to return a ring that I had given to her months earlier. Why I requested that your mother to return something as insignificant as an inexpensive ring, I was not certain, other than the fact I was upset and grieving about what had just taken place. Willow looked surprised, but gave the ring to me. Once outside, I summarily threw the damn ring either on to the lawn or in the bushes.

Nevertheless, it would be the last time I ever saw Willow and her family. As I was going out the front door, Willow, without any expression, offered her hand—why I did not know. I took it, shook hands with her, but said nothing, and summarily left. Why Willow wanted to shake hands is still a conundrum. Frankly, I believe it was a dismissive gesture, and somewhat insulting. It appeared Willow simple shook hands with me as a means to acknowledge receipt of the money. She then said in a low, almost sad voice, "I'm sorry" to whom though I was not certain. I had no idea as to whether she made this remark to her father or to me. I did not respond to what she said. It did not matter at that time, though, later, her comment bothered me.

I am not certain why, but I could not forget Willow's apology. While Willow and I were undertaking the last gesture of decency between us, her father simply surveyed what was going on. I then walked out the front door. When I left Willow's house, I remember that I felt the pervasive hatred from within the house metaphorically following me out the door. I also sensed that Willow was in danger, but from what and who I was not certain. I got the feeling, however, that her father was manipulating her for his purpose(s), not for Willow's well being or your right to come to term. To this day, I still believe that what took place that Friday evening when I gave Willow the money put her in great peril. I loved your mother and you Pilgrim, but had failed to protect either of you.

I got back into the truck, and without looking in the rearview mirror tearfully drove away. At the same time, however, I was relieved that contact with Willow and her father had been minimal. There had been no altercation; I was not shot or assaulted; the police did not have to come to rescue me; and Willow and her father got their money. I hoped I would never see Willow and her family again. I had enough pain and chagrin to last a lifetime; but, later on, I had to live with the additional anguish of finding out you had been aborted.

Moreover, anger was an indication of grief, frustration, and pain. Pilgrim, you would die because I could not prevent you being aborted. I had failed to convince Willow not to abort you. The ball was now in Willow's court. Yet, by giving your mother the money, I possibly validated her reason to abort you.

Pilgrim, later on, I even asked myself how Willow would have felt had I demanded that she come over to Craig's and Laura's alone, if she wanted the $500. What if I had Craig and Laura silently watching while I required that Willow put her hands out as I counted the money, and then told her to leave? I could not have done that to your mother—let alone to anyone else. If I had done anything like that to her, I would have felt so ashamed. I could not have ever hated your mother enough to hurt her the way she and her father did to me that Friday night.

Laura and Craig were relieved when I returned—I was relieved as well. They asked how things had gone. I told them of the setting that faced me as Willow and I undertook the "blood money" transaction. I went on to tell them of my emotional and spiritual fear for Willow. Repeating what I said earlier, I believed that Willow's father was running the show. And one reason that he made his presence known was that he wanted to make sure that Willow got the money, and to prevent any further communication between Willow and me. No doubt, Willow's father was afraid that I would attempt to convince her not to abort you. Pilgrim, frankly, I just did not have the energy to talk any longer with Willow. I loved her, but that was all. I was too numb to do anything but hope Willow would not abort you.

I mentioned to Laura and Craig that I believed Willow and her father wanted to humiliate me as a means of deflection regarding the abortion. I also told them that Willow's father controlled her as he always had—and what took place that Friday evening was a cardinal example of that.

Had I done the unconscionable by leaving California without having given Willow the $500, her parents still would have, without hesitation, paid for the abortion. Sadly though, Willow would likely have been required by her parents to make restitution for the abortion, and possibly forced to move out. Though it was extremely traumatic for the two of us to have confronted one another regarding the money, I did not hesitate to give Willow the $500. I would not allow your mother's parents to hold over her any comments about how they personally paid for the abortion. No matter what Willow thought of me, I at least came forward with the money—though feeling deep emotional and spiritual pain—knowing how the money was going to be used. The primary regret was how the money was ultimately used; but my remorse was subsequently transcended by my fear that something terrible could happen to your mother during an abortion procedure.

I was frightened for both you and your mother—because I did not want to face the inevitable—that being your eventual death. Pilgrim, I loved both you and your mother; that is why I was so frightened about the abortion.

The next day—Saturday—was one in which I did nothing other than ride my bike to the beach, sit on the beach, and think about your mother, and whether she had aborted you or would the following week. I decided that I would phone her father during the middle of the next week.

It was with a great deal of angst that I made the decision to phone Willow's father the following Wednesday to find out whether Willow had the abortion. I dreaded doing that. However, regardless of what Willow thought of me, I had the right and responsibility to know what happened to you and to her.

Even after forty-one years, the phone call I made to Willow's father remains firmly etched in my psyche. It was one of the most horrible days in my life. Pilgrim, I was going to find out what had happened to you—at least I thought so. I phoned Willow's father and asked if she had the abortion and how she was. He said with little emotion, "We've taken care of everything." Neither of us said anything more. That comment wrenched at my heart. I knew what it meant; Willow had likely already aborted you! More important now was whether your mother had any physical problems after her abortion.

Regardless of where Willow's parents would have taken her for an abortion, it would have been a dangerous undertaking in 1963. Medical butchery was not unheard of in California in 1963. I had no indication that things had gone smoothly or otherwise. I was frightened for Willow. I could only hope and pray that she had no complications. To this day, I cannot fathom how Willow's parents could have rationalized putting her life in danger by advocating that she abort you. Pilgrim, I felt very ashamed and angry that Willow's parents showed little respect for your mother's safety by going through with the abortion. After having phoned Willow's father and getting his disturbing news, I remember that I went home, got a blanket, went to the beach, sat on the blanket; I wept for a long time thinking of you and your mother. I felt very much alone, and I remember that I felt dirty.

Numerous people went by; however, I paid them little heed. I was only thinking about you and Willow, and whether she was all right. Pilgrim, it was too late to worry about you. I knew that the angels had taken you swiftly, yet gently and lovingly to Heaven. However, in my mind, and even aloud, I kept asking Willow and her parents why they aborted you. The three of them knew there were other viable choices—at least I thought they did.

The longer I sat on the beach, that day, the more angry and distraught I became, and the greater my disconsolation. You and Willow were the only things I thought about that day. I had lost the both of you. I believe that I attempted to pray between tears and my anguish. It seemed prayers had no purpose. I kept asking myself what I could pray about. After all, prayer was not going to return you to the womb or Willow back into my life. I remember that I became illogical in my prayers and asked that Willow change her mind and bring you to term, or that if she had aborted you, that she would have the decency to tell me. They were selfish, desperate prayers. The prayers, however, were not answered—at least not to my satisfaction. Why should my prayers have been answered? I was a hypocrite and had been immoral! I believed that I had put Willow in the untenable position of contemplating an abortion. While sitting on the beach, I recall that I almost began to believe that Willow had actually told me that you were going to be brought to term, and she would tell me when you were due, and that I could be there when you were born! Emotionally, I was a mess.

Continuing on, Pilgrim, while on the beach that day, I knew that you were now in the bosom of the Lord, but I wept thinking how you suffered while being aborted. I wondered if, when your mother aborted you, did she know the fact that you cruelly died, with pain, and no maternal love whatsoever. You did not deserve to die such a horrible death. Meanwhile, I still worried whether or not Willow had undergone any complications. I continued to be concerned for her, and yet I sensed that Willow was very much alone and frightened while on the gurney. Though this sounds foolish, I still loved your mother. Yet, as I earlier intimated, I was overcome with rage regarding your mother and her parents' decision to abort you. Yes, I was your father and equally responsible for your conception, as was your mother; however, though you were unplanned, I believed you had the right to have been born.

A woman acquaintance, upon hearing I was writing this book, said that I should not have concerned myself about you being aborted. I would refute that rather disingenuous comment by the fact that as the father of an unborn baby, I had every right to be emotionally and morally involved in attempting to have saved you Pilgrim. It did not mean that I could or should have tried to physically prevent you from being aborted. I did have the right, however, of moral persuasion—regardless if you were aborted. Pilgrim, the fact remained that your mother's and my lack of morality brought about your conception.

I had to face the fact that the Lord held Willow and me accountable for our not having you brought to term—no matter what the circumstances of your conception. Tragically, Willow and her family showed their possible disdain for the life within her womb. This meant, Pilgrim, that you were suddenly and savagely aborted. There was no compassion shown to either you or Willow while she aborted you. Your mother, fortunately, did not lose her life on the abortion gurney the day she aborted you; she did, however, lose a part of her soul—figuratively speaking—as I did. I daresay that after Willow aborted you, there were no longer the trappings of logic and cogency that she could hide behind. She and her parents could, and possibly did, hate me with an unbridled rage—but they also likely had little remorse regarding their decision not to bring an unborn baby to term.

I did not want you aborted nor would I have agreed to you being aborted, Pilgrim. Nevertheless, there was the strong likelihood that Willow and her parents believed they had to blame someone for what they did. According to them, I was the logical perpetrator. I have talked with a number of clinicians who told me that one glaring thing that happens regarding an abortion is the need for blame to be mandated by one person on to someone else. Thus, there is often the victim and the victimizer. The reader may make up his or her mind as to which description best fits Willow, her parents, and me.

As I have written the above sentences, I asked myself if your mother believed you were insignificant while in her womb and, therefore, it mattered little if you were aborted. I found that possibility to be so repugnant, as to have hoped your mother aborted you for some other reason, such as

undue pressure by her parents . My darling Pilgrim, because of our foolish, immoral, and immature behavior, your mother and I did not deserve
the gift of you as our child in her womb. Yet, God, allowed you to be in
your mother's body as a gift. In reference to an earlier comment, the Bible
says in Jeremiah 1:7, "Before I formed you in the womb I knew you." But
people who did not see you as a wonderful star of life—given to us by the
Lord—took the gift of life from you.

I am sorry if I am unable to, "cut any slack" regarding the abortion
of you Pilgrim. I can ill afford to feel or act "politically correct" when
your life in the womb was arbitrarily taken, because it was an obvious
impediment to your mother and others. Nevertheless, I am certain that
had I been the one to have vociferously and adamantly demanded that
Willow abort you, most people would not have hesitated to hold me in
reproach for my actions.

The tragedy of an abortion is that there are only losers. Those involved in the decision-making process regarding abortions, very seldom
live comfortably with what they do. How can they? Often, these people
become angry and blame the party or parties who did not agree to the
abortion.

They also emotionally "grandstand" by stating that the abortion had
or has no psychological or spiritual impact upon them, or they emotionally
acquire numerous reasons why they had to have an abortion. It never seems
to be their fault as to why they abort unborn babies.

Two mantras heard are, "If only_____ had not gotten me pregnant
or if he had only used a condom!" The second mantra stating, "If she had
only wore a diaphragm" has also been heard. The above behavior happens
every day in this country. It seems that no one wants to claim the author-
ship of a pregnancy or an abortion. Having said that, I know the Lord
forgives us, but guess what, we are still accountable for our sin(s)—otherwise known as "suffering the consequences." The irony is that people
often look at forgiveness by God as the spiritual quick fix. The Lord is
a God of justice and mercy. However, the death of one or more innocent
unborn babies has to be punished. All of us involved in any way with the
abortion—including me—had to pay for your death. Perhaps, Willow
and I initially believed we could escape our Heavenly Father's requirement
of justice and retribution. The two of us would, nevertheless, find out we
had to, "pay the piper."

I sadly doubted if Willow and her parents weighed the tragedy and consequences of your death. They possibly thought it to be far easier to live with destroying you than having allowed you to be brought to term. I also asked the question as to how Willow and her parents dealt with one another after aborting you. I wondered if they maintained a conspiracy of silence whereby they never dealt with or discussed your abortion, or did Willow and her parents amply program a scenario that put the blame entirely on me?

Willow was not likely to indict herself, nor confront her parents for their role in your death. Pilgrim, your mother probably was not willing, or maybe would not have dared to accost her parents for their role in the abortion. Indeed, for Willow to confront her parents for their part in your death might have been a difficult undertaking. It would have necessitated honest, painful, bitter, and open communication between Willow and her parents—something not likely to occur—because it would have entailed three individuals having to acknowledge their roles in your death.

Yes, even back in the dark days before *Roe v. Wade*, Willow had the ultimate right to abort our unborn child—though she had to do it illegally. However, Pilgrim, human beings ultimately get into serious trouble when they "play God." As a reminder, our Heavenly Father did not grant people the right to become, judge, jury, and executioner when it came to His laws—particularly concerning the rights of unborn children. People, however, decided to assume the above roles, and when they did, you died.

Perhaps, Willow initially handled your abortion, as being a requisite to her future happiness, and left it as that. Conversely, my reaction concerning the abortion, Pilgrim was that of a father who lamented that he would never hold or know his daughter. As I have mentioned before, I also was apprehensive that Willow could have suffered a terrible infection or a procedure gone awry while aborting you. I thought if Willow and her parents had only taken some time to realize that if allowed to come to term, you could have been their greatest source of joy—or at least someone else's.

My sister Anne put in proper perspective my role in the abortion. She told me in a telephone call that I made to her shortly after the likely time of the abortion, that unless I had forced Willow to have an abortion or told her to have one, or had taken her to have one, that I had no responsibility for her actually having the abortion. Anne was right; Willow had to own her role in her decision to get an abortion. Yet, I was still traumatized by your death Pilgrim, because I was your father.

Until I heard Willow's voice on the phone before I left California, I had no indication as to whether or not your mother was all right. This was not projected thinking on my part; what I worried about could easily have been a reality back in 1963 because of the illegality of abortions. Many women died from botched illegal abortions in the 1960s. Fortunately, your mother was not one of them. Nevertheless, I raise the question as to whether any of the people actually involved in your abortion even discussed what could go wrong with it. Up until 2004, I was quite angry with Willow's and her parents for their obvious selfishness and thoughtlessness. They had taken unwarranted risks with your mother's life.

I remember that in 1963, society looked upon abortion as anti-societal behavior. What evolved was the, "Don't ask, don't tell" scenario, whereby Americans did not face or address the issue of abortion in the early 1960s. Abortions seemingly happened to someone else. Any woman who had an abortion before *Roe v. Wade (1973)* usually denied that she had one, or kept it a secret, and certainly did not show her grief or pain. Whoever was involved in abortions were expected to "tough it out." Speaking of "toughing it out," I would like to relate an incident that took place shortly after Willow's abortion. Pilgrim, I was feeling depressed and needed to talk things out about your tragic loss of life and my pain dealing with it. Hence, I went to a local mental health clinic in Southern California to talk with someone. It was the wrong thing to have done! The woman social worker, with whom I spoke regarding the abortion and its effect upon me, and my concern for Willow, castigated me for even attempting to deal with my feelings about the abortion.

She told me something to the effect that, "Why are you even worried about the lady aborting her fetus? That is her right to do with the fetus whatever she wants. Just get on with your life and be glad that you don't have to pay child support." The social worker's monologue indicated that I was to "tough it out." Honestly, that conversation took place! I was not saying who was right or wrong; I just needed someone to talk with about my confused feelings. But, obviously, as a male, I was simply to, "tough it out."

Meanwhile, the summer of 1963 could be aptly described as the "summer from hell." I realized that it was imperative that I leave Southern

California to begin life somewhere new. My sister Anne pressed me to come back to New York. It was a timely suggestion. I made the decision to head east—though I had generally enjoyed my years in Southern California. I knew that leaving California had its good sides.

I could begin a new life and refresh and repair my psyche. Darling Pilgrim, I now could slowly begin the healing process—though knowing it would take time to overcome the cruel circle of events that had taken place during the summer of 1963. Darling little daughter, you were now safely ensconced in my psyche. Though you were in the loving arms of our Heavenly Father, I knew that you would be with me as I traveled life's many paths. Therefore, as I am writing this story, I will bring you to earth—metaphorically and spiritually—because I need you and love you.

Of course, you will always be the little girl spirit that went to Heaven. But, you will also be with me as I write this story about us. I was twenty-six when I met Willow and when you were taken to Heaven; now I am seventy-years old, and though an old man, the Lord has given me the recall—no matter how painful—to take you on an odyssey that you and I might have taken together as father and daughter, had you lived. I think the Lord will allow us to do that. Darling Pilgrim, as I write about you and the period of time in which you would have lived had you been brought to term, I will no doubt imagine what you might have looked and been like had you been born. Yet, I still want you to be the lovely little spirit that the angels lovingly and tenderly took to Heaven—because I believe that is where you truly belong.

Pilgrim, speaking of lovely spirits, I had a wonderful woman friend who was of great comfort during my rough period. I think you would have loved her. She taught at the same college your mother and I had attended, and I had known her for a number of years. Sandra was her name, and she had a wonderful little terrier by the name of Chula who was as adoring as Sandra was a great friend. Sandra was from Illinois, and as me, a diehard Cubs fan! Go Cubs! I introduced Willow to Sandra during the spring of 1963 and Sandra thought she was nice, but believed Willow somewhat aloof. Sandra told me later, she thought neither Willow or I were suited for one another.

She was correct in her assessment. Sandra, however, thought she had no right to intervene as far as expressing her feelings about Willow and me. I can remember that her remarks moved me to tears, because though

Sandra told me what she did, she realized that I had loved you mother very much, and that I never meant Willow to become pregnant and to eventually abort you. Sandra let me cry on her shoulder. I needed that opportunity.

The following day I bought a ticket to fly back to New York City (NYC). Frankly, Pilgrim, I was apprehensive. I certainly had every right to be anxious. I had no idea what the future held, but it had to be better in NYC than it had been the last few months in Southern California. Pilgrim, I knew that I had made too many mistakes in the past and a change of venue was warranted. Darling daughter, your father was going to begin what would be a sojourn over many years.

As I was preparing to leave California, I made a checklist of people to whom I would say goodbye. Practically all of them had been close friends or those I had known in my college days. By the way, I decided to phone your mother and say goodbye to her! Was I brave or stupid? I will let the reader decide. One reason I wanted to phone Willow was to be certain that she was not injured or ill. Pilgrim, I see that you were raising your eyebrows, and when a female does that, I know that means you disapprove! Allow your impulsive father to illustrate beyond a doubt that he could be the quintessential fool.

As I said earlier, I wanted to phone Willow to make sure she had not suffered any complications from the abortion. I also wanted to make amends, if possible, and say goodbye. I still loved your mother, though I know she had little, if any, feelings for me. Darling daughter, it was time to go where angels decided not to set foot.

Off I went to a phone booth in Bellflower, California and phoned Willow's house. It took but a nanosecond to realize the mistake. I should have quickly hung up; instead, I let the phone ring. It rang but a few seconds until someone picked up the phone and said hello. It was Willow! I still had time to simply hang up.

Guess what though, I said hello! Did Willow hang up? No. There was a momentary silence; then a loud angry voice began screaming over the phone. It was Willow's mother yelling, "How can you call after what you did!" She subsequently berated me for getting Willow pregnant, and insinuated that I caused your mother to have an abortion! As expected, Willow's mother did not refer to Willow's role in becoming pregnant or to the events leading to the abortion. I just listened to what Willow's mother had to say, and made no effort to interrupt her.

I was not going to get into an argument with her, so I just waited until she stopped talking; then I told Willow's mother that I was leaving California, and that I had phoned to say goodbye to Willow. I then hung up.

I was greatly relieved that your mother was apparently well. However, by her comments, Willow's mother indicated that Willow and her parents had likely already constructed the imagery of perpetrator and victim concerning the abortion.

There seemingly was little ownership to any part of the abortion by Willow and her parents. That should not have been a surprise. Their anger, though somewhat misdirected regarding the actual aborting of you, was understandable. They were unable to claim responsibility for the abortion—to them it obviously just happened—or I had been entirely responsible for it. As expected, Willow and her parents were protecting each other

Yes, I got Willow pregnant, but she was not raped, cajoled, or adversely influenced to having sex with me. She and I slept with one another because we wanted to. There was no sexual aggression whatsoever. I did not, however, abnegate my responsibility for the pregnancy. Nonetheless, I was not going to agree to compound one wrong with another one—that being to have agreed to Willow having an abortion. Yet, she had the right to have an abortion; in turn, I had the moral justification not to want you to be aborted.

Continuing on, Pilgrim, the time came to say goodbye to other people. The day before I was scheduled to leave California, I said my final farewells to a number of friends. One good friend named Stephanie, with whom I had gone to college, drove me around to say my goodbyes. Pilgrim, none of these goodbyes were easy, especially saying having to say farewell to Craig, Laura, their children, and to Sandra.

All of these folks were amazing people. Sandra and I tearfully hugged one another and she told me to take care of myself. I thanked her for her wonderful friendship and kindness throughout the years. Stephanie and I then drove to say goodbye to Craig, Laura, and their family. When I left California in 1963, I knew I would never have enough time to thank this family for all it had been for me and done for me. Pilgrim, you would have loved them, and they, in turn, would have loved you. I had never met such an amazing family. I knew that I was greatly blessed to have had them in my life—particularly when I had to deal with Willow's pregnancy and abortion. That family had been the buffer against many storms.

We spent a few minutes on their front porch reminiscing about our friendship and describing some humorous anecdotes. I then hugged each member of the family and tearfully told everyone that I loved them.

Laura then gave me one last hug, and said that her family had turned me over to their Heavenly Father for a safe trip and protection in the future. Stephanie and I then left. Later, Stephanie and her roommates had me over for dinner the night before I left California. Stephanie then drove me home, and said that she would pick me up at our scheduled time the next morning for our drive to the Los Angeles Airport. I was to leave Southern California wearing the only suit I owned, and a shirt and tie. I owned some dress shirts and a few incidental casual clothes—all of which I put into a small trunk. I also had a small box of books. The next morning was the time to take a plane ride.

I love you so much,
Dad

"LEAVING ON A JET PLANE, DON'T KNOW WHEN I'LL BE BACK AGAIN"

1963

I flew from Los Angeles to New York on September 13, 1963—which was on a Friday. That morning, Stephanie came over, and after I put all my things in the trunk of her car, I took one last look at the apartment where your mother and I had spent a lot of time. I did not stay very long so as not to have to think very much about the past. I locked the door, gave the key to the property owner, said goodbye, got in the car, and then we drove away. The day was hot and humid, but the drive to the airport was pleasant and the freeways were not crowded. It was obvious darling daughter that I was going to begin a new phase of my life. Though uncertain of the future, I knew that it would bring about important changes in my life. Later on Pilgrim, I referred to my moves to new places and new situations as "milieu therapy." I knew there would be new opportunities, along with new experiences, and hopefully a modicum of bumps in the proverbial road of life.

Stephanie and I arrived at the airport; I checked in and Stephanie walked me to gate from where I was leaving. We talked for a while; then she and I said a rather tearful goodbye to one another. I boarded the United Airlines four-engine DC-8 and took my assigned seat—a window seat behind the wing.

At noontime, the DC-8 took off from the Los Angeles International Airport, headed west over the Pacific Ocean; then made a sharp left turn over the California coastline; proceeded eastward while climbing to its cruising altitude; and then it was on to New York. I recall that the flight was full and the captain said our flight to New York should take about four and one-half hours. He also told us the weather system across the entire country was good. So Pilgrim, I settled back in my seat, but something happened: I began thinking about you and Willow, and then my eyes began to water. For being an adult male, I thought I had better control of myself. It was obvious, however, that you and your mother were metaphorically along for the trip—at least cerebrally. I wanted you with me on the plane, but I did not want your mother along for the flight. However, I realized at that time, you and Willow came as a pair. Oh well. Though I spent most of the flight staring out the window at the blinking strobe light at the end of the wing, at the same time you and your mother might as well have been in the adjoining seats! Pilgrim, the two of you were on my mind the entire flight from Los Angeles to New York—though figuratively as non-paying passengers.

I undertook diversions, such as reading, talking with my seatmates, eating lunch, looking out the window at the ever-changing landscape beneath the aircraft, and I even walked throughout the cabin a couple of times. I finally returned to my seat, lapsed into silence, and then continued thinking of Willow and you.

Simultaneously, I attempted to keep your mother's parents out of my train of thought. Thinking of them angered and depressed me—and would for many years. Darling Pilgrim, it was odd that at about 33,000 feet, on a commercial jet flying about 500 miles an hour, I was immersed in my continual thinking of you and your mother, and grieving for the two of you. I guess I was not meant to be able to extricate myself from spending most of the trip being teary-eyed and angry.

Even as we eventually flew eastward over the Great Plains with their slowly lengthening evening shadows, there was no respite from thinking of the two of you. With two hours left in the flight, I settled back and stared out at the now green navigation strobe light blinking intermittently as the evening sky surrounded the plane. It was with a sense of resignation, I that allowed you and Willow to dance across the imagery of my mind. Pilgrim, you have now earned your first frequent flyer miles!

Pilgrim, I arrived in New York two hours later to begin the rest of my life! My sister Anne and her family met me; we had not seen one another for almost seven years. The last time we were together was when coincidently Anne saw me off at the same airport (Idyllwild-now Kennedy) as I embarked on a flight to Los Angeles after I was discharged from the Marine Corps. It was great to see everyone again. After exchanging pleasantries about the flight, then getting my trunk, we all got into the car to drive up to Westchester County. Your Aunt Anne and I began talking about Willow's pregnancy and the abortion. Anne brooked no excuses from me about what happened—therefore I kept my mouth shut. She correctly nailed both Willow and me for our irresponsible behavior regarding Willow's pregnancy and the abortion.

Anne and I, however, cleared the air, and her input was what I need. Anne felt pain because she had seemingly not been successful in talking your mother out of aborting you. I told Anne that Willow likely had made up her mind a good while before Anne had phoned her.

I stayed with Anne and her family until I moved into the city and found a job. Do you know what I began doing shortly after I moved into the city? I began making mental and emotional notes about what would have been your due date—which would have been March 1964! Darling daughter, not only is it the mothers of aborted babies who make calendar notes about when a baby would have been born; many fathers do the same.

Often the mother and father of an aborted baby unknowingly integrate their pain and grief—even though they are thousands of miles apart from one another. It would not surprise me if Willow and I did that, though I have no real way knowing if that actually happened.

Speaking of Willow, I found out that she had transferred to a different college before the fall semester of 1963. Yet, it was possible that Willow was dealing with the identical feelings I had regarding your due date. Having said that though, human beings are an odd lot; they tend to be evasive when it comes time to dealing with harsh subjects, such as abortion. I will give an example.

In 2004, a woman friend told me that when I am writing to you or about you, since you are now a heavenly spirit, that you would have no idea about being aborted. She went on to say that as I write to you, I should not talk about abortions! To me that is hogwash. I am certain you were very aware that people were going against the plan of our Heavenly Father who had placed you inside your mother's womb. I know that after you were aborted, as the angels were quickly taking you to Heaven, that you took one last look down at your mother lying on the gurney, smiled at her, and tearfully blew her a kiss as you did also to me. You cried for Willow and me. Pilgrim, my dear, I certainly have wept for you through the decades since your death.

Pilgrim, I refer to 1963 as "The year of death." You were aborted. The wonderful Catholic Pope, John XXIII died; President John F. Kennedy's newborn son tragically died; and President Kennedy was assassinated in November 1963! The year was a sad one.

Pilgrim darling, once away from California, I was able to think with somewhat more clarity regarding your mother. I really believe that some of the reasons Willow aborted you was because she was confused, pressured by her parents, and angry, Willow and I, however, were no less selfish than other partners who conceive babies who are aborted. Instead of seeing how important life is, we only see how significant *our* particular lives are. Willow and I used sex as a means of recreation; we certainly did not plan for procreation. Therefore, we forgot that our Heavenly Father put you in Willow's womb because He had a wonderful plan for both the baby and its mother. Yet, babies are aborted when the father or mother—or both—conveniently forget that abortion is a direct sin against the Lord's handiwork.

Darling Pilgrim, do you know that the sin of abortion goes all the way back to almost the beginning of the Old Testament? Abortion is just not a 20th or 21st Century phenomena. Maybe, someday, we will all get it right, and not abort babies. However, I doubt it.

I forgot to ask you if you enjoyed the plane trip from Los Angeles to New York. I realized it was your first trip, but you really seemed to be an old pro during the entire flight. Did you see any of your other spirit baby friends that you knew from Heaven, who were on our flight busily comforting their mothers or fathers? I know it is silly that I should ask. Speaking of due dates and blessings, I believe that it really is a blessing—though maybe initially a painful one—that we remember our baby's due dates and birthdays. I think that to do so is to honor our Heavenly Father for his original gift of a baby to the mother's body. This is a way for the Lord to remind us of our lost babies.

Thanks to the Lord, I was able to stay away from falling back into old habits. I felt good about my newfound discipline. Pilgrim, I was, however, still undergoing grief, anger, despair, and shame for what happened. I went to see a psychiatrist, and began long term therapy sessions. We looked critically at the abortion of you, why it likely happened, and the dynamics of Willow's and my relationship. The psychiatrist brought to my attention the fact that what Willow and her parents had done regarding you being aborted, was simply to them, a logical defense mechanism, that morality had nothing to do with what they did. Willow and her parents believed that her having a baby was "simply not acceptable" (my words). They likely determined that it was expedient to kill you. According to the therapist, by aborting you, Pilgrim, the three of them were concealing their respective agendas regarding the reasons for your death. In essence, Willow's parents protected her from her plight, by either suggesting or agreeing that you be aborted, and she, in turn, protected the family's social status—by aborting you.

The psychiatrist also said that Willow and her parents did not want me involved in any part of the abortion equation. He said that the Friday night scenario where I had to deal with giving Willow the money was not a spontaneous endeavor, but likely an orchestrated effort to dehumanize me, for purportedly causing the perturbations relative to their decision to abort you. The therapist did tell me during one of our discussions that both Willow and I were immature, irresponsible and selfish, and would not have been good parents. The psychiatrist was accurate in his assessment of your mother and me. He, however, did not condone the abortion, but suggested that we should have brought an innocent baby (you) to term—and then made the "appropriate" decisions. The psychiatrist was sympathetic but tough. He was from the "Reality Therapy "venue.

For a while, your mother became somewhat of a cerebral and painful annoyance, but for most of the time while living in New York City, I was able to keep her image at arms length. If I spent too much time thinking about Willow and her parents, within time I became angry enough to force her out of my mind—at least for a while. However, I still missed and loved your mother. No doubt about it, I was helplessly maudlin and/or unrealistic—likely both.

The therapist gave me some pointers by telling me the best way to reduce the role of Willow in my life was to not to dwell on the pleasant aspects of the relationship—but instead examine the dynamics of the pregnancy and the abortion, such as the grief, pain, anger, separation, humiliation, and denial. This also meant facing the reality of my impotence in trying to get Willow to change her mind, and the apparentness of being dehumanized by Willow and her father as their deflection from her role in the pregnancy.

The psychiatrist also suggested that I not be afraid to deal with my pain and grief of losing you and your mother. And he suggested that I accept my negative emotions toward Willow and her parents—as being necessary—and part of the healing process. No longer did I allow my mind to wonder to the extent that Willow was a nostalgic part of my life. Instead, it took only a short time before I looked realistically at her and her parents concerning your death. I got away from using euphemisms, such as "termi- nated, ended, extracted," etc, and used in their place harsh, but applicable terms such as, "killed, murdered, executed, and butchered."

The technique was a kind of aversion therapy regarding Willow, her parents and the abortion. The issue was not whether I liked or loved Wil- low; instead, it was to accept the horror of what took place, and remove myself from thinking that I had to have positive feelings or compassion for those responsible for your death. What this finally meant was that I did not have to like, love, or respect your mother and her parents. I did love Willow, but no longer did I respect or like either her or her parents. To this day, I believe that my feelings were honest, logical, warranted and healthy. I had every reason to be angry and grieving over what took place earlier in California. This did not mean that I would always entertain the negative feelings that I had. However, what would and did take place was a lengthy period until I forgave those who insensitively brought about your death. Yet, I still had to be held accountable for getting Willow pregnant, which of course factored into the subsequent abortion. I had been careless, irresponsible, and lacked moral judgment.

I had to claim additional ownership to not setting a good example as a person. I had not set appropriate boundaries, nor did I provide examples of being the type of person that Willow would have been proud of. To this day, I still regret the above.

I knew that healing and forgiveness regarding such a horrible thing as an abortion took time—and in fact, it took quite a lot of time. Thus, the aversion therapy helped me work through the actual events and behaviors that brought about your death. I became honest with my pain, remorse, anger, and grief, and even with my denial. I no longer paid attention to how Willow and her family might feel about me—but instead how I felt about myself.

I knew I could not change Willow's feelings toward me, or her ra- tionale for aborting you. The psychiatrist told me that I should not even worry about Willow and her parents' feelings about me. Darling, Pilgrim, what I attempted to do instead was to reinforce the ideas that I was worthy of self-respect and that for most of the time, I was a decent person—albeit not a perfect one. In fact, something happen Pilgrim that tested my ability to not overly respond to a coincidental unpleasant reminder of the past.

In the spring of 1964, while living in New York City, I purchased a nationally known magazine that I usually bought on a monthly basis. I was sitting at the neighborhood drugstore, having coffee and a Danish. I began paging through the magazine when I came across the "Letters to the Editor" section. I was perusing the letters when what popped up at me at the end of one of the letters was the signature with Willow's name! I almost spilled my coffee and dropped my Danish! To be honest, at first I was shocked; I thought to myself, "Can't I ever get rid of this woman?" However, I recovered, read the letter, and after reading it, laughed at myself for my initial reaction. I knew that my response was normal and even healthy—in that I could gauge my feelings based on the stimuli presented. Does that make sense, Pilgrim? I think you understand what I am attempting to say.

However, I noticed that while living in NYC, it did not take much for me to begin crying when I thought of you and Willow. The pain and grief of losing you and your mother never went away. They were only muted at best. Many people cannot or will not fathom the fact that a great number of fathers of aborted babies suffer immeasurable pain, grief, and anger. Society, back in the 1960s, and in my opinion, still today, has no perception of what abortions do to men. My sense of grief and depression matched the winter grayness of New York City in late 1963 and early 1964.

The tough month of 1964 was March, That would have been the month that you would have been born! March was the month that winter was beginning to give way to the first signs of spring. Therefore, it was difficult to face the reality that you were not going to be brought to term.

I imagined what it would have been like to see you born and to hold you in my arms shortly thereafter. Willow and I for one brief period were possibly united in the pain and loneliness associated with your hypothetical due date. Pilgrim, I felt sad for your mother. I believe she thought it would be easy to justify the abortion. However, I think in order to mitigate her and her family's responsibility, Willow attempted to repress anything associated with the abortion.

Conversely, the loss of you and your mother burned irrevocably in my mind. Pilgrim, I am certain that when your mother was alone, she might have occasionally cried for you as only a mother who lost a child could weep.

Tragically, Pilgrim, as I mentioned in the previous letter, I never saw your mother weep because Willow learned that to cry meant she would have to show her vulnerability, and thus to have wept meant that people would have seen the "real" Willow. She could not allow people to know that she had the same frailties that most individuals have. Pilgrim, certain people who should have affirmed your mother when she was young never did; I also should have also validated Willow's worth. Instead, I was too busy dealing with my own demons. I think your mother learned from the time she was young that it was better that she not ever show her real feelings. Because to have allowed others to see her genuine emotions meant that she had to deal with possibly having been rebuked, embarrassed, ignored, and emotionally hurt. I believe that Willow also might have undergone some form of abuse when young.

The psychiatrist brought to my attention that one reason that your mother likely hated me was that I apparently mirrored her in many ways. Thus, my behavior was identical to hers. The divergent ideas between Willow and I regarding her pregnancy and the subsequent abortion illustrated, however, that we had not thought of one another as people of worth, but instead perceived each other to be the enemy. No one told the two of us that it was the baby who was important—not our selfishness and immaturity. Pilgrim, Willow and I can presently have all the spirituality in the world, all the wealth, all the prestige, and education—but we cannot reverse our respective roles regarding your death. As I said earlier, the Lord can forgive us for our sins; however, the two of us still have to bear the consequences of our actions. Pilgrim, I purposely issue the above mantra regarding consequences throughout the book as a reminder of the severity of what Willow and I did to bring about your abortion—and how we have to be held accountable for our misdeeds. Yet, it was during March 1964 that I decided to affirm your birth and existence by giving you a body replete with the most beautiful little face, and wonderful personality. Many people—particularly women—believe that a man is not capable of nurturing, loving feelings toward the child we lose to an abortion. Willow never knew the extent of my heartbreak and grief; nor did she likely care. I doubt if she could ever gather the tears that I shed for both her and you. However, I could never hate your mother.

March 1964 was rough though, because life was going on without you. Darling, Pilgrim, your mother and I subsequently have had children; however, we both have had to acknowledge that you were and always will be our first conceived baby. Speaking of babies, I have an anecdote to relate: it was on Easter Sunday, 1964 that a woman friend and I were walking arm-in-arm down New York City's Fifth Avenue, swept along by the storied regalia of the Easter Parade. We had not walked very far when coming the other way was a young couple pushing a baby carriage. The young man was pushing the carriage; the young woman had her arm in his; and they talked and laughed as they looked at the baby in the carriage. Pilgrim, I can still remember that upon observing that scene, I felt a temporary sense of sadness wash over me. I thought of you, your mother, and me. Fortunately, I regained my composure and continued my jaunt with my friend. However, I still remember the pain precipitated by that chance event.

Otherwise being in New York City was great. I had the opportunity to meet many interesting and enjoyable people. Pilgrim, the city had a great deal of charm as far as its history and cultural opportunities. I was able to go to the Metropolitan Opera, and buy inexpensive standing-room only tickets to see the wonderful operatic performances. During my stay in NYC, I went to Broadway shows, and numerous sporting events at Madison Square Garden, and at Yankee and Shea Stadiums. I bought books and read voraciously. There was never enough time to spend at the great museums, such as the Metropolitan Museum of Art—from where I sent Willow a poster—the Guggenheim Museum, and Museum of Natural History. They were amazing places to spend either a Saturday or Sunday afternoon. Pilgrim, if we had stayed in NYC, and as you would have become older, you and I would have had a great time going to all these places. Guess what darling Pilgrim, I believe we would have had a great time at the Bronx Zoo, and the Central Park Zoo! I would have put you on my shoulders so that you could have gotten a bird's eye view of all the animals, birds, and reptiles, etc. Central Park is beautiful any time of the year—especially in the fall. You and I would have been enthralled with the multi-color leaves on the trees. Speaking of the trees, they are so pretty during the fall. Do you know what would have been fun to do? We could have ridden the subway. Does that sound rather corny to you? I hope not. Pilgrim, when I lived in NYC, it costs only fifteen cents to ride the subway. And you, as a baby, could ride to all the five boroughs for free. We could have observed all types of people. Let me tell you about another interesting ride: that would have been the Staten Island Ferry. It was free, and you could ride from Battery Park to Staten Island in about twenty or twenty-five minutes.   As an aside, I kept in touch on a regular basis with Laura and Craig during the time I was living in New York City. I wrote them short letters and phoned them every other week. They always said I was in their prayers and thoughts. We spent very little time talking about what had taken place back in the summer of 1963. To say the least, it was great to hear from them—either by phone or by letter. I sent them mementos of NYC.

During the stay in NYC, I met a number of very attractive and interesting women. I met them at work, in church, a few times on a subway of all places, even when I was working part time as a sales manager at Macy's Department Store. I also became acquainted with some in Central Park when I was jogging. I even chanced across one very lovely woman who was taking a Ph.D. in English Literature at Columbia, University. She and I became acquainted at a Chaucer exhibit at the New York Public Library. She had graduated from the University of California at Berkeley a few years before and had been living in the city while attending Columbia. We got to be good friends, and did a number of things together. However, I was wise enough not to attempt to become emotionally involved with any of my women friends.

During the spring of 1964, I was attempting to decide whether I wanted to stay in NYC. It was a great city and I had enjoyed the time I was there. New York was a type of milieu therapy. If I had to grieve during the month that you would have been born, I would rather that I do it in New York City. The city was a palliative of sorts along with the attendant therapy. I had many friends and acquired a measure of emotional stability there. Yet, Pilgrim, I believed it was time for the two of us to go elsewhere.

I had earlier thought about beginning graduate work in New York City. Thanks to the Lord, I was feeling confident. I was slowly becoming focused, and maturing. There were no magical moments of transformation, but instead the slow, though at times, seemingly imperceptible lifting of the clouds of doubt and despair. Though things were going well for me in NYC, I believed it was time to find some other place to live. It was not the call of the wild or that the west had to be conquered that activated my cerebral transmitters; it was simply something viscerally telling me that there were other experiences to be a part of, and other people to be in my life. I believed it was that simple darling daughter. Some friends had mixed feelings about me leaving NYC. They believed, however, that I could handle such a move if I also incorporated some psychotherapy wherever it was that I settled.

Leaving New York City was not easy, Pilgrim. Nevertheless, leaving the East Coast would be far less traumatic than had been the exit from Southern California. Because of warm feelings for the city where I was born, I would return to it numerous times in the future.

Let me segue into asking you, where do you think we should go? This is your time to provide input into a major decision. After all, we are on this odyssey for the long haul. Should I throw darts, while blindfolded, at a wall map of the United States? You could agree that wherever the dart landed, that is where we would go. It is a great idea with one exception: that being what if the dart landed on Southern California? Pilgrim, I would have to throw the dart again until it landed somewhere else. I am not really cheating. Pilgrim, it would just be so absurd to return anywhere near where your mother and her family lived. Remember my comment about not having respect for Willow and her family because of what they allowed to take place? Well, after my part in the pregnancy, I am certain that I would not command any semblance of respect from Willow and her family. However, that is no longer an issue. Instead, Pilgrim, what is of importance is that you and I continue to look for a new area of the country to move to, and a place in which to live. I know what I will do; I will let the spirit move me. I have confidence in our Heavenly Father to love a sinner such as I am enough to move me where He can keep an eye on me. I feel that there will be great opportunities and wonderful people where I will be going. Pilgrim, it is time for another letter. Hang on, because it is windy where we are going!

Hey, little girl, I love you so very much,

Dad

"GOING TO KANSAS (CITY), KANSAS (CITY) HERE I COME"

In the late spring of 1964, I had decided to move to Kansas! Until I actually moved little one, I was not certain why I was doing so. I had never been to Kansas, and I had no ties in the Jayhawk State. However, one cannot hesitate where adventure beckons. I see your cherubic smile. I think you are actually looking forward to our new experiences. Pilgrim, let me interject a question. Do you think that any of your spirit baby friends are taking similar trips with their fathers? I am certain there are countless fathers who grieved the loss of their infant sons and daughters who died tragically by abortions, and who miss them so much as to figuratively want to have their children with them as they (the fathers) go through life. We just might possibly run into some of your friends and their dads!

Well, one hot, humid day in the summer of 1964, you and I took the flight from New York to Kansas City, Missouri. It was about a two-hour and one-half-hour flight, but a rather uneventful one as opposed to the trip the previous year from Los Angeles to New York. I had better control of my emotions, and only you and I were on the flight to Kansas City—not Willow. This time, Pilgrim, I also had a larger box of books than I had when I left California in 1963. After landing at the old downtown Kansas City Airport, I changed planes and flew to Topeka, Kansas the capital of Kansas. I flew on an old DC-3 plane, which was as old as Methuselah. The flight from Kansas City to Topeka was a thirty-minute flight, and it seemed that we flew at treetop level before we set down at the municipal airport in Topeka. Dorothy in *The Wizard of Oz* had more direction than I had—and she already had been blown off course by a tornado!

Topeka was a very nice mid-sized Midwestern City. Kansans were of mostly central and northern European stock. It would not be long, darling Pilgrim, until I found that Kansans were friendly, somewhat reserved, but extremely generous and very down-to-earth. Well, what do you think so far? I have to admit I was a bit apprehensive; I, however, was adventuresome enough to look forward to another set of experiences.

I took a taxi to a downtown Topeka hotel where I checked in for the evening. I settled into a comfortable, but sparsely furnished room, and after a while, I began examining the local newspaper for rooms or apartments to rent. I even briefly examined the job opportunities that were listed, but decided to wait until I found a place to live before looking for work. Pilgrim, it did not take very long to conclude that Kansas was different than either New York City or Southern California. I went out that evening to eat, and found a small, but nice restaurant. While eating dinner, I talked to a few of the other patrons. They were friendly, but somewhat curious as to why I had come to Topeka. I may have said that life was obviously good in Kansas and I was here to partake of it.

The next morning, while having breakfast, I read the want ads in the local newspaper, and found some ads for rooms and apartments for rent. I asked the desk clerk where I might find a nice residential area. She told me of one across the street from Washburn University, the municipal university. I then walked about two miles before I found the address of the woman, who rented rooms in her house. After a friendly discussion, I was offered a room to rent. I could look out the window and see the university across the street. I returned to the hotel, got my things, paid my bill, got a cab, and went to my new quarters. Upon arriving back at the house, I met my new roommate, a young man from Kansas City, who was going to school at Washburn. We became good friends.

Pilgrim, moving from NYC to the Midwest had not been as difficult as I originally believed it would be. Topeka was a city with a great deal of history—some of it going back to the pre-Civil War period. It was an urban area surrounded by an ever-apparent agricultural realm; yet, Topeka was an easy city to get around. However, I realized that I needed an automobile; so guess what, Pilgrim, I bought my first car in three years! I bought a used 1955 Buick sedan, which, though large, was quite comfortable. Since gas was only about 25 cents a gallon at that time, I could readily afford to fill the gas tank.

It was time to find work. It did not take long to find a job as a lifeguard at a large municipal pool. It was very enjoyable. I swam a lot, got a tan, and occasionally saved a few swimmers. Every so often, I would look back on the previous summer with its attendant trauma. It would bring about some temporary sadness. If I saw mothers with very small children, I sometimes found myself thinking about you and Willow. I remembered what the psychiatrist told me: that if I found myself missing your mother, that I should look long and hard at the harsh reality of what actually had taken place in the summer of 1963. Though it was not easy, I did what he had suggested. The success rate of such an endeavor was about fifty percent at best. Pilgrim, I still missed Willow the other fifty percent of the time.

Pilgrim, before leaving New York City, I looked at college catalogues at the New York Public Library. One caught my attention: it was the Kansas State Teachers College in Emporia, Kansas—later to be Emporia State University. I had read about Emporia, Kansas and its famous newspaper editor, William Allen White, and the influence of the town on American History. The college itself was famous for having been one of the early such teachers colleges—having opened in 1863—two years after Kansas had become a state. The college had several thousand students, and was diverse enough to have its requisite college of education, along with other college departments, a library school, and a fine small graduate school.

While still in New York City, I wrote a letter to the college asking for their requirements. I was required to take the Graduate Record Examination (GRE), send transcripts of all previous undergraduate and graduate work, and to officially apply for admission. Pilgrim, it seemed so easy, but to the contrary, it was not because of my low grade point average. Other graduate schools had without hesitation turned down my applications because of my apparent lack of academic achievement. There was no one to blame but me. The earlier years of minimally average work were obvious.

I was embarrassed. I think the Lord jarred me by gently rebuking me with all the rejections by graduate schools. This was his way of letting me know that I was not using the talents he had given me. Frankly, I had been too busy fouling up my life to be aware of such abilities. Here I was in my late twenties and had nothing to really show for it. It was time to forsake the hitherto immature attitude toward life. Pilgrim, I understand why your mother saw me as a loser. Now it was time to face life and no longer make excuses.

The college responded to my application and made the decision for me: if I did well on the GRE, I would be admitted initially only for the spring semester of 1965 as a probationary student. Continuation of graduate school would be predicated on meeting or exceeding the subsequent requirement: while on academic probation, I had to maintain a B average throughout the entire semester—if not I would be summarily removed from the program anytime during the semester. It was strictly up to me to succeed. Push had come to shove. Pilgrim I think that not only were the college administration and graduate dean putting the bite on me so to speak, I believe the Lord also had issued a challenge. I know that the Lord was dusting me off so to speak, and putting me back on my feet, and telling me to once again start running the race of life.

Fortunately, I had the endurance to run the race darling daughter. Failure is something that most people do not like to admit or face. I had failed much of my early life, so whatever success I subsequently had I would savor it, and be thankful for it. Since I was unable to begin the Kansas State Teachers College until spring semester 1965, I had to find a job in the interim. What would you think, Pilgrim, if I told you that I found a last minute teaching job at a small, two-room school in the northeastern part of Kansas? Since I did not meet requirements for teaching certification for the State of Kansas, I could only teach for one semester—which actually was fortunate for me—because I eventually went back to school in the spring of 1965. Pilgrim, I had no idea that such a school existed in the 1960s. Let me tell you up front, it would be one of the most wonderful experiences that I would have in my entire life. The school was about 75 miles north of Topeka, which meant that I moved to a town near the school. I rented a furnished apartment over the hardware store. The town had 2100 people living in it.

To think, darling daughter, that it was a year to the day that I had left Los Angeles for New York City. What a contrast in time, places, and events! I really believed the Lord had his hand as to where I was and why. I am not certain why I lived in a very small town in northeastern Kansas many years ago. Nevertheless, I would never relinquish that time Pilgrim. One reason was that in the evenings I had plenty of time to think of you and Willow. What I found was that when I thought of the two of you, I was able to do so with not as much anger or anguish, but instead with more of a sense of sadness about what had taken place the previous year. What was unusual was that I spent more time thinking of you and Willow as mother and daughter. This did not mean that I had forgiven Willow and her parents, but instead it meant that I was coming to terms with what had taken place. I knew that if I acknowledged you as my very own daughter, then I had to accept Willow's claim to you as your mother. I did that with love for the both of you. At the same time, I was comfortable to memorialize you having been in Heaven; but you are now on loan to me by the Lord.

It is wonderful to know that you were free of pain, and above all, to know how blessed I am to have you as my beautiful daughter. By the way, it was somewhat normal for people in the small town in which I lived to ask if I was married and had a family. I always answered no, though knowing that was not entirely the truth.

Pilgrim, the first day at the little country school was a revelation. It was a darling little school. It looked like something out of a 19th Century photograph. The school was back from the road surrounded by trees, and with a play area with gym equipment, an outdoor basketball court, and a softball diamond—all in an expansive farm field setting.

The school itself was surrounded by farmland on three sides; it was a bucolic scene. I never forgot that picture-like scenery. I could tell that you enjoyed the scenery. Though living on a farm for a number of years, while at a boys' school, I had never seen or been in a one or two-room school-house. Pilgrim, though you would have been an infant at the time I first arrived at the school, it would have been a wonderful experience to have carried you into the school so that the two of us could have checked it out (You would have then been six months old). This school had a great deal of history to it. Just think darling daughter this school was almost one hundred years old in 1964. Imagine all the boys and girls who had traveled these halls and rooms of the school these nearly one hundred years.

Pilgrim, I am certain all these boys and girls grew up to become adults, and it is not incomprehensible to think that many of these boys fought in our nation's wars such as, the Spanish American War, the First and Second World Wars, and the Korean War. I daresay that many of them sacrificed their lives, and left grieving families and loved ones. My darling daughter, I can still remember with clarity the sense of awe and expectation that overwhelmed me as I went up the steps of that school the first day.

A board member greeted me at the school and introduced me to my fellow teacher; she was a very nice-middle-aged lady (I was still in my late twenties in 1964) who taught grades first through fifth in a classroom across the hall. I was to teach grades six through eight. The school had thirty-three students. I was also accorded the position of acting principal. This was the first administrative job that I ever had. There was also a school library replete with many wonderful books—some of which dated back to the 19th Century and were classics. The library was a treasure trove of literary classics. One such book was *Vanity Fair* by William Makepeace Thackeray, and was written in the mid 19th Century. This particular copy in the school library was an original first edition that had been brought over to this country by a young lady who had the book signed by the author, and had later in life endowed it to the little school. Speaking of history, the school was not very far from the old Oregon Trail on which thousands of people traveled as they migrated west. In the school hallway, there were paintings and photographs of the Kansas governors and the American presidents—including Lyndon Baines Johnson—the incumbent president in 1964.

Pilgrim, I met my fifteen students. They were the quintessential farm kids. You would have enjoyed them. They were unassuming and eager to learn. Darling Pilgrim, these students ranged in age from ten to thirteen, most of whom had never really traveled very far from where they lived. Yet, I felt that they offered me such a refreshing outlook on life. Pilgrim, these were wonderful children. You would have been proud to have them as friends. They were loyal, unselfish, kind, and considerate. I know adults that could have learned from them—me included.

Guess what I did, Miss Pilgrim, I gave the students a brief oral history of my life and where I had lived. The fact that I had been born, raised and later lived in New York City, and previous to my time spent in New York City, had lived in Southern California, and had surfed impressed them. As expected they asked many questions, two of which were: was I married and did I have children? I answered no to both questions.

So few people had the privilege of teaching where I did in 1964 Pilgrim. I learned to teach the students the subjects I was required to teach them. In turn, I hoped they became educated, and best of all, I learned from them as well. For example, I learned the students and their families always went to the Kansas State Fair; that the boys in the class enjoyed hunting and fishing; and all of the students enjoyed going to the movies.

Speaking of significant events, one of the students had actually gone to California by train and had visited Disneyland. Other than the above, what the students learned about the world came primarily from television. It would not be long before these students' world would erupt in violence such as the Vietnam War, Civil Rights, and the crashing of American morality. I hope that none of the male students ever had to go to Vietnam, but if they did, I hope they made it back alive and in one piece. Pilgrim, to this day, I will always thank our Heavenly Father for the indelible impression these boys and girls made upon my life.

Sometimes, the entire school took a walking field trip around the surrounding area to see bits of Americana, such as old road markers, wheels from covered wagons, as well as the gently rolling country of northeast Kansas. These were great times when the entire school would survey the countryside. Guess what, darling Pilgrim, I would have bundled you up, and put you in a baby back carrier, and taken you on such a walk. Of course, it would have meant having the requisite diaper bag with all the attendant logistical support, but it would have been fun for everyone. Though to some people, it might have seemed difficult at best to geographically and emotionally make the transition from the mammoth city of New York to the farmland of Kansas, and to a town of 2100,. however, to have done so was a wonderful change. I began to settle down emotionally and spiritually during the fall of 1964.

One thing I enjoyed doing was to take the back road from the town in which I lived to school. It was about a fifteen-minute drive from town to school on this road, and it the road winded through a valley wherein laid deserted homesteads and traces of barns and fences. The trip was always peaceful, but somewhat melancholy, because as I drove to school, I had the opportunity to imagine the lives of those who had lived and toiled on these homesteads.

Their dreams, aspirations, joys and heartaches were in all likelihood not much different than those of people in the 1960s—and even later generations. Thus, I acquired a quiet sensitivity as I drove down this road to and from school. I would normally see but a few vehicles on the road, and the occupants would wave to one another. In fact, after a while, I recognized the vehicles and their occupants as we passed each other. It was the "road less traveled." Pilgrim, I believe you would have enjoyed the back roads as well.

Pilgrim, I believe you will get a kick out of this. There was a telephone in the classroom where I taught. So, one day, I asked the students if they would like to be able to phone information in some large cities throughout the country. They were excited to undertake such an endeavor. We looked under "Information" in the telephone book, each student selected a city to phone, and they were to ask the information operator for the phone number of city hall or some municipal entity. The boys and girls phoned information operators in cities, such as Washington, New York, Los Angeles, Denver, Chicago, etc. Some students even asked incidental questions dealing with weather, time, and other tidbits of information. Their phone calls expanded the breadth of their knowledge and interest of the outside world. It was a wonderful experience for all of us in class that day. Pilgrim, to this day, I get teary-eyed but amused as I think of this classroom experience.

We discussed what had been learned from the phone exercise. All of the students were excited and appreciative of the opportunity to call other cities. The students said they got a better understanding of other people and places. Most of them said that they planned to visit each of these cities someday. Bravo, I told them for a job well done.

Another facet of this little country school was its dining room/kitchen set up in the basement. All of the students and the teachers would eat lunch together. Pilgrim, it was a wonderful time to interact with each other, and it did not take very long to establish a real sense of friendship with all the students, and the other teacher, the custodian/bus driver, and the kitchen help—most of whom were mothers of the students. Little daughter, I am sharing these anecdotes to give you some idea that these students and their families were wonderful, unassuming people who welcomed every day as a gift and lived it accordingly. They lacked pretension, incivility, and materialism, but instead took pride in their word, their work ethic, and in their faith—all of which were genuine.

Quite often, I would drive down to Topeka for the weekend and stay where I stayed during the summer. I guess I thought that I would get that big city ambience. I began dating during the previous summer—but on a cautionary basis. I just wanted to enjoy the company of women in general. I did not have to get myself in any entangling alliances darling Pilgrim. Occasionally I would drive to Kansas City, Missouri for the weekend. There was a lot to do there. It was great, however, to come back to school after spending a weekend in the bustling metropolis of Kansas City..

Finally, though with some sadness, both the semester and 1964 were ending. I would be leaving the students, my wonderful experiences, and northeastern Kansas. Another milestone would end Pilgrim. I had been accepted to go to graduate school beginning with the spring semester of 1965. I was enthusiastic about the opportunities that lay ahead of me. The school board had already found a replacement for me—a retired certified schoolteacher. The students would be in great hands. Before leaving for the Christmas vacation, the students from the two classes put on a Christmas play for their parents and families. It was a warm, well done play—and one that I would never forget. After the completion of the play, the school board gave to me, as a going-away present, the book *Vanity Fair*. I was moved by the gesture. I said goodbye to the students, my fellow teacher, and the staff—which as might be expected was difficult. I would really miss the students. They were great. I was so blessed to have the experience of teaching them, and having them as a most important part of my life for several months. Darling Pilgrim, I know you would have missed the students as well. Pilgrim, even after the many years, I still think about them.

I went to Houston, Texas for a wedding during the Christmas vacation. It was a wedding of a young woman friend from my college days in Southern California. Her wedding was very nice. I was happy to see many old friends from California. My friend Stephanie was to have come, but she was unable to get away as she planned. But in all honesty, being among these friends was somewhat difficult because it brought up vivid remembrances of the past with Willow and the summer of 1963. Pilgrim, one really cannot run away from the past. I can attest to that.

Meanwhile back in California, your mother was likely completing her undergraduate work. Having said that did not mean that she was not on my mind. Yet, when Willow was moving about in my psyche, she had to play a secondary role to you. I remember that I was looking forward to what would have been your first birthday. The month of March 1965 would be when you would be a one year old. Though you mother might not make a conscious effort to remember your due date and birthday, I am certain she would not be able to completely, if at all, erase the above significance. As your father, I also have that right to remember all the pertinent things about you, though many people—particularly women—often think that the father of an aborted baby should not spend any time thinking about his child. I disagree, because thinking of you, Pilgrim, is what got me through the horrific events of 1963. No matter if no one else acknowledged you, I would have affirmed you, and I did. You are my daughter.

Darling daughter, the tragedy that beset you was the fact that you were conceived in a decade that the American fabric of life was torn apart by domestic violence, drugs, and war. During this time, there was a generation of young Americans who reveled in their hedonism, and lack of respect for life. Willow and I were the early members of this movement. Having said that darling daughter, I will end this letter. It will soon be a new year.

I love you so much,

Dad

A NEW LIFE AND GUESS WHAT—A WIFE!

1965

Happy New Year darling Pilgrim! It is January 1965 and what would have been your birthday will soon be here—in fact in March 1965. I have left northern Kansas and am now down in Emporia, Kansas, where I have begun my first year of graduate school at Kansas State Teachers College. Eventually the college will be given university status as part of the state university system. It will then be known as Emporia State University. Emporia was a small college town with two colleges, and was known for being the home of the famous American journalist, William Allen White, who had been the publisher and editor of *The Emporia Gazette*—a renowned part of Americana. The town was also on the main line of the then Santa Fe Railroad—itself a part of American history.

Well, Princess, you and I have undertaken another sojourn of sorts I will admit that I was initially anxious because I was certain that I could marshal enough confidence to deal with an unknown future. Guess what, I knew the Lord was carrying me part of the way until He was certain that I was ready to take my first "baby" steps. It is all right to admit that I did not have the boundless self-assurance regarding the future. Well, there you and I were in Emporia, Kansas. For some reason—possibly going back to my belief that I had to meet Willow's approval in order to be a verifiable good person—I began second-guessing myself about my ability. Finally, I talked myself out of my self-induced anxiety, and stepped forward to meet *my* challenges. I signed up for 12 hours of graduate work in history and political science. I actually enjoyed the stimulation of class work, and realized I did have the ability to work hard and get good grades. The classes were tough and thorough, and all my professors were PhDs and sharp. Most of them were graduates of Big Ten schools. I was also able to transfer six hours of graduate credit..

The department chairperson met with me when I first got on campus, and in friendly but firm manner told me, I was going to have to prove myself. I thanked him for the opportunity he had given me to either prove myself capable of being a graduate student or to prove myself otherwise. I could not render any excuses about the past or not knowing how to spell the word "focus." I added a bit of levity, Pilgrim, to see you smile.

Well, it was time to head southwest down the Kansas Turnpike to Emporia in January 1965. I did so Pilgrim with some trepidation. However, I was determined to finally achieve some significant goal in my life. No longer could or would I allow other people's comments influence my efforts and abilities. I met with my major professors and the Chairman of the Social Science Department. They laid down the framework for my being able to matriculate and hopefully succeed. The central theme was "study and review." This meant that every six weeks there would be a review by the above professors as to my work. I also had to be carrying no less than a B average throughout the entire semester. The Department Chairman, in a firm but polite manner told me that if I did not meet or exceed academic expectations, anywhere throughout the duration of the semester, I could summarily be removed from the classes and dismissed from the college.

These requirements did not seem harsh dear daughter; they conversely appeared to be a worthy challenge, and one that I was going to do my best. In fact, the chairman was encouraging in that he told me that he believed I could succeed. It had been a very long time since anyone had registered any faith in my achieving any goals. I think you understood that I had to get away from making excuses for non-performance. Willow and her parents may have rightly criticized me; but now I had the opportunity to prove that I was a better person than they had given me credit for. It was time to move out smartly.

I shared a furnished house with several other fellows—including another graduate student. I liked all my housemates. They were good people. Pilgrim, I was learning to spend many hours in the library studying and working on papers, so did not see much of the house or the other students. Darling daughter, I was anxious to show that I was capable of doing graduate work, in turn, my professors were encouraging, helpful, and motivated me by their interest in me. I believed they realized I was not the failure that I thought myself to be. One of my favorite professors, in fact, laughed when I told him something to the effect, "I had no excuses, but only hope at this stage of my life." The professors appeared to have some understanding of whatever it was I was going through—and in fact were supportive of me.

Pilgrim, I wish that I had undergone some magical transformation, whereby I would have been an instant success in life. However, darling, that does not happen—nor did it ever. Most of us plod along taking one step at a time, and doing our best without being overwhelmed by life. I was no exception. I also had to remember that as flowers, life blooms slowly. However, Kansas State Teachers College was good for me. The school had about 4000 students. It was a mix of a regular college, a graduate school, and a school of education. The town of Emporia was small, but was only thirty-five miles southwest of Topeka via the Kansas Turnpike—now I-35. Both on campus and in the town people accepted you for who you were. Pilgrim, Guess what, it was not long before I began going on dates, which in itself was an interesting endeavor. I dated mostly women who were either seniors or graduate students. They were enjoyable, stimulating women. However, in all honesty, I still missed your mother.

While doing graduate work, I decided to go into further therapy. There was a campus-counseling program, in which I spent time seeing the college clinical psychologist. Pilgrim, it was a great opportunity to look at my feelings, as I got closer to what would have been your first birthday in March 1965. Though having been geographically removed from California since 1963, it was imperative that no matter where I was that I validate what should have been a most exciting and happy event—that being the celebration of your first year on earth. As expected, however, the forthcoming anniversary would have been a melancholy one. Perhaps to some people, it would have seemed far more logical to put you out of my mind. That was not going to happen. However, Pilgrim, few, if any people who have had to deal with an abortion really dismiss it.

I have no idea what was going on in your mother's mind in early 1965, but I was going to deal with my pain, anger, and grief—particularly as they applied to your forthcoming first birthday. The clinical psychologist and I discussed the tendency that often men and women believed they are immune to post-abortion problems. Their rationalization for an abortion was comfortably affirmed by those who talked them into having an abortion or agreed to it. However, as a woman and a man who have had to deal with an abortion go through life, the support is usually no longer there, at which time they often face alone the reality of having aborted a baby.

Therefore, your mother might not have paid as much attention to your birth month as I did—at least that first year. To be remembered is that Post Abortion Stress Syndrome was not even a politically correct or a medical term in the 1960s; however, this is not to say it did not exist. Though I was busy and productive in graduate school, there were not enough distractions that could have caused me not to think of you. The most monumental of birthdays—that being your first one—never was to take place in March 1965. Neither Willow nor I had the opportunity to take pictures of you sitting in your high chair, while you attempted to make up your mind what to do with a birthday cake, and its one lit candle, as we sang Happy Birthday to you. There were no family members assembled to dote over you with love and affection. Pilgrim, there was no photograph taken of your mother, you, and I together on your birthday. Your mother and I were never granted the cherished opportunity of ever knowing what you would have looked like.

One of the saddest things was the fact your mother and I never had the opportunity to thank the Lord for having given you to us. I eventually thanked God that no matter what had physically happened to you in 1963, that you still were and would always be Willow's and my daughter—and other than the time you are "on loan" to me, you were with the Lord. In fact, Pilgrim, I can see you toddling toward me with your blonde hair, light blue eyes, and your beautiful cherubic face with your full smile. I can feel you cheek against mine and your chubby arms around my neck. I believe you would not look either like your mother or me; you would have your own beautiful countenance. However, since March 1965 has just arrived, I want to wish you a very Happy Birthday my darling Pilgrim—and many more! I look forward to other birthdays. I am the proudest father in the world and I love you so much.

I will refer back to therapy. I liked this college clinical psychologist because he was kind, sensitive and interacted with his patients. He also helped guide the discussion toward meaningful directions. I had the impression that he had dealt with abortion issues before. However, I did ask him if he got very many male students who had to deal with their grief and anger regarding abortions. Pilgrim, I was one of the very few male students who obviously had come forward to deal with their emotions about abortion.   The psychologist told me that by dealing with my pain and sorrow over the loss of you and Willow, I was exhibiting growth. Darling Pilgrim, I owed it to you to face my pain and loss concerning you. As had the psychiatrist in New York told me the previous year, the psychologist said that by realistically looking at the negative actions of Willow and her parents—both toward you and me—that I would be able within time to be more objective in my assessment of the abortion. He stressed that I would heal and forgive within my time—not anyone else's. He was right.

One thing that was beneficial was the fact that I was seeing this psychologist while I was in school, so he also served as a sounding board for my class activities and work. He provided confidence in how I was doing, and said he believed I had potentialPreviously, no one had ever told me that. However, the psychologist mentioned that part of my problem regarding disastrous relationships, such as with your mother, was that I lacked the confidence to be myself, and instead attempted to meet other people's criteria. He suggested that I learn that was all right to be me, and not to blame myself for what Willow and her parents did regarding you being aborted.

Pilgrim, March came, but with the help of therapy and my being busy with classes, I actually welcomed what would have been your first birthday. The psychologist helped me deal with your first birthday by telling me that no one can or will be able to take you away from my heart; and that my celebrating your birthday was a confirmation of your existence and my love for you. I felt so much better when he told me that. There was of course pain because you were not actually allowed to have life; however, Pilgrim, you do exist—in my heart and mind—and always will. Of course, you will always be my precious daughter. Once again Happy Birthday Pilgrim.

Pilgrim, guess what, one day in early March, I was doing research in the library stacks of the main library; and I literally bumped into a beautiful woman student. We were doing research for papers in our respective classes. Her name was Jessica and she was a senior. Jessica was tall, lithe, with striking features and long black hair. Wow, suddenly, and unexpectedly, I acquired a new appreciation of life. Darling Pilgrim, I was not certain as to my emotional state; I, however, believed this beautiful brown-haired person had been angelically placed into my life! My purported analytical and intellectual abilities quivered and then were smashed into smithereens. I was infatuated. After leaving California in 1963, I did not think that I would ever have such feelings again.

Jessica was beautiful, and she was very sophisticated, plus having a vibrant sexuality. She looked nothing like Willow. Pilgrim, I had promised myself that after dealing with the past tragedy of 1963, I would be extremely cautious when it came to women. I broke that promise in a hurry. Fortunately, my memory bank was strong enough that I instinctively maintained enough emotional restraint not to do anything stupid. Nevertheless, all kinds of irreverent thoughts cropped up when I thought of Jessica. It seemed my self-control might go by the wayside if I were not careful. I was like the apostle Paul in the New Testament asking the Lord for deliverance from my "thorns in the flesh." However, unlike Paul, I did not believe I was given an answer. I was going to have to work out my own plan of dealing with temptation.

Pilgrim, I believe Jessica would have fascinated you. She commanded everyone's attention because she was beautiful. Jessica had an aura of mystery about her that I had not seen in any other woman. Jessica came from a large family comprised of her parents and five siblings. She was the second oldest of the children. Jessica had a sister a few years younger than her, with whom she was quite close. Her parents were gracious and caring people, who I always held in high esteem.

Pilgrim darling, what do you think I should have done? I wondered if I should be reticent about my past, or if asked about it, just give vague or evasive answers. Most of us tend to hide those things we think will make us appear to be unattractive or inconsequential. Your mother and I had done that with one another—with obvious tragic results. It was time to get help from an expert. I went to the therapist. The psychologist told me the following: go slow, be honest, and do not put the relationship in jeopardy. I clearly understood his suggestions. They made sense. He also suggested that I make a concerted effort to go slow with the physical side of Jessica's and my friendship/relationship.

For a comfortable opener to our friendship, Jessica and I spent time discussing a class the two of us were taking from a specific professor—though not at the same time. We both enjoyed this professor and the class, and so spent our time comparing and contrasting our thoughts about the class, of course the professor, and the contents and objectives of the class.

Jessica was honest with her emotions—there was no subterfuge—which in itself was quite refreshing. I did not have to be on guard with her nor did she with me. We liked one another too much to do anything to cause havoc with the blossoming friendship that later became a healthy relationship. Darling daughter, Jessica and I were not only very much attracted to one another, but we were comfortable with each other as well. We were able to be affectionate without being sexual.

Jessica and I were able to talk and laugh about many things, and share our most personal feelings. It was not long before I was comfortable enough to be with Jessica and share with her what had happened between your mother and me. Jessica was understanding and supportive, and bore no judgment as to the abortion. She said that under the same set of circumstances, she would have had the baby, and then decided whether to keep it or give it up for adoption. Jessica's answer was a thought-provoking one—and one I wished that Willow had considered and implemented.

Pilgrim, it was wonderful to have a special person such as Jessica in my life. She was caring, and showed interest in what my professional and academic plans were. I had not volunteered any information regarding the above plans because I thought I would come across as being unrealistic in my appraisal of my abilities. However, Jessica pressed me one time to share my plans with her. When I finally divulged my aspirations to get my masters degree and eventually go on for a Ph.D., in order that I could become a college professor, Jessica was genuinely supportive of me. It was great to have an advocate in my corner. Jessica wanted to get a masters degree in Social Work, which she eventually did. She was extremely intelligent without being showy. In fact, she was low-keyed about it.

Jessica and I thought about getting married. After what Willow and I had gone through, I had ambivalent feelings about being man and wife. However, Jessica and I had begun to fall in love with one another, and marriage was an appealing idea. Before we decided that we wanted to get married, we thought it was imperative that we discuss whether we wanted children, and if so when. I was still mourning the loss of you, Pilgrim, and both Jessica and I decided that maybe having a child was not logical.

We both had educations that we wanted to complete; we also planned to travel; and most important was the fact that it was important for us to get to know one another. Well, having shared all of the above with you, it was time for another shock; Jessica and I had decided to go to the county court house and get married. However, we first had to get a license, and a physical. We did both, and we purchased new clothes for the wedding. Jessica bought a beautiful pink suit with a small box hat—which was stylish in the early to mid 1960s. I purchased a dark suit replete with a vest. Two of our friends—a young married couple—were to be our witnesses at the wedding. We kept our decision to get married as much as possible a secret. Even my roommates did not know about our decision to get married. However, I must admit little one that I was nervous. Bridegrooms tend to be anxious about many things. I was apprehensive. But, I gained my composure and we got married on a Friday afternoon, spent our wedding night at a motel, then the next morning we drove to Jessica's family to share with them the 'glad tidings." Well, Pilgrim, as expected, Jessica's family was shocked, but recovered, especially when reassured that she was not pregnant. Since the birth control pill had been on the market for a while, Jessica had time before we got married to get used to the pill, so there was not a likelihood of an "accident." Second, we had not been intimate until our wedding night.

It was but a short time before the shock dissipated and Jessica's family recovered, though Jessica had to comfort her next youngest sister who needed reassurance that our being married would not bring about any exclusion or reduction of the relationship between the two sisters. Jessica and I spent the day with her family at their home, but spent a second night at a hotel. We then left the next evening and drove back to Emporia.

Since we had no apartment to go to, I took Jessica back to the house she shared with her girl friend and I went back to my place. I told my roommates the good news. They congratulated me, and said that since they all went home on weekends, Jessica and I could have the house for the weekends. Jessica and I enthusiastically accepted their offer. Since, it was near the semester, when we got married, we were able to "tough it out" during the week as far as being able to spend nights together. Jessica and I sometimes drove to her folk's where we spent the weekends. Let me put it this way, Jessica and I were always able to spend quality time together.

Jessica graduated from college after the spring semester of 1965. Pilgrim, I was so proud of her, and she looked beautiful walking across the stage with her diploma. I had a very successful semester with over a B average. I had proven my mettle, thanks to the encouragement of my professors, some good friends, and above all, because the Lord blessed me by providing the talents and work ethic to succeed. Darling Pilgrim, my professors told me that I was approved to continue in the graduate program.

My major professor said he was impressed how well I had done. I mention this because I found myself thinking why had I not done this before. However, I realized that my maturation took longer than I expected, and would be an on-going process. Jessica, however, had been instrumental in my academic success that spring semester. She constantly was reassuring me that I had ability, and not to let the past be an obstacle to a successful future.

After graduation, Jessica and I moved to Topeka, where we found a nice, but small, furnished apartment. Jessica got a job with the State of Kansas; I went back to working as a lifeguard; and took two summer school courses back at Emporia. Thanks in large measure to Jessica's mother, the papers that I was assigned to do for the two courses turned out quite well. She accomplished this by editing and typing the papers on her electric typewriter, and by doing so, my mother-in-law made the papers excellent in quality. My mother-in-law was a wonderful woman. Jessica's entire family was an amazing unit. They were a cohesive, loving family.

Jessica enjoyed coming to the municipal pool with me when I worked on the weekend. Pilgrim, Jessica was a beautiful woman, with an amazing figure, and looked stunning in a bathing suit. I was flattered that men glanced at her. After getting married, Jessica and I settled down being a married couple. Though being married, Jessica and I tended to have our own stubborn personalities, but we were a very affectionate, intimate couple, and we learned to eventually accept one another's obdurate attitudes. Even through the heady days of marriage, you were on my mind quite often, darling daughter.

Jessica would have been the ideal mother for you—at least in my mind. She not only was quite beautiful, but a very, caring and loving person. She related well with children. I could have seen the two of you laughing as you would toddle over to her, and she would pick you up and twirl you around, then hold you as you cradled you head on to her shoulder. Both of you would be immersed into one another—as only a mother and daughter could be. I remember once that Jessica and I discussed what it would have been like to have incorporated you into our lives had you lived.

Well, the fall of 1965 came and I returned to finish my masters degree. Several of other married male students who lived in Topeka took turns driving from Topeka to Emporia throughout the week. We would leave early in the morning and return in the early evenings. Jessica and I became friends of the other couples and socialized with them. Guess what, Pilgrim, Jessica and I got a female kitten that we named "Do-be" after a character from a television show. You would have really enjoyed her. She was very affectionate, liked being handled and petted, and was playful. Do-be enjoyed sleeping at the end of the bed. When it was cold, she would get into bed with us, and then crawl down to the bottom of the bed and sleep. Guess what, Do-be was a silly cat, in that she enjoyed biting our toes when she wanted us to get up. She was our feline alarm clock! Jessica and I enjoyed taking her down to Jessica's folks for weekends when we decided to spend time with her family. Do-be of course was always spoiled and had the run of the house. Pilgrim, we would probably have had to watch you with Do-be, because no doubt, you would have been rambunctious with her until you learned how to play with Do-be without frightening her or teasing her. Little children, such as you have to learn to be with pets. Do not worry darling daughter, I know you would have been very good with Do-be.

The year 1965 was almost over as Jessica and I were working through our first year of marriage. It was a year of change, adaptation, and some emotional roller-coaster activity. Jessica and I were very much in love, but we had to work through residual insecurities from past relationships. Sometimes, as many newlyweds, Jessica and I took turns vying for control of various facets of our marriage. Nevertheless, we were able to work through most of our issues. Jessica was a multifaceted woman, who was an artist, writer, intellectual, and uncannily logical. She was also very affectionate, and had an emotional depth that I had seen in very few other women. Thus having said the above, I did not have to worry about "walking on eggs" when it came time to showing my emotions. Jessica encouraged me to express my feelings; in turn, she did not hesitate to speak her mind. Sometimes we had heated discussions, but we would stop the argument by giving one another a "time out" and letting our emotions subside. We agreed to disagree, while respecting each other's views.

One area that we agreed on was that we would eventually like to have children of our own. We planned that after I completed my doctorate, she in turn, would do her graduate work. Then, darling Pilgrim, after Jessica and I were finished with our degrees, you perhaps might have had younger brothers and sisters. I know you would have been delighted to have siblings who would look up to you and adore you. Unfortunately, Pilgrim, the 1960s was not the best of decades. The Vietnam War was becoming more of a political and emotional issue; civil rights divided the country; morality was something no longer believed to be a significant part of mainstream America. Young Americans purportedly did not trust anyone over thirty, and free love and the drug culture were alive and well. I thought I would keep you up to snuff regarding what was going on in life.

Guess what, Pilgrim, I graduated with my masters degree in Political Science in 1966. It had been a busy, but remarkable year and a half. Thanks to the Lord, Jessica, her mother, the tough, but fair professors, and some latent ability on my part, I had proven to be a capable person and good student. I started planning to send applications to universities for further graduate study toward my Ph.D. I had earlier made up my mind that I wanted to be a college history professor, thus it was necessary that I have a Ph.D., in order to meet the requirements for an assistant professor at either a small college or a major university. Jessica and I discussed that after I had finished my doctorate, we would find a college where I would teach, do research, and write; buy a small home for ourselves and whatever cats we had; and she would get her Masters of Social Work. Then we could plan to start a family. I could not believe it, Pilgrim, just three years before my life was in complete shambles with little, if any, promise for the future. Thanks to the Lord and others, I began turning things around—however, I still had a long way to go. Hey, Happy Second Birthday my darling daughter!

Please know that you are uniquely with me no matter where I go; Pilgrim, I am realistic about my life, but to not have you tag along as my first child would be reprehensible. I need you as the daughter you are, and I believe you want me always to embrace you as my child. When you were aborted and quickly, but gently taken back to heaven, I initially believed you were lost to me, and despaired of ever knowing you. How I got you back with me was to incorporate you and Willow into my psyche and life. I could not ever love you any less than any subsequent child I might have. You never died—you just moved to another place.

Pilgrim, Jessica and I had an interesting summer in 1966. Along with a number of other recipients of graduate degrees, I was offered the opportunity to teach summer school to high school students who had emotional problems, and lived in a hospital environment. What an oxymoron, because all high school students have emotional problems—and I certainly knew something about emotional issues!

I was assigned to teach several social science classes to a number of high school students—most of who were seniors. The classroom where we gathered had bright colors and the tables and chairs were in a semi-circle, whereby the students and I faced one another. The unit psychologist told the teachers that the classrooms were so arranged as to mitigate the students' feeling intimidated by having an authority figure directly in front of them. This was a new approach to teaching, but it seemed to lessen stress between the students and the teachers.

Darling Pilgrim, I taught students who were from broken homes, abusive parental relationships, or who suffered from depression and were suicidal. Guess what, darling, as a small child, I had been emotionally where these students were. I will discuss the above in a later letter. In some ways, I was a subject matter expert regarding their pain.

The young people that I taught were very bright, but apparently very confused. Heretofore, they had gone through their lives lacking direction, or self-esteem, and had built walls to keep out other people. The teachers were instructed to teach these adolescents the same way we would instruct conventional students. We used this method of instruction to give our students the opportunity to believe that they could and would finish high school.

Though daunting at times, teaching was enjoyable and most reward-ing. One thing we noticed was that in order to survive the pain that eventu-ally had them hospitalized, these adolescents had conveniently learned to emotionally shut down in order to survive. My colleagues and I remarked during one of our first staff meetings between the clinical personnel and us, about the presence of pain in the eyes and expressions of these young-sters. Their pain, anger and grief were apparent.

Remember when I had earlier commented as to what was happening to our society in the 1960s? Well, this was the prime example of society turning away from nurturing and guiding its children. Most of the teenag-ers on the ward where we held our classes were from white middle-class or upper-class backgrounds, with at least one college-educated parent. They could have been from Orange County, California or Westchester County, New York, as well as from urban or rural Kansas. Nevertheless, these boys and girls had lost their direction and purpose in life; they believed no one loved them or cared about them. Pilgrim, you would have only been two in 1966, so you might not have understood my comments. I am, however, sharing my observations with you to let you know, in a somewhat oblique manner, that there were parents who essentially had emotionally aban-doned their children. Unfortunately, as the result of the abandonment, these adolescents had lost their point of reference, and confidence in life; they believed no one loved them or cared about them.

These students needed structure, affirmation, and a sense of trust in the adults who were in their lives—in whatever capacity. Jessica and I would discuss my summer school teaching, and I would bounce ideas off her to help me become a better teacher. She would help by "brainstorming" ways that I might be a more effective teacher to my students and be able to gain their trust. Pilgrim, I do not know what I would have done without Jessica's support. She was non-judgmental, quite perceptive, offered great suggestions, and instilled confidence.

Dear daughter, allow me to draw an unusual parallel by referring to the fact that you died a horrible, but quick death; however, you were quickly retrieved by the angels and taken to Heaven. Yet, most of the students taught during the summer of 1966, however, had metaphorically died countless emotional deaths throughout their lives. Some had even attempted suicide more than once before being hospitalized. They had no angels to take away their pain, and wipe the tears from their eyes. Whatever psychological demons beset the teenagers they were difficult to be excised. The students were given the best medicine of the era; yet in our daily meetings, the hospital psychiatric staff did not indicate the prognosis was good for these boys and girls.

Pilgrim, people may think they are great teachers warranting titles and awards. Unless, however, they have known what it is to serve and teach young men and women who do not have the same opportunities as most of us individuals, they cannot call themselves "real teachers." Though I received a Ph.D. several years later, and was blessed to teach on the university level, one of my finest teaching experiences ever was the one I undertook during the summer of 1966. However, darling, though I have had essentially a wonderful life, nothing can compare to having taught these students who heretofore believed they had nowhere to go but down! It really does not take much to think that you are better than others. However, it sometimes takes a great deal to realize that you are no better than the "least of those who you serve."

Pilgrim, I could have easily been where those young people were. I was fortunate that maybe it was the luck of the draw that kept me from ever having to go to a mental hospital as a child or as an adolescent. Darling Pilgrim, it is always easy to judge when you do not have to endure what others go through or when you know that circumstances favor the likelihood of you not having to undergo the misfortune of others.

One thing my colleagues and I noticed were these adolescents tended not to be not unlike their peers in the "normal" world. As their fellow adolescents in every day life, these teenagers bonded with one another; tried to play the system; and attempted to ignore us adults if they believed we were being too confrontational or giving them grief.

Nevertheless, my classes were generally free of noticeable behavior problems. This was partially because I kept a tight rein on my students, and only "cut them enough slack" when I believed they could handle it.

There was one student, however, who believed I was her nemesis. Her name was Nina and she was eighteen. She was a very attractive young woman who had the "usual" mental health illnesses that had put her in the hospital. The clinical staff said that Nina was very intelligent, but if not verbally restrained, she would eventually attempt to disrupt the class. Nina and I jockeyed for control regarding, not only our relationship in the class but, who would prevail over the other. She "conformed" for about two weeks, but then during the third week of our class, something triggered Nina to act out in class.

I remember that one day a male student made some seemingly innocuous comment to Nina before the class actually began. She jumped out of her seat and attempted to hit him. I quickly separated Nina and her intended victim, and got her back to her seat. I then tried to calm her, but she was angry as a hornet and disruptive. I realized that Nina was done for the day as far as being in class. I then sent her back to the ward, but told her in the hall that upon completion of the class, I would discuss the episode with her social worker. The following day, after the altercation in the class, a subdued and contrite Nina returned to class. I accepted her apologies and nothing more was said. Nina was a model of decorum for the remaining weeks and contributed to the class. What impressed me about the saga of Nina was that she was not unlike most of us. She wanted to believe that she was a lovable, fallible human being, yet vulnerable—as we, all are. Perhaps, all of us who purport to be "normal" are not as emotionally healthy as we believe we are.

Though hospitalized, Nina certainly was redeemable in all ways. She was a Child of God—as we all are. I remembered her look of sadness that, however, could and did change under certain circumstances.

One day, Jessica came to pick me after my classes were finished. We had earlier decided to meet at the hospital's snack bar. When Jessica arrived, she and I sat down to have coffee with another teacher. Shortly, thereafter, Nina and a couple of her friends came into the snack bar, so I invited Nina to come over to meet Jessica. Guess what, darling daughter, the two of them got along splendidly. The other teacher and I simply disengaged from the conversation while Jessica and Nina talked about everything from "soup to nuts." Nina was quite effusive—which I had never observed her to be—and it seemed that Jessica and Nina enjoyed one another's company. It was a wonderful experience to see Nina being animated and apparently happy.

Unfortunately, the conversation ended because Nina had to return to the ward, and Jessica and I had to drive home. People were always comfortable with Jessica. She was empathetic, warm, and caring. She was not pretentious. Upon my return to the class next morning, Nina told me how much she enjoyed talking with Jessica, because she thought Jessica accepted her and was not condescending toward her. I was flattered by Nina's remarks and later shared them with Jessica, who briefly became teary-eyed upon hearing Nina's comments.

The hospital had a strict policy against unwarranted fraternization between staff, teachers, and the patients, so Jessica and Nina did not have the opportunity to expand their friendship. Though Nina and Jessica had no further contact with one another, I believe they were both the better for having spent about an hour talking with one another.

The emotionally disturbed teenagers, with whom my colleagues and I had contact with during the summer of 1966, constantly dealt with trying to understand their own actions. Sadly, they often did not comprehend that there were appropriate and inappropriate behaviors and choices. Many of them had learned to strictly react to physical, psychological, sexual, and verbal abuse. They never had been allowed to confront their tormentors. These children could do nothing but attempt to protect themselves the best they could. They did this by tuning out their pain. These adolescents had no advocates. Life was lived minute-to-minute. They trusted no one—not even themselves.

Pilgrim, I had been where these youngster had been—only at a different time in my life. I knew their pain and suffering very well. However, unless they were convinced by therapy of their sense of self-worth, these young people were often unable to make any choices at all—let alone the right ones. Where Willow and I had not hesitated being cruel and critical to one another because we were immature and selfish, these adolescents would become devastated by any rebukes or negative assessment of them or their behavior. In other words, these young people might show the same kinds of behavior that Willow and I had implemented in 1963, without really knowing why. What it took, Pilgrim, was involving these youngsters in the decision-making process, whereby they acquired self-assurance, and a sense of accomplishment regarding the choices they made.

By doing this, the students slowly began to become accountable for their actions and feelings. Speaking of feelings and actions, Pilgrim, how about a change in the venue, with some unexpected excitement? Okay darling little one, here we go.

Guess what, during the early summer of 1966, Jessica and I made the remarks that we would in all likelihood leave Topeka, and possibly Kansas without ever having been in a tornado. Well, having said that, Pilgrim, our prognostications went awry several days later. What happened one evening was that the "mother of all tornados" skipped across Kansas, from a line west of Wichita, up to Manhattan, Kansas, then east to Topeka. The tornado was referred to as a "skipper." The skipping action made it difficult to pinpoint. It earlier had cut a devastating swath across the state with numerous injuries and deaths. The weather stations had gauged this tornado to be the largest one ever to be moving toward Topeka. I forgot to tell you what a tornado is. Well, it is a funnel of wind and air that moves rapidly across the ground at speeds up to 200-300 miles per hour, destroying everything in its path.

We lived in a house with a storm cellar. The landlady and her dog lived in the back of the house and were the closest to the storm cellar. Upon the tornado's approach, she quickly knocked on our back door and told us to get into the cellar with her and her dog. Jessica, being the good mother she was, wanted to take our cats with us—we had another cat. However, I told her that we did not have time to be chasing cats around the apartment to attempt to pick them up and carry them down to the storm cellar. In fact, the cats were under the bed, and I am certain there was no way in thunder that I could have retrieved them. So, Jessica and I ran out the front door and around to the back, when we both looked up and saw the massive funnel cloud wending its way toward our section of the city. Wow, it was something to behold Pilgrim!. For a second I stood transfixed watching the huge twister coming into sight from the southwest.

Jessica, quickly grabbed me, and into the cellar, we went. I quickly double bolted the doors from the inside, Jessica and I sat on one bench, holding one another, and our landlady sat across from us on another bench. If I remember correctly, her dog was by her side and surprisingly quiet. Were you with us that evening, Jessica and I would have had you sitting between us and would have covered your body and head with our arms, and held you tightly.

Gasp, Pilgrim, it was but a very short time before we began to hear the tornado's wind and rumbling—which sounded like the proverbial "100 freight trains." The landlady had her transistor radio (remember them?) so we were able to hear the local CBS television station narrative by Bill Kurtis—later to be a famous television journalist—as he told everyone to take cover. Jessica and I were holding one another when she smiled and whispered, "Hey, this is romantic!" Her comment added some unexpected levity. However, our attention quickly turned to the fact the tornado was coming closer; its crescendo and accompanying winds had an almost sur-realistic quality about them. Then suddenly, the tornado was gone! It was eerily quiet. Then the all clear sounded. After several minutes, I unbolted the storm doors, told Jessica and the landlady to stay where they were until I checked to see if there were downed power lines, branches, etc. I went outside. It was strangely silent, but there was no damage to the houses on either side of the block—other than some downed tree limbs. People be-gan slowly coming out of their houses to assess the damage and to check on their neighbors. When I started to turn around to get Jessica, our land-lady, and her dog, they were already standing behind me taking measure of what happened. Eventually, the landlady and her dog returned to their side of the house, and Jessica and I went into our apartment, which faced the street. Upon hearing us opening the door and coming into the apart-ment, our cats, Baby-Baby and Do-be slowly emerged from under the bed. They were not any worse for wear, but wanted to be picked up and held. In fact, Pilgrim, when Jessica and I went to bed, it was but a very short time before each of us had a cat curled up by our heads—as if to make sure we were not going anywhere. They did not move the entire night—nor did we. Because of the trauma of the tornado, Pilgrim, we would have had you in bed sleeping with us.

Of course, the tornado made the national news. Craig and Laura back in Southern California attempted to call us right after they heard about it and seen it on the evening television news from Los Angeles. They were unable to get through nor were Jessica's family or Anne in New York. The phone service from Topeka was down, so when we got through to all of them, and reassured everybody that we were not injured, they all remarked about seeing the tornado and its accompanying destruction (18 people killed and hundreds injured) on national television. Laura said that she and several of her children were at a mall in Orange County, California, at which time she heard about the tornado—close to 5:00 p.m. California time. Laura quickly drove home, contacted Craig who was working at his fire station. He told her that he had already seen the devastation on the fire station's television set, and attempted to contact her, but that no one was home.

The next day, I was able to take Jessica downtown to her job, after which I drove to the hospital and my classes. Nothing fortunately had happened to any of the buildings nor was anyone hurt. In fact, according to their ward staff, the students embraced the excitement of the tornado, but were kept in an interior classroom that had no windows, as to ensure their safety from flying glass or objects. I allowed the students to discuss with one another their feelings about the tornado. However, though not in eminent danger—because the tornado was on the other side of the city—discussing their feelings about the tornado served as a catharsis for the students. Then it was time to return to the classroom.

As the summer school session began winding down, I noticed the students seemed more subdued and reticent. There was no acting out, and the class periods were uneventful. I observed that Nina seemed more into her own feelings, but as usual, she contributed to all the discussions. I realized, my darling Pilgrim, that all of us were dealing with separation anxiety—including me. These students had become a part of me. I remember discussing with Jessica about my observations and feelings. She listened, made some comments, and rendered some suggestions as how best to deal with the impending goodbyes. Ironically, Jessica later would have the same feelings—but for a different reason.

Finally, the summer school ended. It was difficult to say goodbye to colleagues, the staff, but most of all the students. I believe that the interaction between the students and the teachers had enriched all of our lives. Indeed, I felt that I had become a more compassionate, less judgmental, and better person for having had the wonderful opportunity to teach these students. In turn, they taught me as one famous philosopher had said, that, "Life was not meant to be fair, but to be lived." These young men and women were attempting to live life, as they knew it.

They had not been dealt a good hand in life, but they did the best they could with the cards they were given. All of us teachers admired them for their courage. Kudos also had to be given to the wonderful staff of clinicians, nurses, and orderlies who supported these troubled children, and helped us in so many ways. We teachers were not allowed to show physical affection to the students—such as giving hugs—so we gave each student a perfunctory handshake. Nina and I were the last to shake hands and to say our goodbyes; I think that as we did so, we both became teary-eyed. Nina was almost crying when she turned to go to her ward. I had a lump in my throat. I do not like to see people in any manner of pain; I know very well what pain does to people, relationships, and the spirit. I just had to look at the youngsters that I taught that summer of 1966. They knew pain well.

The evening of the last day of summer school, some of the psychologists, psychiatrists, and social workers, and all the teachers—along with their spouses—had dinner at one of our colleagues' homes, in Lawrence, Kansas. Her husband was a professor at the University of Kansas. Pilgrim, it was a wonderful evening; the food and company were great, and the conversation stimulating. After dinner, we chatted about numerous things, during which time, the chief psychiatrist commented that the summer school program had been far more successful and challenging than initially expected. We all felt quite pleased, yet humble, because we had gained as much, if not more than our students. These young men and women had enriched all of our lives.

During the evening spent together with colleagues, their spouses, and hospital staff members—including the chief psychiatrist—a pleasant revelation was made by the above psychiatrist: he said that several students would be allowed to go to a college or university within commuting distance. Nina was one of the students who would be going to college. The psychiatrist did not tell us to what colleges the students would be going. I was, however, delighted that Nina would be able to continue her education. Pilgrim, Nina and her fellow students deserved the opportunity to begin their journey through life. I was proud to have been her teacher.

What I almost forgot to do Pilgrim was to keep the reader apprised of the fact that in 1966, you would have been walking, talking, of course into everything, chasing the cats, and enjoying being a gorgeous two-year old. If you had been with your mother, I would have sent her a camera with film so that she could have taken pictures of you; after which time, I would have asked her to send me the film to be developed. She would have gotten the originals and Jessica and I would have received duplicate copies. Had you been living with Willow, I might have had to go to court to ensure that I would have visitation privileges. However, there would have been no stopping me.

After having finished teaching summer school, Jessica and I began packing our furniture, clothes, and the two cats to move to Jessica's hometown. We planned to spend a brief time with her family before we got our own apartment. Jessica would return to working for the state, and the Boeing Aircraft Company in Wichita was preparing to offer me a job. Jessica and I decided to make plans eventually to buy our own house—and guess what, Pilgrim—we even discussed the possibility of starting our own family within several years. Unfortunately, however, Jessica and I were not ever to have a family together.

Jessica, the cats, and I left Topeka on a typical hot, humid summer day in 1966. As we drove down the Kansas Turnpike that day, Jessica and I realized we were beginning a new chapter in our lives. Pilgrim, Jessica and I believed we would in all likelihood live in Wichita—which was a nice middle-class Midwestern city. Jessica was understandably close to her family and wanted to be geographically close to them. Jessica's family was very kind to me and I had a special affinity with them. I felt as if I were a worthy member of her family. Jessica and I looked forward to living in Wichita where we believed we would begin another phase of our life.

Jessica, the cats, and I returned to her hometown. We stayed with her family, and then I began looking for a job. I applied at Boeing Aircraft in Wichita, and since I had previously worked for a large missile firm in California in the early 1960s, the Boeing Company took an interest in me. I had the experience that Boeing could use. However, I had to wait until Boeing did some initial investigations into my background before I would be notified as to whether or not I would be hired. Meantime, Jessica began looking for apartments. It appeared it would be but a short time before Jessica and I would be settled into our new life in Wichita.

Well, Pilgrim, something happened that was unexpected. As I was completing my master's degree, one of my professors suggested that I apply for a position as a college instructor in the field of history and/or political science, while deciding where and when I wanted to begin my Ph.D. During late 1965 and early 1966, I sent out a small number of resumes to colleges and universities throughout the country. I received only a few responses—none of which were encouraging. I surmised that I would not be offered a teaching position—let alone an interview. Therefore, Jessica and I decided to go ahead and pursue a new life in Wichita.

Unknown to Jessica and me, the Chairman of the History Department at the University of Alaska had received my resume, took an interest in it, phoned my former chairman, and upon talking with him decided to contact me. We had not left any forwarding phone number, but my chairman gave the department chairman at the University of Alaska Jessica's family number, which he obtained from student records. The professor phoned me from Fairbanks, Alaska. He had originally wanted meet me in Portland for an interview; he changed his mind, however, because it would have been a long flight for him to make from Fairbanks to Portland. The interview, therefore, was done by phone—which was an interesting undertaking Pilgrim.

Finally, a couple of days after the phone interview, the chairman from the University of Alaska called and offered me a teaching job at the Ketchikan Community College, Ketchikan, Alaska. The college was part of the University of Alaska system. Jessica, her parents and I spent a long time discussing whether or not I should accept the opportunity to teach in Alaska. It was a good distance from Wichita and Jessica's family.

Though I was initially excited about the possible offer, I wanted Jessica to make the final decision because a move to Alaska would have been one whereby we would have been away from her family. A trip home would normally have been by plane, and a rather long flight. Jessica's happiness was important, because this is the woman with whom I planned to spend the rest of my life. Jessica, however, said she wanted to go to Alaska. Ironically, the same day I accepted the Alaska offer, the Boeing Aircraft Company phoned offering me a position. I declined the offer after explaining what had earlier transpired, and thanked the personnel representative for having considered me. Well darling daughter, it is time to go, "north to Alaska." Jessica and I are taking you with us.

I love you so much,
Dad

NORTH TO ALASKA IN 1966

Pilgrim, Jessica and I packed for the move to Alaska. We sold the car to Jessica's father. Sadly, we had to leave the two cats with Jessica's family. Saying goodbye to Jessica's family was not easy. I knew it would be difficult for Jessica to say goodbye to her family. I found it difficult as well. I had become close to her family. The family had accepted me as one of its members. In a few days Jessica and I were to fly from Wichita to Denver, then Denver to Seattle, where we would stay overnight, then fly on to Ketchikan the following morning. I talked earlier by phone with the college director, Mr. John Tyler. We had an enjoyable conversation, and he and I would have a warm professional relationship.

The morning came when we had to leave Wichita for Ketchikan. Our goodbyes were difficult. We got on the plane, and since Jessica had the window seat, it was easy for her to wave to her family as the aircraft taxied away from the tarmac. Pilgrim, We were both subdued. Guess what, little one, other than having you and your mother on the flight to New York City in 1963, this was the first time I had actually taken someone on a plane with me—and it was Jessica. She and I began talking once the plane became airborne. We discussed what it would be like in Alaska. John Tyler told me that Ketchikan and southeastern Alaska had as much as 150 inches of rain a year. Mr. Tyler, however, further told me the scenery was beautiful in the region.

We arrived in Denver's Stapleton Airport, where we eventually boarded our connecting flight to Seattle. The flight was a two-hour flight, and so we were given lunch. Neither of us had been to the Northwest, so the flight time was spent looking out the window at the verdant scenery and mountains below us. We arrived in Seattle, where we stayed overnight, and then left for Ketchikan the next morning. The flight was full, and was scheduled to be approximately two hours in duration. We had breakfast on the plane. Jessica was sitting by the window, so she had to see the beauty of British Columbia and southeastern Alaska.

We landed at Annette Island across the sound from Ketchikan. Annette Island was where the large jets landed. The weather was overcast and cool as opposed to the day before when we left sunny and humid Wichita. Upon debarking from the aircraft, we noticed several converted World War II Navy PBY seaplanes. They would be our source of transportation to Ketchikan. Along with several other people who had deplaned from the flight from Seattle, Jessica and I got into the PBY and off we flew to Ketchikan.

Pilgrim, it was not long before we guessed why we were flying in a seaplane. Guess what, we were going to land on water, About fifteen minutes later, we landed and taxied over to the Ketchikan seaplane terminal. John Tyler and his wife Betty met us. They warmly greeted us, and after exchanging pleasantries, they took us over to a modern apartment building known as the Tongass Towers, where we were able to rent a large furnished apartment. As to be expected, Jessica and I underwent a culture shock. Ketchikan had a population of about 10,000 people, including a Tlingit Indian community. The primary industries were fishing, logging, a paper mill, and tourism. Ketchikan had the basic amenities, such as a hospital, library, post office, public school system, bus company, a local radio station, and of course, the community college. There were also some decent restaurants. There was even a movie theater, and a foreign film festival held bi-weekly at the high school.

Gosh Pilgrim, I am thinking what it might have been like if Jessica and I brought you up to live in Ketchikan. You would have been able to see Bald Eagles, bears, whales—including killer whales—porpoises and salmon. Southeastern Alaska was an almost indescribably beautiful area—remote, but awe-inspiring.

The people of Ketchikan were wonderful people. They were warm, friendly, and down-to-earth. They enjoyed having a great time, which they did at the local bars. Unfortunately, Ketchikan had a rather high rate of alcoholism. It took a special type of person to live in Ketchikan and southeastern Alaska. People had to be independent, self-sufficient, somewhat of an outdoorsman, and be able to make their own lives. They also had to be able to adapt to the extreme climate. Most important was the ability to insulate oneself against isolation, and the harsh weather—otherwise one could have problems with depression and alcoholism. Did I tell you that Alaska was the largest state of the fifty states? Yet, back in the 1960s, it had only about 220,000 people. Its population now (2005) is about 640,000 people. Regarding the weather extremes, the first year that we were in Ketchikan, it rained 140 inches, and during the month of July 1967, thirty inches rain accumulated. During the summer of 1967, it even rained when the sun was shining!

Jessica and I settled into our apartment, and the first thing we did after moving in was to order telephone service so we could make phone calls to the "lower forty-eight" as the continental United States was called. Because Alaska was actually separated from the American continent by Canada, it made those living in Alaska feel isolated from what was going on in the continental states. Yet, sometimes it was to our advantage to be alone.

A couple of days after Jessica and I moved in to our apartment, I began teaching my college classes. The classes were rather small, and I taught both day and night sessions. The students were interesting and friendly. They lacked the pretension of students on the mainland in that they were not into drugs, demonstrating against whatever, or overwhelmed by materialism. They were well grounded in their value system, and were determined to get a good education. Most of the students upon completing one or two years at the community college level would either go north to Fairbanks, where the main campus of the University of Alaska was, or to colleges or universities in the continental United States. The students tended to be bright and ranged in age from seventeen to mid forties.

By taking you ethereally with me, I strengthened our bond that would have existed, had you lived. Many mothers who abort their babies for whatever reason—are often driven to reclaim them as part of the healing process. Fathers have the same right and inclination. I hope the reader acquires an understanding that parents of aborted babies may initially believe once an aborted baby dies, that the memory of it dies as well. Such is not the case—nor will it ever be—regarding you. An abortion is a sin for many reasons, but one apparent reason is that an abortion is the willful destruction of what God has made and deigned to be His will. I have no idea what your mother is dealing with as far as acknowledging you; however, I cannot reject you in any way. Therefore, taking you with me and recognizing what would have been a seminal work by our Heavenly Father—that being you—is a most delightful undertaking. I am and will always be blessed that I was your father. If I am maudlin, darling Pilgrim, please accept this from an individual who had a piece of him die when you died.

Back to something more pleasant. One Sunday, Pilgrim, along with about twenty other people, including children, Jessica and I took a cruise around the Island of Ketchikan, and through the fiord-like waters of Dixon Inlet and the back of the Tongass National Forest. You would have enjoyed this excursion. We were blessed to see large Humpback Whales sounding, a small pod of Killer Whales, many eagles sitting on tree limbs staring at us, and doll sheep climbing the steep sides of the fiord as we went through it. I would be holding you so you could see God's handiwork. It would have been wonderful to see your expression as you gazed at everything I just described. Gosh, even after almost forty years, I cannot forget the pristine wilderness of Alaska. I am certain you as well would not have ever forgotten the beauty of southeastern Alaska. While on our cruise, we had the opportunity to see one of the giant Alaska State Ferries sailing up the inlet. The vessel was impressive to watch.

Guess what, Pilgrim, do you remember Nina from when I taught summer school in Topeka at the state hospital? Well, Jessica and I received a very sweet note from her. She had enrolled at the University of Kansas, and was enjoying her classes. Nina and several other students commuted to Lawrence, Kansas where the university is located. I was very proud of Nina, and she seemed well grounded in her determination to do well with her life. Pilgrim, I hope Nina is alive, well, and that she has had a wonderful life.

Pilgrim, might I wax a bit philosophically? After 1963, I found that as part of what would be a life-long healing process, the Lord put me in positions where I served other people—particularly young people. I had been so extraordinarily selfish with my life, that by the time I met Willow, this negative behavior seemed to be a comfortable facet of my being. I unfortunately, would still occasionally fall prey to this inclination. However, I have worked hard to minimize such behavior. I believe God decided after you died that I would be successful and happy only when I would be serving others. To this day (2005), what I have achieved, I owe to others and to the Lord. Whatever talents I have, my darling daughter, have been given to me by our Heavenly Father. I cannot claim them for myself. Therefore, I have been so blessed by having to give to others—without thought of others giving to me.

However, being in Alaska alone was not easy for Jessica and me. We quickly came to the realization that we had no familial support close by as we had in Kansas. The two of us had to learn that we were several thousand miles away from physical or emotional contacts with families or friends. We could no longer take a timely respite from one another or our problems by driving down the Kansas turnpike to spend time with Jessica's family. Though we had been married going on two years, our earlier life in Kansas was markedly different than the one we now embraced in Alaska. No longer did we have the cultural or intellectual amenities that we had in Topeka. Besides, we had no car.

The reason that we had no automobile in Ketchikan was that the town was closely compact, thus people could practically walk everywhere they needed to go. Ketchikan even had a bus system that was efficient. Pilgrim. Jessica and I were now required to play "adults." This meant Jessica and I had to learn to live in one another's space a lot of the time. Since I was making a good salary, Jessica decided not to work. However, within time, Jessica became bored, which later translated into resentment and depression. I was also to blame for her unhappiness, because I was busy with my teaching and course preparations, plus I was teaching both day and evening classes. Sadly, I did not leave enough time to be with Jessica. Pilgrim, that was not intentional; it insidiously happened.

Pilgrim, Jessica and I were not selfish or self-centered as I and Willow had been. We were not mean-spirited, but we simply had not spent enough time growing with the marriage. The two of us had always had been there for the other. We had been able to provide the means to make one another happy. For some reason, we were unable to do this in Alaska. Pilgrim, Jessica and I truly loved one another. We just did not have the skills to adjust to the changing circumstances of life.

We began verbally and psychologically sniping at one another over the next several months. Jessica and I had the weekends to ourselves, and should have spent the time emotionally recharging our batteries; we, however, began closing down with one another. Pilgrim, tragically, Jessica and I fell into somewhat of an emotional coma, in that we seemingly ignored one another's insecurities and issues. We forgot to listen to each other. I should have been a subject matter expert on this type of behavior, because this is what took place between your mother and me several years earlier. I am not certain as to why this unfortunate and bizarre behavior took place between Jessica and me. Nevertheless, I was no less at fault than Jessica in the implementation of this psychologically tiresome behavior. Ketchikan did not have a mental health facility; therefore, we would have to fly to Seattle to get counseling.

A colleague of mine had spent a week with her husband in Seattle getting some much needed marital therapy on what might be referred to as an emersion basis, whereby, the couple spent several intense sessions during the week with a therapist and social worker. I suggested to Jessica that we take off and to Seattle, and spend the week getting counseling. Jessica responded by saying she did not want to spend the money. It would be but a few months before the marriage, metaphorically, exploded. Jessica and I would not be able to be put it back together again. It does no good to heap blame on anyone. The two of us were equally at fault. We both knew we had nowhere to go but down.

I did make a final suggestion that we fly down to her folks' for Christmas. Jessica again said no. From December 1966 to the middle of the summer of 1967, Jessica and I implemented a type of "cold war" with one another. However, during the time our marriage was falling below the proverbial radar screen, we found two kittens that became a source of great joy, and our surrogate children. The female's name was "Ollie" and the male was called "Patrice." They accepted us for our countless quirks, and they gave us undivided love. The two kittens did their jobs well. Pilgrim, they reduced, somewhat, our mutual despair and depression. Jessica and I had to stop being selfish and allow Patrice and Ollie to become our objects of affection. Ironically, though, Jessica and I could, and would, often be affectionate and intimate with one another.

The spring of 1967 was your third birthday darling daughter. I want to wish you a Happy Birthday, Pilgrim. You, no doubt, would have been growing like a weed; and you would have by now a wonderful personality and love of life. I must, however, tell you that Jessica's and my marriage had run its course; there was nothing any longer to retrieve or hold on to. Jessica and I were simply in a non-verbal manner getting ready to disengage from what, by 1967, was an untenable situation. No longer were the two of us spending much time talking with each other. It was a pathetic way for a couple to live. The divorce was imminent. I was working for the forest service for the summer season, when Jessica said that she was going home to Kansas for a vacation with her family, and that I should fly down a couple of weeks later. By the time Jessica had told me of her plans to go to Kansas, the two of us had no feelings or emotional assets left regarding whether our marriage was worth saving. Jessica and I were unable to transcend the emotional trauma of our marriage coming apart. Reflecting on that period of our marriage, the two of us only wanted relief from the pain and the grief. I was hoping that Jessica would tell me that she was going to get a divorce. However, she did nothing.

I would not have challenged Jessica in any way, if she wanted a divorce. However, Jessica said nothing about a divorce. Even up until the time Jessica left to go back to her folk's, we alternated between periods of silence or saying very little to one another. When I saw Jessica off at the dock, we gave each other a perfunctory kiss. After Jessica left, Pilgrim, I just walked back to the apartment feeling washed out. I spent the next week doing nothing but working, coming home, taking care of Ollie and Patrice, and staring into space. Neither Jessica nor I phoned one another the first week, though she sent a card stating that she looked forward meeting me at the Wichita Airport in a week or so. I made no response. . There was nothing left to salvage. It would have been foolish to continue the pain. I decided it was time to get a divorce. No recriminations were necessary. Jessica and I loved one another, but we apparently no longer liked each other. This was a tragic commentary, Pilgrim, for a marriage, that two years earlier, had been very promising.

Pilgrim darling, I love you so very much,
Dad

THE DIVORCE AND A NEW TRAIL OF TEARS

I went to see a lawyer in Ketchikan who discussed with me the rami-fications of a divorce. They were not pretty. I weighed them carefully. I de-cided to go ahead with the divorce. The lawyer wrote to Jessica that I was filing for a divorce on the grounds of irreconcilable differences. The lawyer told Jessica that if she wanted to contest my actions, she would be required to return to Ketchikan. Jessica contacted the lawyer that she decided not to return to Ketchikan. The lawyer told Jessica that he would honor any requests she made regarding settlement of property, bank accounts, etc, and that I was required by Alaska law to split assets on an equal basis.

Pilgrim, no divorce is neat—even when there are no children involved. What divorce so well illustrates is the fallibility of human beings in inter-personal relationships. Often, so many things get in the way of a successful marriage, and no matter how well intentioned a man and a woman might be, unless they work together for the good of the marriage, it invariably fails. Our marriage was such an example. Years later, darling Pilgrim, I was to find out why I did not epitomize the tenets of a good marriage partner. My problems began with my troubled early childhood.

I sent Jessica half of the money in our savings and checking accounts, along with her clothes, and whatever incidentals she wanted. Jessica wanted Patrice, so I got an animal carrier; sadly put him in it; and sent everything, including Patrice, by air to Jessica. She received all that she asked for. Pilgrim, our marriage was now formally over. There was no joy in being divorced—let alone separated—from Jessica. She was a great person and, in many ways, had been a wonderful influence upon my life. She had been very much a part of me. No matter what problems we eventually encoun-tered, Jessica and I had a rather lengthy period that we had enjoyed being married to each other—and that was when we lived back in Kansas. I loved Jessica's family, and I owed so very much to them. Her family had provided stability and love.

I felt an overwhelming sense of guilt during and after the divorce. Yet, I was a better person for having been married to Jessica and having been a part of her family. All I now had, Pilgrim, were you and Ollie. You and Ollie were my constant company. I was several thousand miles away from Laura, Craig, and my sister. I kept in contact with all of them and they lovingly commiserated with me. I even phoned my former in-laws and thanked them for having allowed me to be part of their family.

I wanted to get away from the trauma of the impending divorce. I had never been to the Canadian national parks, so the summer of 1967 was an ideal time to go. I took a trip to Jasper and Banff national parks in Canada. Though I had a wonderful time seeing the wonderful flora and fauna of the parks, I felt isolated. Jessica and I had done so many things together and I wished she could still have been with me. It did not take long at all before I realized the same emotions dealing with an abortion also existed with a divorce. Grief, anger, denial, love, and rejection were integral to both a divorce and an abortion. As opposed to what had taken place between Willow and me, Jessica and I did love one another and had respected one another. Jessica and I shared many wonderful times, emotions, interests, and plans. She and I, for a long time, had complemented each other in many ways. However, toward the end of our marriage, we spent too much time seeing the shortcomings in one another, rather than in ourselves.

Pilgrim, the remainder of 1967 was difficult because of now being alone in Alaska and the trauma of the divorce. I only had to look around the house and I saw countless reminders of Jessica. I sensed her everywhere. Friends asked about her. However, when they did, they were very compassionate and attempted to be unobtrusive in their questions. It was not out of the ordinary for me to reach out for Jessica while I was sleeping—expecting to find her next to me. I missed every aspect of her. I thought about her constantly. Meanwhile, life continued in Ketchikan—though with great effort. I would dutifully teach my classes, just to be happy to have contact with other people. Pilgrim, my other roommate, Ollie the cat, was not only my roommate, but she was my soul mate as well. I always enjoyed holding her and talking to her. She was a wonderful companion.

Pilgrim, quite unexpectedly, I began thinking about your mother. As opposed to the previous emotions regarding Willow, this new round of thoughts about her was almost devoid of the broad spectrum of feelings that many months before had caused great pain. What took place was a curiosity that one might have about someone who they had known in the past. I became inquisitive as to what was going on in Willow's life. This, however, did not mean that I had forgotten that you were aborted nor did it mean that I had forgotten or forgiven your mother and her parents for their part in your death. Nevertheless, I wanted to hear Willow's voice, possibly because I was feeling vulnerable, but more likely, because I was curious to see what was going on in her life.

I was not anxious nor did I worry about not being civil. If upon hearing my voice, Willow would have slammed the phone down or hurled expletives at me, I would simply have hung up. It was nearly five years, Pilgrim, since I had last spoken with your mother I certainly did not expect any immediate conciliatory conversation or behavior—so I felt that I had nothing to lose by phoning Willow. This time, the only cost of making a phone call would be financial. Willow and I eventually talked one Sunday afternoon in early 1968—which would have been your fourth birthday. Earlier, I had called the local operator in Southern California, and asked if there was a phone number listed under Willow's name. There was a published number, so I phoned her. When she answered, I simply said hello. She recognized my voice and said hello in return. As I expected, your mother seemed surprised, guarded, and awkward with her responses. Her voice sounded harsh—which did not surprise me. Though having caught Willow unawares, it was apparent that she was curious as to why I phoned and what I was doing, I sensed your mother knew that I was no threat to her, nor did I think her to be a source of intimidation to me. Neither of us alluded to the abortion. We tactfully skirted the issue. The tone of Willow's voice was such that I was able to perceive that she was still in denial about everything—including me. Though Willow's and my conversation was brief and bland, when I got off the phone, I felt a great weight had been lifted off my shoulders. No longer did I feel humiliated. Willow and her parents were simply people who had been a part of a very unhappy and tragic period of my life. Yet, I still felt the pain, grief, loss, and anger regarding your death Pilgrim. However, these emotions were not as debilitating in 1968 as they had been in 1963.

A wonderful thing that did happen as the result of that phone call to Willow in 1968, was that I became more determined to acknowledge your right to having been born, darling Pilgrim. I validated your life, your death, and your spirit—all as my daughter. Pilgrim, I could not bring you back to life; however, I could and have brought your spirit into my life for four decades. I love you so much, and thank our Heavenly Father for putting you in your mother's womb. No matter the fact you were briefly in Willow's body, your spirit has transcended the evil and bitterness that destroyed you. No one could deny the Lord's love for you little girl—or my love for you.

Let me return to Ketchikan. The divorce was difficult to deal with—which is the story of most divorces. Seldom is there a real winner. There may be an ostensible legal winner; however, everyone in a divorce loses. Jessica and I had no children. Therefore, there were no issues dealing with custody or child support—two acrimonious points of discussion. There was, however, still the ambience of Jessica present in the house—and there would be for some time. The divorce had taken place but a short time, when I underwent a depression. No doubt, its causes were many. People remarked that I looked thin, depressed, and in a world of my own. I still assumed my life and continued teaching—though somewhat robotically. I final went to a local physician who diagnosed that I was depressed, and made an appointment for me to see a psychiatrist in Seattle. A week later, I flew down to Seattle, and a couple of days later, I was able to see him. We had a long discussion. He suggested that I take a hiatus from teaching as a means of milieu therapy.

Pilgrim, the doctor's rationale was that I had no support structure to mitigate the loneliness of an isolated area such as Ketchikan, and the related feelings of the divorce. The psychiatrist said that as long as I was where I had no means for healthy emotional and cultural distractions, I would likely become depressed. I had nowhere to go as far as having a job or future waiting for me. Nevertheless, I felt that being better educated and more employable than when I had left California five years before, I was not as uncertain about the future as I previously had been. There was the possibility that I would be criticized for not "sticking" it out" as far as remaining in Ketchikan. Such criticism was understandable and no doubt justified—though I gave Mr. Tyler enough notice to be able to get a re-placement. In the 1960s, people were expected to stand tall, be brave, and weather any and all life's storms. Unfortunately, I had not quite reached that capacity. That capability, however, would eventually emerge.

I left Alaska with you and Ollie in January 1968 and flew to New York to spend some time with Anne and her family. I left Ollie with Anne, because Anne had a woman friend who wanted a cat because hers had died. I was in tears when I held Ollie for the last time and felt her face against mine. I had been so blessed to have her as part of my life for over a year.

She had really been a source of comfort when I was divorced. However, not knowing my future, I decided that Ollie needed a new home, and this woman would give it to her. Even now, Pilgrim, I vividly remember Ollie—and of course, Patrice.

I returned to Seattle to "find" my life and work. The intent was not to stay in Seattle very long, but to eventually go to graduate school once more—this time to do a Ph.D. in history. I chose to live in Seattle because of its location and its beauty. Another factor that influenced the decision to live in the Northwest was because of the cultural diversity. For once, I could be laid back as far as spending time to, "find myself," Pilgrim. I realized, however, that with just a master's degree, I might not have an easy time finding employment. I was not discouraged, even when it took a long time for me to find employment. I did not apply for unemployment insurance, simply because I did not need it, and others were in need of it more than I was. As opposed to when I had left California five years before, I was a bit more secure than in 1963. I was neither naïve nor stupid—maybe a bit quixotic. Though having been a slacker as far as my spirituality and church going, I still believed that Jesus had assumed my sins by His death on the cross. I knew, however, that I would have to answer for them. I realized I would never be a perfect Christian or free of sin and pride. Actually, I was probably less inclined to suffer hubris, as opposed to still dealing with every day sin. Yet, I believed that the Lord was watching over me and had a purpose for me, Pilgrim. You were with me though, and I sensed the two of us could weather any problem.

Looking for work was not easy, because teaching positions were not plentiful during the middle of the year. Guess what, darling daughter, I was hired as a substitute high school teacher. I was called practically every day of the remaining school year to replace people who were ill, pregnant, or had other reasons for being out. I substituted in all areas of the educational spectrum, and actually had times in which I actually taught an assignment—as opposed to baby-sitting students.

Pilgrim, as I was wresting control of my psyche and emotions over the five-year period since your having been aborted, I began to slowly believe that in spite of traumatic and sad events, such as Jessica's and my divorce, I was able to exist. Do you know, I believe that I began turning my life slowly around because you became the impetus for my wanting to be successful. The Lord had put you front and center into my thought process, and, as Ollie, the cat, had been, you became my soul mate and co-pilot.

The city of Seattle, by its beauty and diversity, caught my attention and interest. The surrounding water, distant mountains, verdant forests, and an exciting way of life in the city, peaked my interest. There were so many things to do in Seattle, and what better person to do these many activities than with you.

We could have hung out in so many neat places, and done countless things together. Darling daughter, we could have ridden the ferries, gone to the Space Needle and the zoo, dug for clams, etc. Well, since I was once again without a car, we would have used public transportation or walked to some of these places were they close by. We could have gone to the coffee shops on 4th Avenue for a bite to eat and to observe the people coming into these shops. Pilgrim, it also would have been fun to spend some time at the Public Library.

I will give you some idea where I lived while in Seattle. I lived on top of the hill on Madison Avenue going toward the University of Washington. I rented an upstairs room in an old, large house from an elderly brother and sister. They were genuinely wonderful human beings. I liked them very much. Darling Pilgrim, once again I was being blessed by the fact that amazing people were being placed in my life. This further reinforced my belief in a loving Heavenly Father who places people into one another's lives to help them become better, giving, happier, more loving, productive human beings. I believed this couple was put into my life to assist me in accomplishing the above. We are all put on this earth to serve our fellow men and women and our Lord. Sadly, as most human beings, especially in my early adulthood, I did a pathetic job of serving my neighbors and strangers. The post-1963 events and years finally brought me out of my selfish ways, and made me realize that I was no better than, "the least of those" who I served. That was a mantra that I have taken with me throughout the remainder of my life.

Pilgrim, it was apparent that the Lord had His hand on what was going on in my life. The tragedy and ignominy of 1963 were becoming passing memories etched in muted colors on a tapestry that was almost indiscernible within the confines of my everyday life. No longer would I be able to blame others for how I lived my life. I decided that I would be the master of my own destiny.

The 1960s were anything but a glorious decade. Society was still being driven by materialism and false promises of uniting the diverse racial, ethnic, and economic groups that dotted the fabric of America. Sadly, Pilgrim, we were becoming a nation that criticized the misfortune of others, while loudly trumpeting our sense of charity. Instead of following the biblical axiom of, "the right hand not knowing what the left hand was doing," Americans made charity a public pronouncement as opposed to being unpretentious. Even education in the 1960s was no longer valued as a means to truly educate, enlighten and pique the curiosity of students, or to enhance their skills in areas in which to serve their fellow human beings. It instead became the platform for mediocrity and political correctness. Classes were to be taught that offended no one, but cheated everyone as far as the quality and purpose of them. A few years later, as I was pursuing my Ph.D., a professor told us doctoral students that we had no business in graduate school if we could not be true to the discipline of history, and to the teaching of it. There were no better words spoken.

Meanwhile, Pilgrim, your father was learning in Seattle to do "more with less," to use the storied military axiom. I barely had enough financial and emotional resources to keep me going. However, having said that, I acquired friends and numerous acquaintances. Therefore, I was a wealthy man. There was no time to indulge in self-pity. I was too busy being caught up with the experiences associated with living on a daily basis. Yet, I enjoyed myself immensely, darling daughter. I would go to bookstores to peruse books and read newspapers, because I had little money to buy them. I spent hours in bookstores having a wonderful time. Instead of taking a bus or trolley bus, I usually walked almost everywhere I went. I went to museums and art galleries, and brought small, hopefully unobtrusive bits of food in with me, so I would not have to buy food at the facility. Shame on me!

Austerity was the name of the game. I even had a small heating element in my apartment, whereupon I heated cans of food as I needed them. I also often bought day-old sandwiches at grocery stores. Though I was apparently poor as a church mouse, I was rich in so many other ways. Maybe what I did was to cancel out those things that would or should have bothered me. Actually, Pilgrim, what I believe happened was that the Lord instructed my guardian angels to keep close tabs on me, and guide me. Figuratively speaking, these angels earned their pay doing that.

Darling Pilgrim, though I was an individual of little means, I was markedly blessed in 1968. I am certain that no matter what my state of being was, you loved me as unabashedly as I loved you—now and forever. I know you love Willow as you do me, and that makes me happy, simply because she was, and will always be, your mother. One thing, darling daughter, a child's love for his or her parents is total and unassuming—regardless how the parents or parent treat their offspring. Once again, no matter what our feelings are toward each other, Willow and I are forever linked with you by your complete love for us. Love transcends death, Pilgrim, and I know that our love for one another has overcome the veil of death and will always live—as will our spirits. What happened to you in 1963 forever changed me in so many ways. For one thing, the terrible events of that summer served to make me able to cry. I have cried for you many times and for your mother as well. Another spin-off from the horror of you being aborted was that I did not hesitate to show anger as to what happened to you. I have sometimes even felt abject rage for the cruelty of those responsible for your death—and I know that it was all right to do that—in fact, I believe that anger was warranted.

Well, it is time to move on to something that will be the start of a new and wonderful phase of my life. I believe my next letter will make you smile.

I love you so much,
Dad

THE JOIE DE VIVRE 1968

Pilgrim, in the spring of 1968, while living in Seattle, I met the woman who would become the mother of your younger sibling! Our first contact was far different than those that I had with your mother and Jessica. I met "Carol" at a hotel lounge where a friend of mine and I had stopped for a small snack.. We happened to sit next to her and a woman friend of hers. We engaged the women in conversation, and, of course, immediately introduced ourselves to one another. Carol was a very pretty, mature, and a very nice person. And, guess what, she was a truly interesting person.

As opposed to the antecedent relationships with Willow and Jessica, Carol and I were noticeably restrained when we first met. I actually was relatively low-key, and seemed to be without appreciable social skills. For example, when Carol went to light her cigarette, instead of offering to light it for her and then gazing into her eyes as I lit it, I just sat across from her with my Alfred E. Newman look of "what me worry," appearing stupid, while she lit her own cigarette. In the 1960s, smoking was in vogue. I think that Carol just glared at me. My actions, or lack thereof, should have been a portent of what I was truly about. Pilgrim, having divulged the above, I found that I felt comfortable with Carol—even though she had already drawn a rather condescending opinion of me. I think Carol was amused that I did not do well attempting to be a "stuff shirt." However, it was in the not too distant future that I found out that Carol had a great deal of confidence in herself. She had great people skills, because she was a registered nurse, and did a decent job of determining what people were all about. Carol initially, however, saw few redeeming qualities in me. She had dated far more mature and successful men, and would have made any mature man a wonderful wife.

Possibly, as the result of attempting to go slow with Carol—simply because she was not encouraging me—I maintained my own lifestyle. What this meant was that on weekends, I would walk downtown and hang out at the bookstore or coffee shops, or see a movie, do cultural activities, jog around the reservoir, and just enjoy my own company. I had no choice but to do what I just mentioned, because Carol was aloof.

I even asked myself, Pilgrim, why I was bothering to drive on with my unrequited acquaintance with Carol. As the result of my previous failures, I thought what I would do was to simply go on for my Ph.D., immerse myself in it, and then upon graduating, look for both a teaching job and a relationship—all in that order.

Yet, Pilgrim, Carol did not completely discourage me. She fed me bits and pieces of hope. I got the impression that her other male friends were probably more emotionally, socially, and possibly physically attractive than I was. Thus, better the reason for me just to plan to return to graduate school and, at best, have "non-entangling alliances." However, what began taking place was that Carol was willing to allow me into her life on a gradual basis. She and I eventually established somewhat of a comfort level regarding our relationship. We found that we could talk comfortably about our families and our pasts. I told Carole about my previous marriage and about you, Willow, and the subsequent abortion. Being a nurse, Carol understood the likely abortion procedure you endured. She comprehended my emotions and was sympathetic as to what I had gone through. I appreciated Carol not being judgmental; in actuality, she was supportive of my feelings.

While I was dating Carol during the spring of 1968, I had the opportunity to apply back to the US Department of Agriculture's Regional Office in Ketchikan for a summer position with the Forest Service as a Visitor Information Specialist (VIS). This was a new position whereby the two people selected for the position would do such things as answer questions about the Tongass National Forest, the flora and fauna of Southeastern Alaska, the Indian culture and the Tlingit Totem Park in Ketchikan. The VIS personnel were also to describe the demographics of Southeastern Alaska, and to show a slide presentation on the national forest and surrounding area. We were of course to answer incidental questions, and be of whatever assistance possible to the tourists.

I had been aware of the tentative VIS positions the previous summer when I was doing trail work for the Forest Service. Pilgrim, something went right the summer of 1967 when I had received a high evaluation for my summer work on the trail. The Regional Director of the Tongass National Forest invited me to apply for one of the two future VIS positions. I wrote him from Seattle applying for one of the positions. I received a letter from the director a week later offering me one of the two VIS slots.

Pilgrim, I was elated to receive an offer; if I forgot to thank the Lord then, I certainly do now. I went to the regional Forest Service Office in Seattle to do the required paperwork, get a physical, then to go to a local tailor shop to have my summer uniforms fitted. I did the above, and was told to report to Ketchikan around the last week of May 1968. I was given a plane ticket to fly back to Ketchikan.

Do you remember that when Jessica and I had begun living in Ketchikan in the fall of 1966, that we had in a fanciful manner taken you on the cruise around Ketchikan Island? Well, now you are four years old, and I am certain you would really enjoy Ketchikan, and meeting the thousands of tourists. Once again, darling daughter, you and I are going to share Ketchikan. Having discussed my anticipation of the two of us back in Ketchikan for the summer of 1968, I will return once more to my relationship with Carol.

The spring of 1968 was coming to a close, and apparently my ties with Carol as well. It seemed the two of us were unable to make up our minds as to how we felt about one another. We vacillated between being in love and becoming frustrated with each other. Pilgrim, your father was not certain as to whether or not he could make a commitment, and, in turn, Carol thought I might not really care for her. I loved Carol, but my heretofore failures with your mother and Jessica served as a portent of what the future might be like. Carol took matters into her own hands by telling me to get out of her life. She obviously made the right move. I thought I would never hear from her or ever see her again. Frankly, I resigned myself to being by myself once again—this time for a very long duration.

Well, little one, the school year was over as was the job as a substitute teacher—which in actuality had been a wonderful experience. I subsequently prepared to leave Seattle for Ketchikan. I packed two small suitcases along with my carryall for my VIS uniform and hat. My landlord and his sister allowed me to leave my small box of books and the remaining few clothes I had in the attic until I returned from Ketchikan after the end of the summer. A friend in Ketchikan, with whom I had maintained contact while in Seattle, had already gotten a post office mailbox for me, so I had an address where I could be reached.

On the last Sunday of May 1968, I said goodbye to my landlord and his sister, and took a taxi to the Seattle-Tacoma Airport. The flight to Ketchikan was not scheduled to leave for a couple of hours, so I bought a newspaper to read. While reading the paper, I thought it be only proper to phone Carol and say goodbye to her. As suddenly as I thought the above, I quickly quelled that impulse. Pilgrim, I daresay the reader knows why. However, I was sorry that Carol apparently no longer wanted me in her life. I believed I would never see her again—which was sad to think about.

It was finally time to board the flight to Ketchikan. Well, once again, Pilgrim, you and I were back on a flight to Ketchikan. The flight was an early evening one. It was light both when we took off and when we landed in Ketchikan. We landed in Ketchikan about two hours later. Pilgrim, I guess that you knew that I was looking forward to returning to Ketchikan—even if it was only for the summer. I still had friends in Ketchikan, and my hiatus from Alaska had been a beneficial one. I had learned a great deal about myself: I was not perfect, but I was a decent caring person who tried not to hurt people. I was greatly aware that the Lord's grace was sufficient for me. I had nothing to be ashamed of as far as returning to Ketchikan.

Upon returning to Ketchikan, I was met by some friends of mine. They were Jim and Cora Allison and their twelve-year-old son Jimmy. Jack was a high school teacher; Cora was a nutritionist for the state; and Jimmy was in 7th grade. You might have remembered them. They invited me to stay with them for a few days.

On the following day, which was Monday, I reported to the Forest Service Office in Ketchikan, at which time I was warmly greeted by my former supervisor, who introduced me to the office staff, and to my VIS colleague, a local school teacher by the name of Nancy. She and I were decked out in our uniforms and hats, and could have been poster children for a Forest Service ad. We exchanged pleasantries, then our supervisor, a field ranger, and Nancy and I walked over to the Visitor Information Trailer—which was brand new. It was a wide-bodied trailer, replete with a welcoming booth and material, about a number of chairs, a slide projector and slide program with sound narrative. The slide program talked about Southeastern Alaska and was very informative. We also had pamphlets and other handouts. Pilgrim, I know you would have enjoyed the slide presentation and talking to the tourists. In turn, darling daughter, the tourists would have been pleased to talk with you.

The trailer was open seven days a week, and Nancy and I worked in shifts or quite often together. Nancy was from Ketchikan, but she had gone to college at the University of Washington, and upon graduation returned to Ketchikan to teach. The supervisor suggested she be the lead VIS because she knew the area so well and, thus, would be able to teach me a great deal more about the regional flora and fauna than I heretofore had known. She was a great lead VIS, and thanks to her, I became a competent Visitor Information Specialist.

Pilgrim, it was only a few days before the start of the tourist season, and Nancy and I were excited about meeting the countless tourists. The summer was a wonderful one with ideal weather and temperatures. By the beginning of the tourist season, I had moved into an old hotel in Ketchikan, whereupon the owner, having previously known me, offered me a free room—especially when he found out I was planning to go back to graduate school in the fall for my Ph.D. He told me to save my money and use it for school. I thanked him for his kindness—such a nice man. Pilgrim, you would have enjoyed the summer of 1968. I would have taken you on the huge Alaskan State Ferry, the *Matanuska* from Prince Rupert, British Columbia back up to Ketchikan, which was about a six-hour trip. We could have flown down on one of the commercial commuter seaplanes, such as the PBY down to Prince Rupert; we then would take the ferry back to Ketchikan. Pilgrim, you could have seen how crowded the ferry is with tourists and their automobiles, because it goes all the way up to Haines, Alaska where it connects with the Alaskan Highway to Anchorage and Fairbanks.

Many old friends came by to renew friendships, including my former supervisor, John Tyler. It was great to see him, and the two of us spent some time at a local café where we had coffee. I apologized for letting him down; he told me, however, that he understood what I had gone through, and that taking time off from full time teaching had been the best thing for me. Some former students, and fellow faculty members stopped by the trailer to say hello. Mr. Tyler and his family came down several times to the trailer.

The trailer had been open a few days, and Nancy and I were quite busy meeting the tourists. I took a lunch break one afternoon, walked over to the post office to check my postal box, and upon pulling out the mail, lo and behold, Pilgrim, there was a letter from Carol! I was surprised, if for no other reason I had thought that Carol wanted nothing more to do with me. For a minute, I was apprehensive about opening the envelope because

I thought it would be an angry letter. Well, I finally opened it, began reading, and was almost floored by what was an incredulous statement.

Carol said that she missed me and loved me. Darling Pilgrim, what a surprise! I was astonished, to say the least. The last time a woman had spontaneously and unexpectedly told me that she loved me was in 1963. The occasion was a college dance, to which I had taken Willow. I believe the dance was at the Twentieth Century Plaza Hotel in Los Angeles. Willow looked gorgeous that evening, and, as I recollect, it was during the evening, as the two of us were dancing, that she looked at me and said, "I don't think that there is a woman that could be any happier than I am tonight." Willow's comments moved me to tears then. Even now, I have a feeling of sadness as I recall that occasion. By the way, that would be the last time Willow either said or implied that she loved me.

Well, I read Carol's letter often and with deliberation. Carol told me, Pilgrim, that she had gotten my address from my landlord. She said she knew she loved me, but initially had been reluctant to tell me her feelings. Carol went on to say that she wanted to see me. I wanted to see her as well; however, after my failures with your mother and Jessica, I lacked the assurance that I would be able to have a viable, happy relationship. However, I told myself to "get off the stump" and be willing to take risks. I knew I loved Carol. Therefore, it was time to show some valor and be a mature man—neither of which were easy undertakings for me. Having said that, and missing Carol so very much, I decided to quickly write a letter to Carol telling her that I loved her and wanted to see her as well. I wrote to Carol the next day; I then became intrepid enough to call her two days after I wrote to her. We had a wonderful conversation, at which time we established the plans for Carole to fly up to Ketchikan to spend an extended weekend with me.

Meanwhile, Pilgrim, the first of the great numbers of tourists began arriving in Ketchikan—and I would say that almost all of them stopped by the VIS Trailer. The tourists arrived either by the giant state ferries that came up either from Seattle or Prince Rupert, British Columbia, or by the cruise ships that began their summer cruises to Alaska. Nancy and I found out that many people also flew up from Seattle to visit Ketchikan and Southeastern Alaska. It was not out of the ordinary that when Nancy or I opened the trailer for business, there were already a large number of tourists waiting to come in to see the slide show presentation, the exhibits, to get information about Southeastern Alaska from us, and to see the salmon swimming up a local creek to spawn The tourists also signed the guest book, and it was interesting to see from where they had come. By the time, the summer was over, Nancy and I discerned that people from every state in the country, Canada, Mexico, also from Europe and Japan had visited the trailer. We were quite often busy from the time we opened until we closed in the evening—even on weekends.

The trailer became a social happening, in that Nancy and I would exchange pleasantries with the tourists about where they lived, why they decided to visit Alaska, and where they were going. They, in turn, would ask us why we lived in Alaska; what the weather was like; how much things cost, etc. Tourists often took pictures of Nancy and me. People might come in strangers, but left as friends. In fact, I met people who lived not too far from where I had lived in Southern California.

My dear Pilgrim, I have a most unusual anecdote to share with you: one afternoon, I was working the desk in the trailer while Nancy was at lunch. A very nice older couple came into to see the slide show, exhibits, etc. They both signed their names and wrote where they lived. I happened to glance at the writing indicating their hometown. They were from the upper Midwest. I noticed the name of a small town where this coupled lived. I remembered that name, because Willow had told me several times that her father had been raised in or near that town, and that her paternal grandparents still lived there.

Without any hesitation, I asked the couple if they knew a family with Willow's last name. I told them that I had been "acquainted" with the family, and that a member (Willow) of it had mentioned the name of the town from where her father came. Much to my surprise, they told me they had known both her father and his family! They further shared with me that either her paternal grandmother or grandfather had recently died. The couple told me that Willow's family or her father had returned for the funeral. I made no further comments about the above information, but continued to take the couple around the trailer to the exhibits, and showed them the slide presentation. The three of us visited for a while, because there were few people in the trailer during lunchtime. I enjoyed my time with them, and bid them goodbye and a safe trip north to Anchorage. Pilgrim, I really enjoyed talking with these people. They were very nice, and what they told me drew some interest, but otherwise little emotion from me. I later told Nancy about my chance encounter with my past, and the two of us had a good chuckle about it.

Carol was coming to Ketchikan the following Friday evening. Jim Allison had a truck that he told me to use as Carol's and my transportation during her visit. Nancy offered to switch schedules with me, but told me that she wanted very much to meet Carol. I promised her that I would bring Carol to the trailer.

Well, Friday evening came, and Carol flew from Seattle to Annette Island, and then took the PBY seaplane to Ketchikan. When she stepped out of the plane, she looked stunning, and as in a soap opera, my heart was racing. We ran into each other's arms, hugged, and kissed one another—which people do, Pilgrim, when they have not seen a loved one for a long time. I still remember it was wonderful to see Carol and to hold her. Seeing Carol get off the plane was an experience I would not forget. Gosh Pilgrim, it had been only a few weeks before that I thought I was out of Carol's life. How wonderful that statement, "hope springs eternal!"

Carol and I had several wonderful days together. I took her all over Ketchikan Island to places such as Totem Park, where I took some pictures of her in front of the Abraham Lincoln Totem Pole, the largest totem pole in the world. We frequented the local stores and quaint bars to partake of the local ambience. I also took Carol to the VIS trailer where she and Nancy got to meet one another. They got along famously, and later on, when Nancy and I were in the trailer, she told me that Carol was the one for me. Pilgrim, I knew that, but in some ways, contemplating the possibility of another marriage was frightening. After all, Pilgrim, I had reason to be apprehensive. Bur, what I did was to conveniently not think about what Nancy had said—at least at that time. Instead, Carol, the Allison's, and a young couple who had just moved to Ketchikan from Arizona and I spent a wonderful afternoon on a local beach. We broiled freshly caught salmon on a grill, prepared corn on the cob, other types of food and drinks and had a great time. We all marveled at seeing some Killer Whales swimming up the channel no more than a hundred yards off the shore. Pilgrim, had you been with us that day, I would have held you up so that you would have been able to see these magnificent creatures. We also saw some bald eagles perched in the trees. The drive from Ketchikan through the beautiful Tongass National Forest was breath-taking. The majestic fir and evergreen trees formed a canopy over us as we drove on the Forest Service road to the beach.

Two days later, I sadly had to put Carol on the plane to Seattle. Pilgrim, it was very difficult saying goodbye to her. We earlier had discussed the possibility about getting married. Yet, we both had reservations about undertaking such an important step. Carol said that once she got back to Seattle she would think about getting married. She certainly did the right thing in light of the fact that my record concerning interpersonal relationships was not anything to write home about. I could sense the anxiety as I kissed Carol goodbye. I was afraid I might not see her again. Carol got on the PBY to fly to Annette Island to get the jet to Seattle. I already missed her as the seaplane was taxiing out to take off.

After Carol left, I immersed myself in my work. The summer was very busy with the flood of tourists visiting Ketchikan; thus, the summer went by rapidly. I earlier discussed some aspects of the tourists coming to the trailer. If you had been four years old, I believe you would have been very comfortable with all of the tourists who came to visit the trailer. You would have gotten to know a little bit about every tourist who came into the trailer, signed the book, and visited. Both Nancy and I observed that each tourist shared a little piece of his or her life with us. As I said earlier, tourists often took our pictures—why mine, I do not know—but Nancy and I enjoyed the attention.

During the preceding spring, I had begun applying once more to graduate schools where I could work on my Ph.D. I was ready to go on with the rest of my life. I felt that our Heavenly Father was prodding me to be more confident in what I wanted to do. Pilgrim, I was both ambivalent and yet eager to storm the bastions of academia to fulfill my dreams to become a college professor. I no longer felt chastened about even thinking or believing that with the Lord's help I could and would succeed.

I applied to a number of schools for further graduate study. Some turned me down; others agreed to accept on either a conditional or probationary status. I could accept the latter schools' criteria. After all, my earlier slovenly undergraduate endeavors—though offset by a good Graduate Record Exam (GRE) score and a very good grade point on my master's degree—as expected did not exude a complete sense of confidence by academic deans or department chairmen as to my ability.

Pilgrim, your father was learning that it was all right to have to prove himself once more in an academic environment. If there was one redeeming quality that emanated from my relationship with Willow, it was the realization that I no longer had to hide behind excuses as far as my previously poor performance while an undergraduate. A few years later, I became a very good marathon runner, and like time spent in college, a runner had to show his mettle. He or she simply did not begin running the 26.2 miles from the very beginning; he had to train slowly and often, before ever running his first marathon. Such would also be the case regarding the pursuit of the doctorate. Whereas I had been so defensive with your mother regarding my apparent inability to accomplish anything of note, thanks to the Lord and others, things were changing—and I was undergoing modification of sorts.

Pilgrim, I give thanks to the Lord, because for so many years of my life, I acknowledged no one but myself. I had seemingly learned to live in a self-destructive mode most of my life, and never had a difficult time getting into mutually destructive relationships, e.g., your mother and me. However, your tragic death made me realize I had no talents or abilities except those given to me by God. The abortion, however, made me understand what happened when your mother and I completely walked away from our Heavenly Father's plans for us. We and a few other people allowed evil into our respective lives long enough to bring about your death. Yet, our Lord took compassion on us to allow us to go on with our own lives. If nothing else had happened, I still would have given God the glory. To be able to work toward the fruition of the dream to be an historian and teach was the Lord's will. Thus, darling Pilgrim, I give our God the glory—not me.

As opposed to the earlier application to Kansas State Teachers College, it was not imperative that I present a cogent plea as to my ability; what was necessary, however, was that I be given the opportunity to prove myself in the graduate school academic climes. I decided to go to the Brigham Young University in Provo, Utah for my Ph.D. in the area of history. BYU—as it was known—was a wonderful university with strong academic, intellectual, and spiritual influences—three things that I knew I needed. I had once before gone to school at BYU, and so I knew it well. It has a large student body for the 1960s—approximately 23,000 students—that included both undergraduate and graduate students. The campus was large and expansive, and set below the foothills of the towering Wasatch Range of mountains. The setting was breathtaking, and I never got tired of seeing it. Pilgrim, I know you would love Provo, the university, the people, and the beauty of both the campus and the mountains.

I was accepted at BYU as a non-degree seeking student, with aspirations to be eventually accepted in the doctoral program in history. No matter under what provisions that I was accepted, I was elated. It simply meant that I would have another chance to prove myself. Pilgrim, guess what, the Lord was providing me with the resources to use; but it would be entirely up to me as far as using what our Heavenly Father saw fit to have given me. I was not certain as to my worthiness; I was, however, full of gratitude for whatever opportunities had been given to me. No doubt, there were more intelligent, more mature, and more successful individuals worthy of getting a Ph.D. However, I was going to do my best to obtain one.

I only hoped by the dint of hard work, and some talent that I might be worthy of obtaining a Doctorate in History, because I wanted to be a college professor and impart my knowledge, enthusiasm, and skills to others. I would, within time find out if I would meet my objectives.

About a week before I was preparing to leave Ketchikan for the last time, I phoned Carol to tell her of the good news about graduate school and to once again ask her to marry me. She gave no definitive answer, other than we could discuss it when I flew to Seattle. Again, I had to wait for any definitive answer that might take place. Nevertheless, it was worth it.

It came time for Nancy and I to close the VIS trailer and to say goodbye to one another. We had a wonderful three months working with each other, and meeting so many interesting tourists. Nancy had been a great friend, and I was going to miss her. As I, she was going to be leaving Ketchikan to go south to teach. She planned to get married the following spring. Nancy told me to give Carol her best and that Carol and I should stop fooling around and get married. I told her that I would do all in my power to accomplish that.

It finally came time to embark from Ketchikan to Seattle. I said goodbye to all my friends, such as the Allison's, the Tyler's, and others, who I would never forget. The summer of 1968 had been a wonderful and eventful one. I would now be entering another part of my life—that once again included a plane flight from an area that I would not see again. Pilgrim, your spirit will be a well-traveled one. In fact, I could venture that you would have qualified for umpteen frequent flier miles. Well, it was a Sunday morning, and time to fly to Seattle. The eventual destination was Provo, Utah—hopefully with an intermediate stop in Seattle—to ask Carol to marry me.

The flight down to Seattle was uneventful; I, however, spent much of the flight mulling over in my mind as to what was going to take place between Carol and me at the Seattle-Tacoma Airport. Approximately two hours later, we landed in Seattle. Carol was waiting for me as I debarked from the aircraft. Carol smiled as she saw me coming toward her. We hugged and kissed one another warmly. We were happy to see one another. It was then that I asked her to marry me, and she said yes—of all places in the Seattle-Tacoma Airport! Darling Pilgrim, I had never asked a woman to marry me in an airport. I guess there is a first for everything. Carol told her family of our decision to get married. Pilgrim, remember the title for this chapter? Well, translated, *joie de vivre* means, "joy of life." How apropos! I believe the Lord put Carol in my life so we would have a joyous life. I had learned a great deal from my first marriage—at least I hoped that I had.

Carol and I decided to get married in Reno and spend our honeymoon in the area. She had a married sister who lived in Reno, so Carol phoned her sister Judy, who was delighted we were flying to Reno to get married. This meant that Carol and Judy could see one another. Meanwhile, back in Seattle, we bought matching wedding bands, and prepared for our flight to Reno. Since it would be time for me to register at BYU after our honeymoon, I would then fly to Salt Lake City, take a bus to Provo, register for my classes, find a small furnished apartment for us, after which time Carol would fly down to Salt Lake City, where I would meet her. We would then buy a car after we got to Provo.

Pilgrim, everything went well. We flew to Reno, where we got married, then Judy, her husband Bob, and their little boy Kevin met us and took us to the hotel where we were going to stay. Carol and I had a wonderful honeymoon, then the day came that I had to fly to Salt Lake City, and go on to Provo to register for graduate school. It was difficult saying goodbye to Carol—though I knew I would see her in three weeks. I waved from the plane as we moved away from the terminal, and then we were airborne, and about an hour later, we landed at Salt Lake City. I then took a bus to Provo, and checked into an small hotel on University Avenue, then walked up to the campus to register.

Provo was the quintessential university town, surrounding the large Brigham Young University campus. As I previously mentioned, the BYU enrollment was 23,000 students. The campus was in the valley right below the towering Wasatch Range of mountains that towered up to about 11,000 feet. The fall colors had already begun blending in with the foothills of the Wasatch Range, and as a pleasant surprise, one mountain peak to the north of the valley already had a sprinkling of snow on it. Provo was referred to as "Happy Valley" because of the bucolic, serene aspect of the area. Because of its location, Provo seemed somewhat insular—which to me it was. Back in the late 1960s, Utah County had a population of about 60,000 people. Its two largest towns were Provo and Orem. The area has since doubled since we left the area in the early 1970s. In fact, BYU now has 33,000 students.

Well, I quickly walked up to the campus, whereupon I saw large numbers of students going in and out of buildings obviously in preparation for their classes, which began the following Monday. I saw the signs for registration at the Smith Field House on the lower campus. Once inside, I followed the sign telling me where graduate students were to register. I went to the table where the Social Science Division was and commenced my registration. It was while registering for the graduate history classes that I met three of my five major professors—the three were to have a major impact upon my future success. Pilgrim, the three men to whom I just referred, were the finest professors I would ever have in my entire college life. I remembered that I briefly visited with them and told them that I just completed my honeymoon, and had sent my bride back to Seattle. The three professors had a good laugh.

Pilgrim, the professor who would be my chairperson told me that I was to have a conference with some members of the history department within the next week to ten days. I knew why. It was time to face an evaluation of my abilities and to simultaneously receive guidance as to what might be given relative to graduate school. I just decided that when confronted by the committee about my marginal undergraduate work, I would make no excuses, but simply tell the members that I believe I could and would succeed. The committee had my GRE record and transcript of my work on my MA. Therefore, I did not have to trumpet any comments about my hitherto graduate school talents.

I met one day with the committee members; most of them were

friendly and sympathetic—including the head of the department. There was one professor who became somewhat confrontational—at least to me—and asked me if I thought I was mature and motivated enough to do the work for a Ph.D. or if I would, instead, embarrass the department. No matter what the reason for the question, it warranted being answered. I politely told the committee member that I would not have returned to BYU if I did not have the confidence in myself and in my abilities. I stated that I would simply accept the department's decision regarding its expectations of me. My chairman bailed me out by saying that he had enough regard for my ability that he would personally be my chairman. I had an advocate—actually several other committee members believed I would do well. Thanks Lord.

The department chairman told me that I would be on a non-graduate student status for two semesters, and every two weeks I would be evaluated to see if I maintained at least a B average in all my work. As had taken place in my master's program, there was a stipulation that the department had a right to summarily remove me from the program if it believed I was not worthy of continuing with my studies. To me, this was a wonderful bargain! I readily agreed to the aforementioned provisions.

Pilgrim, a couple of years later, my chairman told me that the professor who was assailing my ostensible lack of intellectual prowess did it to see if I could accept criticism, and not make excuses, but rise to the challenge. Let me put it in a succinct comment: Thanks to the Lord, the confidence of my professors, Carol, and my belief in myself, I did quite well. Darling daughter, our Heavenly Father was rightly testing me—and I am glad that He did.

Darling Pilgrim, as I talk about BYU, I am so awe-struck that you have been cerebrally and emotionally a part of me. Had you been alive, and able to have been with Carol and me, I know you would have enjoyed Provo and the surrounding area. Yet, though you are alive only in spirit and in my psyche, I still know you would have enjoyed the beauty of Provo and BYU. There are times—in fact many times—that I had looked up at the broad expanse of the universe and thought that Heaven was on the other side of the universe and that you were looking down on Willow and me. Pilgrim, it is so strange that you love your mother and me—though we do not deserve your love. That is why I am so comfortable having you with me spiritually. You have forgiven each of us for what happened to you, yet, please understand, why back in 1968, I was in no way ready to forgive Willow for aborting you—whatever her reasons. Pilgrim, even if you had not been my daughter, but belonged to some other couple, I could not have ever championed you being aborted. I am a sinner, but I could not ever countenance the death of any innocent, unborn baby. During the last thirty-plus years, our nation has become a culture of death, due in large measure to abortion. We have a society that sanctions arbitrary killing of innocent unborn children. That is why I knew that your mother and her parents could never have justified what they did. They simply took an innocent life. Yet, I know that when I came back to Utah, it was for a special reason—it was where the Lord could guide me to do His will through you. This meant that you became the compass as far as what He wanted me to do. Back in 1963, I tried to be everything for Willow, but instead became nothing to her. God, however, softened my pain by letting me know you were in His glory and loved in a special way. I thank Him for that!

There were times that I wished you could have been born in Provo—a truly beautiful place. However, the Lord did so much better by taking you to Heaven—but allowing me to borrow you here in my world—for a while. Pilgrim, it would have been so wonderful if you had been actually alive, to have you wake up every morning and I take you to your bedroom window to look out and see the beautiful Wasatch Range and Mount Timpanogos—the latter which I climbed twice. What glorious sights to wake up to. The Mormons—the dominant church in Utah—and majority of the political infrastructure—have made their mark on American History. They emphasize morality, hard work, close and large families, education, humility, and spirituality. They were, and still are, a wholesome people, who have not accepted abortion as a means to decide whether life was to be sanctified. Mormons are a sensitive, loving people. To me, they are a great culture—and always will be. Pilgrim, for the next four-and one-half years, I will take you with me wherever I go on campus. By the way, your fifth birthday will be coming up in March 1969—and there will be some surprises. I love you.

Well, the three weeks hiatus of sorts from Carol was too long. But she finally did fly down to Salt Lake City. We had talked numerous times during our absence from one another, but phone calls did not replace Carol being with me. While back in Seattle, she packed her furniture and personal belongs, had then transported to Provo, where they were placed in storage. Carol's wonderful colleagues gave her a great going away party, and she spent some time with her family, and then it was on a flight to Salt Lake City. Carol knew the area, having gone to college and nurses' training in Salt Lake City. After we got to Provo, I took Carol to our furnished apartment, which after she saw it, she made me promise that I would never again actively engage in looking for apartments. Fortunately, we eventually found a wonderful apartment that we lived in until we left Provo.

That afternoon, we bought a new car at the local Volkswagen dealership. It was a Super Beetle, and since it was sky blue, we called it, "Blue Baby." We had it for four years. It was a great little automobile and we drove it on many trips throughout the western part of the United States— including several times to the northwest and the west coast. Our first long trip was Christmas of 1969, when we took a trip from Provo to Seattle to spend time with Carol's family and some of her friends. We then continued down the coast to Los Angeles to see Laura and Craig and their family. We then went to the Rose Bowl game on January 1, 1970. It was great to see Laura and Craig, and, guess what, they were now grandparents. Their married daughter Kathy had just had her first child. Carol met the family for the first time when we took our long trip. Craig and Laura however, came up to see us a number of times in Provo.

Well, Carol and I settled into our new life together in Provo. It was busy, exciting, and enjoyable. Carol got a job as a nurse supervisor at the state hospital in Provo. Unfortunately, our respective schedules often did not allow us to spend as much time together as we wanted, but we were able to take advantage of whatever time was accorded to us. When Carol had a weekend off, we would take short trips or attend either a movie or a cultural event on campus.

Well Pilgrim, the first semester in the graduate history program was a very busy one. I will not ever forget the fall of 1968. I took four classes that semester with attendant requirements for lengthy papers. The "fish or cut bait" cliché was alive and well, and along with my other graduate colleagues, I spent what seemed to be an inordinate time in the university library every day studying, reading, researching, and writing papers. All of us went from raucous energy to routine exhaustion after spending the better part of a day on campus. Having described the above though, I looked forward to my classes and going to the library to study and work on papers.

Darling daughter, back in the 1960s, students did not have backpacks to carry their book and essential supplies. The undergraduates on most college and university campuses carried their books in their arms or along their sides. The graduate students usually had attaché cases in which they had books, legal pads, 5X8 note cards, and plenty of pencils or ballpoint pens. There was no such gadgetry as laptop computers, ipods, cell phones, etc. During that era all students had to be ready and able to write, type, rewrite, and retype notes and papers many times over. Noteworthy was the fact that most professors—at least mine—lectured primarily from behind a lectern, and wrote information on the blackboards. When we had graduate seminars, we normally met around a table with our professor at the head of the table. We then would present our papers for discussion and some analyzing by the professor and our colleagues.

Pilgrim, I did quite well the first semester getting a B+ average. I was elated but thankful to my professors for their encouragement, suggestions, and patience. I also owed so very much that first semester—and subsequent ones—to my darling Carol for her love and support.

Above all, I thanked our Heavenly Father for all He was doing for me, and would continue to do so. Living in Provo was great, because we did not have to deal with the troublesome riots, demonstrations, materialism, and callousness that were pervasive throughout the United States in the 1960s.

However, something good came out of what was going on throughout our country during the era of the '60s: I wanted to study Asian history, because that is where the United States had fought its last two wars—the Korean War and the Vietnam War. Throughout two years of course work, I took 21 graduate hours of Asian History that became invaluable—particularly when I was writing my dissertation. During the first year of course work, I was also required to take the first of my two language requirements, which I did successfully. I passed my second language the fall semester of 1969. Passing these examinations were two important hurdles that were overcome.

As I was getting ready for summer school in 1969, Carol and I moved into a nice two-bedroom unfurnished apartment near where Carol worked and fairly close to campus. The area was quite nice with a mix of homes and nice apartments. The neighbors in our apartment complex were wonderful people—a number of whom were retired. We very much enjoyed living there for the time we were in Provo. I was able to walk up to the campus, and did so quite often.

Pilgrim, I made a number of friends while in graduate school; some were pursuing a Ph.D., while others were working towards a Masters Degree in whatever specific discipline of history. We were a tight knit group of students—with most of us being married. We ranged in age from the mid-twenties to the early forties, and were from all parts of the country. Most of the graduate students in history were men; however, we had a small number of women in the program. They were every bit as capable as their male colleagues. The women also brought a great deal of charm, humor, common sense, and strong intellectualism to the program. I learned a great deal from all my colleagues.

During the summer of 1969, I took twelve hours of course work during the two summer school sessions. The courses were challenging, but very enjoyable, and I did quite well in all of them. Pilgrim, remember the apprehension about possibly not being accepted as a graduate student in the history program? Well, one afternoon while walking between my two classes near the end of the second summer school session, my department chairman saw me, waved to me to come over where he was, and told me some very good news. He told me that a committee of faculty members voted unanimously that I be brought into the degree-seeking graduate program! My chairman further stated the committee was impressed with my work ethic, intellectualism, and classroom skills—including the writing of papers. He also remarked that everyone thought I would do quite well as a college professor. I was given a fellowship and a position as a graduate instructor.

Pilgrim, I attempted not to be overwhelmed; however, I thanked my chairman, then phoned Carol, who was elated as I was, and said that I should come home, and we would celebrate. I came home and we celebrated! Pilgrim, I owed all of this to the Lord and Carol. Though I received the above wonderful news, I remembered that back in 1963, Willow, understandably, had little, if any, faith that I would ever amount to anything. Ironically, however, part of the eventual success with my life after 1963 came about because I was no longer worried whether Willow thought I had any abilities. Yet, in a somewhat oblique manner, I eventually acknowledged her part—though albeit somewhat negative—in my becoming a contributing member of society.

Hey, little daughter, remember a while back in one of my previous letters, I referred to the American space program, and the first manned-space vehicle scheduled to land on the moon in 1969? Well, guess what? After a trip into space, Apollo 11—as it was referred to—landed on the moon on July 20, 1969. You would have been five years old when this happened. Carol and I watched the landing on television, and the subsequent first man to set foot on the moon's surface. It was breathtaking! The moon was shining brightly that evening. Carol and I would have taken you out in the front yard of the apartment, and the three of us would have gazed at the moon. We could have discussed the fact that two men were walking on the surface of the moon. In fact, several of our neighbors were standing out on the lawn looking at the moon and discussing it. You would have been able to tell people that you saw the moon on the night the first men ever set foot on it!

Though the above commentary on the moon landing is somewhat sad, Pilgrim, I bet that you had the most wonderful opportunity to see the landing on the moon from Heaven that Sunday night. This meant that you and your other little spirits had a ringside seat along with the Lord, Jesus, the angels, and the rest of the spirits in Heaven.

Allow me to bring you back down to earth and share with you an unusual event relative to Willow that took place during the summer of 1969 when I was in summer school. As I mentioned earlier, I spent a great deal of time in what then was the very large Clark Library, where I studied and wrote my papers. That summer, I was given a graduate carrel and locker on the second floor of the library for my books, papers, note cards, etc. So, I spent most of the time at my carrel. However, late one morning, I went downstairs to the card catalog to check a bibliography. As I walked toward the card drawers, I suddenly heard a voice behind me. I literally froze in my tracks without looking back. The voice eerily sounded like Willow's. I remember that I kept my back to where the voice was coming from, slipped around the back of the drawers, and as unobtrusively as possible, returned to my carrel. It sounded as if a person's with Willow's voice was talking to another woman. I possibly overreacted to a coincidence, as far as the sound of the voice. I remembered that I regained my composure, but never mentioned the incident to Carol.

Carol and I took a trip to Lake Tahoe after summer school of 1969 was over. We had a wonderful time there. We stopped off to see Carol's sister in Reno on our way to Lake Tahoe. After spending several days at the lake and the resort, we then drove back to Provo to prepare for the fall semester. The department chairman had some of us graduate students help with the registering and advisement of students for the semester. I enjoyed doing that. Pilgrim, it was a great feeling that things were going so well. I had to thank the Lord and Carol.

Mormons tend to have large families, so my colleagues would inquire as to when Carol and I were going to begin our "happy brood." In fact, a number of women students told me that they were praying for Carol and I to have a baby. That was a wonderful gesture by these young women. One day when I was in the history office talking with the department secretary, we got talking about families—such a topic was often discussed at BYU. She asked if I had any children, and without thinking, I said something about having a daughter. I quickly backtracked and acted as if I misunderstood the question. I then responded by saying that Carol and I hoped our first child would be a girl. Darling Pilgrim, it appeared that my subconscious became conscious for a moment. No one at BYU ever knew about you. It would have been emotionally painful. No one really needed to know that you had been aborted.

Pilgrim, I should ask you as I begin the fall semester of 1969, how do you like Provo and BYU? I would have enjoyed getting your opinions, suggestions, whatever about the above. I remember thinking that you would have been five years old, and likely in kindergarten. With your precocious ways, intellect, and curiosity, you would have had a wonderful time in kindergarten. I would have immensely enjoyed listening to you telling Carol and me about your everyday activities. Carol and I would have learned so much from you. Darling Pilgrim, I am certain that Carol and I would have enjoyed taking you everywhere we went. You would have gotten to see so much of our beautiful country. I would have delighted to see the expression on your face as you went to new places; saw new things; and met many people—all of whom would have enjoyed talking to you. Darling, do you see why I grieved so very much when your life was taken away? Your death was my loss, because you would never be the human daughter I wished that you had been and you deserved to have been.. Pilgrim, the college year of 1969-1970 was a busy and exciting one. I took twelve hours of course work; taught two classes; and took and passed my final language examination. I enjoyed teaching and the interaction with the students. I had large classes. By the way, Pilgrim, no longer was I in turmoil about my future. The Lord has established and illuminated the path regarding my Ph.D. I say this with humility, because for so many years my life was rudderless. My priorities had not always been the most logical. In fact, it was during the relationship with your mother that I made my first—but unsuccessful attempt—to grow up and to make her proud of me. Growing up, however, came later.

As a segue, I enjoyed teaching the large history classes that I did, because they gave me an opportunity to see the expression on the faces of my young students—most of whom had come to BYU from throughout the United States and other countries. I had the responsibility of teaching students, while activating their intellectual curiosity, and stimulating their enthusiasm to contribute to the betterment of the world. At times, fellow graduate instructors and I would lament that maybe we were not hitting our mark as far as inspiring our students. However, I was reassured by one of my favorite professors that in time I would be a good teacher. I just needed the time and experience—plus scholarship of course. One of the favorite techniques of teaching, Pilgrim, was the Socratic method. It entailed walking in front of the class, from one side of the room to the other while lecturing to the students. I would implement this procedure while lecturing, asking questions of particular students, and inviting comments from the students. This method of teaching kept both the students and me awake and stimulated. Most of the professors used this methodology in their teaching. I still use the Socratic technique of teaching.

As I was finishing my course work during 1969-1970, Carol and I began discussing having a baby within a few years. The two of us were not getting any younger, and when we would have a child, we probably would be in our late thirties. Carol had always wanted at least one baby, and by 1970, I was comfortable enough to become a father once more. Yet, until 1970, I was reluctant to have parental expectations, because as most men and women who have to deal with an abortion, I still dealt with pain, grief, anger, and denial. These emotions mitigated any normal paternal instincts that I might normally have. Through therapy, I had found out that the loss of a baby by either miscarriage or abortion often brings out great trepidation concerning the safety of future pregnancies.

Actually, Carol and I decided there was no reason to plan to have a baby until I had gotten through my coursework, the subsequent five days of written comprehensive examinations, along with my first set of oral exams—all necessary before I was admitted to actual doctoral candidacy. In essence, the baby making would have to wait.

Darling Pilgrim, allow me to share some humorous anecdotes about graduate school in the 1960s. As many doctoral students, as I was completing my course work, I was attempting to read as many secondary works as possible that I might use for my doctoral dissertation. I scoured all the history and political science sources in the stacks—be they books or articles—that might be useful to me. I also did the same for sources that I received from other libraries and universities through inter-library loan. What this meant was checking out books as many times as I could without having to turn them back in, or simply take the books off the shelves, put them either in my carrel locker or actually hide them back in the stacks where I could find them.

Guess what though, Pilgrim, the library staff was always more enterprising than either my colleagues or me. The staff seemed to always find the "lost" books, and every two weeks, the library staff checked the carrels and their lockers for overdue books. This meant that doctoral candidates working on dissertations attempted to be most "enterprising." Most of the time, Pilgrim, our efforts had a minimal success ratio. Therefore, most of the time, we graduate students finally succumbed to using many packages of 5X8 cards on which we either wrote or typed as much information as possible. In the 1960s and 1970s, dissertations were labor-intensive projects—therefore, whatever we could use—we did.

Do you know what else I did, when I needed a break? I would take time out in the Humanities stacks of the library on the third floor, look for a particular literary work or novel, and then sit on the floor between the respective stacks of books and read a book. I would sometimes sit on the floor between the stacks for almost two hours reading a book. After I satisfied my need for "lighter" reading, I would then get up, go back to my carrel, and continue my studies. A hard life indeed!

The fall of 1970, arrived and I completed my course work with a very high grade point. I allude to this, darling Pilgrim, not as a means of boasting, but as a story of contrast of what I was like academically in 1970, as opposed to my 1963 very anemic grade point average of 2.3. The reason for the improvement in the grade point average was a simple one: I had grown up. Of course, I thank our Heavenly Father for that, and Carol as well, because of her support and confidence in me. Pilgrim, unfortunately, your mother never thought me to be a marketable human being—because she was from a family that was impressed by tangible things, such as money, material acquisitions, and status. I had none of these things. However, I did have a dependence upon the Lord who blessed me. I had Carol, who loved and accepted me for me, and wonderful professors and colleagues who had faith in me. I could not ask for anything more.

I was teaching a history class during the fall of 1970 and preparing for the comprehensive examinations that were scheduled for the first part of December. Everything was going smoothly, when late in October 1970, I suddenly found blood in my urine. There was no attendant pain, but Carol quickly took me to the Emergency Room at the Utah Valley Hospital, where, after giving me a complete examination, a doctor concluded I had a kidney stone in the upper kidney. The urologist and a surgeon attempted to pass the stone, but the effort was to no avail. Since it was near the end of the week, the doctors scheduled surgery to remove the kidney stone for the following week. I was given a pass from the hospital to spend one afternoon at home with Carol. We had a wonderful afternoon together. I then returned to the hospital in preparation for the operation.

During the previous week, I had notified the history department of my hospitalization. A graduate student stepped in to teach my classes, and my chairman, some other professors, and a few of my colleagues stopped by to check on me, and also to encourage me. A few students came by as well and said I was in their prayers. The support given to me was wonderful.

Well, darling daughter, the day for the surgery arrived and I was prepped for an early morning operation. However, it was postponed until the early afternoon because an emergency necessitated the doctors to do surgery on someone else. I was given some more of a relaxant as the second operation was finally scheduled for 1:00 p.m. that afternoon. Pilgrim, I still remember being euphoric as I was being wheeled to the operating room; in fact, Carol later told me that I was talking a mile a minute to anyone who got in range of the gurney. She said it was rather humorous. Carol gave me a quick kiss and told me she loved me. I was then wheeled into the operating room (OR).

The surgical team was waiting as I was wheeled in to the OR, and greeted me. The anesthesiologist put my arms straight out from my side as he began inserting the anesthesia into one of my arms. I remember the following rather droll comment I made before I went under: I said, "Well this is as good of a time to appear messianic." The surgical team laughed, and then I fell into la la land. The operation took four hours because the kidney stone had to be removed by an incision through my left side. The OR technicians took me into the recovery room where I stayed for about an hour or a little longer. I then was wheeled back to my room, whereupon being placed in bed, I moaned for what seemed to be an interminable time before I was given a shot of morphine. Carol, however, was by my side.

The operation was successful; however, I stayed in the hospital a week to recuperate. It took several days before I could tolerate the pain without morphine. As an aside, back in 1970, when I had the operation, people remained in hospitals for a longer period of time. With the improvement of medical technology and procedures, were I to have the same operation today, it would likely have been shorter in length, and I would have been home sooner.

Upon my return home, I slowly began to mend, and went back to preparing for my written exams. By the second week in January 1971, I was well, back to running, and ready to take my exams. Well, the week came, and for five days—four hours a day—I filled many Blue Books (test booklets), as I wrote an indescribable number of essay questions. Six professors graded the exams. I found out in two weeks that I had done well and passed my written comprehensives!

Two weeks later, I took a three-hour oral exam of relative bibliography and historiography. I enjoyed this exam much better than the first one. The department chairman and my chairman told me a week later that I had passed my orals and was admitted to candidacy for my dissertation. Carol decided we needed a break, so we drove down to Las Vegas where we enjoyed ourselves. We then continued to Southern California where I had an interview for a position at a local junior college. I later found out that I did not get the teaching job. Upon returning from our vacation, I began working on my dissertation. Well, Pilgrim, it is on to the most eventful letter. You will really enjoy this forthcoming letter.

I love you so much,

Dad

MARK

Carol found out in April 1971 that she was pregnant! Pilgrim, you will be having a little brother or sister in either the following December or early January 1972. The two of us were excited when we found out the great news. We hugged and kissed one another and even cried a bit. We were overwhelmed to say the least. Today, darling daughter, it seems politically correct to say, "We are pregnant." Frankly though, I like to think the woman is pregnant, and that by being so, the pregnancy is her unique gift to the childbearing process. And, that as the father of the baby, I am validating Carol's pregnancy. We were both ecstatic.

Darling Pilgrim, you would have been seven years old had you been alive. Carol and I would have shared with you the news of you having a younger brother or sister. In fact, you would have been the first person we would have told. My darling daughter, as I said at the onset of my letters to you, I was denied the opportunity of anticipating you—and that pain lasts. Because of our sinful and selfish nature, Willow and I never had the chance to have you—our first child. Yet, I sense that you are happy for Carol and me, because our Heavenly Father is going to bless us with your younger sibling; your brother or sister is also a gift to you from God. The three of us can joyously anticipate the new event.

Carol and I began phoning family members around the country—including Craig and Laura—all of whom were excited. I also told my professors the good news, and they were very pleased that we were going to become part of the axiom, "Baby makes three." One of the professors chidingly said that that since we seemingly waited so long to have a baby, that maybe Carol and I were not "spunky" enough in our endeavors to have a child! I told him I was afraid that we at times had been, "too spunky" and had almost run out of gas! That evoked a good laugh from everyone.

Carol and I began referring to her pregnancy as "being big with baby." Carol also gave the baby in her womb the nickname of "Snookums." That was a great name. Imagine, darling daughter, if we had actually named your brother or sister that name. I bet that would have been a real eye-opener. Just think of introducing your sibling to your friends as "Snookums LePore." That child would have been embarrassed all of its life. By the way, Carol accumulated a lengthy list of girls' names; I just had a list of two boys' names. They were Mark and Sean. Carol thought the baby might be a girl, and therefore had plenty of names from which to choose.

Becoming parents-to-be brought the two of us closer. We had invested our time, emotions, aspirations, and money in what would be the third addition to the family. We bought baby furniture, and as a new mother-to-be, Carol excitedly began buying maternity outfits. We painted the baby's furniture and, of course, told all the neighbors that we were going to have a baby. Everyone in the apartment complex became excited when they heard the news. Guess what? We were going to be the first couple in the complex to have a baby! Pilgrim, had you been with us, we would have included you in all the preparations for the birth of your brother or sister. And, even had you been living with your mother in California, we would have phoned you to tell you the news, and sent you pictures of Carol in her maternity outfit, and of the baby's bedroom.

Even when I was on campus, I found that the news of Carol's pregnancy had already been making the rounds. Carol told her colleagues at work. My graduate colleagues and most of the department professors already knew the good news by the time I told them. There were even students from previous and present classes who came up and congratulated me—including some young ladies who told me they had said many prayers for Carol and I to be blessed with a baby. Carol and I were touched by the love and concern shown by so many people.

Darling Pilgrim, as Carol became bigger with her pregnancy, I began to feel a sense of confidence and joy about the baby. In the back of my mind, however, I came to the realization that the Lord was giving me a second chance to be a parent. I hoped at that time that I was worthy of the gift of impending fatherhood. I thanked the Lord for His blessings regarding our baby. Darling daughter, I wanted our Heavenly Father to bless your mother when she had children from her marriage. No matter what our feelings toward one another, I loved you too much to have had really harsh feelings toward Willow. Carol and I took our last trip for a while to California during Carol's first trimester. We drove to Reno to visit with her sister and family, and then we drove on to San Francisco to spend time with Carol's youngest sister and her family. The trip was a bit arduous for Carol, but we took it easy, and made numerous stops.

On the way back to Provo, we stopped at Lake Tahoe for a couple of days, relaxed and enjoyed each other and the beautiful scenery. We had a great vacation. We laughed at the fact that your brother or sister would likely become "Super Baby" instead of the "Blue Baby" beetle that had been wonderful transportation for almost four years—but would be replaced eventually by a larger car. We would need a larger automobile.

During the spring and summer of 1971, I spent some time doing such things as submitting a dissertation proposal/abstract, which was approved. I was given a travel grant to go to major university libraries and repositories throughout the country and to Washington, D.C. to use the National Archives and Library of Congress for research. I would have taken Carol with me to the above places; however, she said that doing a lot of flying would have made her uncomfortable. Guess what, Pilgrim? I flew out to at Stanford University in 1971, to do research as an anti-Vietnam War riot was taking place and the campus had been tear-gassed. I had to run through the remnants of the tear gas to the Hoover Tower where I was doing research. It was exciting, and even humorous. The police were chasing everyone—even me—it seemed. Pilgrim. I found that I could run fast carrying an attaché case! I phoned Carol and told her about it—we had a good laugh.

Pilgrim, Carol and I joined a Lamaze class in 1971, held at Utah Valley Hospital. It was a childbirth training class for expectant couples. It was rather amusing in that out of the twenty couple in the class, we were the oldest—being in our late thirties. The first time we went to the class, the other couples—most of them in their early to mid-twenties—looked at us as if we were in the wrong room. Carol told the facilitator—somewhat sarcastically—that we were in the right room. She then looked at me, and then at the rest of the class, and said something to the effect, "Don't look at me, it's his fault we're in this class!" It got a good laugh. There were, in fact, several former women students who were now married and expecting their first babies. We met one another's spouses and discussed the class. Carol, being older than the other expectant mothers, found that she was not as supple as she once was; it, therefore, was a bit uncomfortable doing the floor exercises. The two of us, however, practiced the art of birthing babies at home.

To be able to augment expenses for the baby, I got a job driving a cab-over school bus for the Provo School District. Practically all the bus drivers were BYU college students. I drove until the time I got my Ph.D. It was fortuitous that I was able obtain this job as my two-year teaching stint ended. I drove both an assigned bus route and took sport teams on trips. The supervisor was very nice in that he told me that if Carol called into the bus garage relative to her possibly going into labor, he would quickly send out a replacement driver so I could get home.

By Christmas 1971, we had everything ready for the baby. All we needed was the 'finished product." Christmas came and went and no baby. We thought the baby might arrive around New Year's Eve or New Year's Day. Nothing happened. We were into January 1972. Things were un-eventful until Thursday, January 13, 1972. I had just completed my morn-ing run when Carol phoned the bus garage. There were no cell phones then, so phone communications were implemented by landlines. Carol said she thought she might be having contractions. Wow, Pilgrim, I jumped into the beetle and drove home as rapidly as legally as possible. By the time I arrived home, Carol had phoned her doctor, whose office was near the hospital. He asked Carol how far apart her contractions were and then told her to come right into the office. The doctor, however, issued Carol a caveat that if her contractions were becoming more pronounced, then to drive right to the hospital. We, of course, had the "baby bag" with everything needed for a delivery and hospital stay. Carol and I arrived at the obstet-rics clinic, at which time the doctor examined her and told her that her contractions were relatively few in number. He told us that the next time Carol had contractions, they would likely be more frequent, and instead of phoning the clinic, to go straight to the hospital and check in.

Darling Pilgrim, as I am doing the narrative about your soon-to-be-born brother or sister, I am not neglecting you. You would have been only a month or so away from being an eight-year-old. Pilgrim. Understand-ably, you might have been a bit confused as to what was happening. If it is any consolation, I was a bit confused as well. Gosh, what if your mother was already married in 1972, you could very well have a brother or sister. Therefore, I should not be so presumptuous that you did not already have one or more siblings. Pilgrim, I am sure the story becomes interesting from here on out!

I stayed home with Carol on January 13, 1972. She rested that day, and took a nap. After she awakened, I bought some hamburgers and fries—that she specifically wanted. I got them and we ate them. Well, as it was becoming evening, two things happened: it began snowing heavily, and Carol once more began having frequent contractions. . Once more, we put both Carol and the baby bag into the car then left a note on the apartment with the date on it, and where we could be found—along with the hospital's phone number. We then drove to the hospital. We drove through the ever-increasing snowstorm to the hospital. The Lord and the angels guided the car through the storm. We arrived safely at the hospital, and I quickly checked Carol in and a nurse took her to the maternity ward.

Carol was put in a room that was fairly close to the delivery room. However, the next three days were not only a blur, but a seemingly never-ending horror story as well. Carol was put in a labor room where she was alone from the time she entered the hospital until she was finally wheeled into the operating room to have a caesarean section done. Carol did get nursing care; however, she was not monitored as often or as well as she should have been.

Pilgrim, I was not only concerned about Carol, but also apprehensive for her and the baby as well. We were told that her primary doctor would be in to check on her during the day on Friday. That did not happen. I will never forget sitting with Carol on the side of her bed and rubbing her back and neck. I also offered Carol encouragement, telling her that I loved her so much, and that we would get through this together. Nevertheless, I was becoming angry, frightened, and almost combative—which was not good.

What was disheartening, Pilgrim, was to have the nurses constantly tell Carol, "Just relax and slowly breathe." It seemed that this was their mantra, though I would like to believe they were just doing their jobs. Their comments were of little consolation to either Carol or me. I could not believe the seemingly non-stop parade of women being wheeled into the delivery room to have their babies. Meanwhile, Carol had not even received a visit from either her primary care doctor or his partner. Damn

Darling Pilgrim, it was during this time that I suddenly had a flashback: I began to think that I was being punished for what tragically had happened to you nine years before. I began feeling almost numb and depressed. I would like to have believed that my thinking became skewed because of what Carol was going through. I certainly did not want a medical emergency to befall Carol or the baby. It was a far rougher weekend for Carol and the baby than it was for me. On Saturday morning, Carol's secondary doctor came in to check her. He apologized that the primary care physician had not come at all on Friday to the hospital. Guess where the first doctor had been? He had been skiing on Friday and was not due back until Saturday evening. The backup doctor apologized for the obvious breakdown in communications. He checked Carol carefully, and instructed the nurses that Carol would very likely be ready to have the baby in the evening. He told me that he would check in at the nurse's station, either by phone or in person throughout the day.

I did something that I heretofore had never done: I attempted to bully the doctor—not physically, but verbally. I will explain, Pilgrim, what I did and why. I told him that if there was any danger to Carol and/or the baby, that Carol's life was the most important point of consideration and should be saved at all costs. There were to be no other considerations made. He nodded when I said that, though he might have thought me out of line.

Pilgrim, what I just did was reprehensible. I was "playing God!" I was no better than Willow and her parents had been, regarding their decision to abort you. I had no business brow-beating a doctor. I had accused your mother and her parents for their sense of relativity regarding the ethics of destroying you; I was, however, just as guilty in making a medical decision that I wanted implemented. I was angry and confused regarding the rights of a mother as opposed to the rights of the unborn baby. What was apparent was that I had made the decision that if Carol was in danger, the baby be aborted! As I mentioned at the beginning of the paragraph, I was replicating what Willow and her parents had done in 1963—that being to imperiously decide what should happen to our baby—if complications should arise. I later had to ask the Lord's forgiveness for my pride and anger.

During Saturday evening, one of the nurses, per direction by the doctor, gave Carol an intravenous injection of Pitocin—a medicine to induce labor. Carol went into shock very shortly thereafter. The needle had to be quickly taken out. Carol yelled to one of the nurses something to the effect, "Stop you're hurting the baby." I was hard pressed to keep my composure. Here, my lovely wife could be close to death, and those nurses were seemingly putting her in mortal danger.

Carol's and your sibling's lives were possible saved by what I perceived to be a miracle by the Lord. Remember, little one, when I commented to you that Carol had instructed me to write a note and leave it on our door that we were going to the hospital. Two of Carol's family members were on their way from Seattle to Phoenix to be at their son's wedding. The male relative was an anesthesiologist who had once practiced medicine in Utah. They had flown to Salt Lake City where they wanted to visit some of their immediate family members; then they were going to rent a car and drive to Phoenix. They planned to stop by our apartment and visit with us. They had stopped by our apartment, read the note, and then decided to drive over to the hospital to check on us.

Carol's family members drove to the hospital, and asked where they could find the maternity word. I had no idea they would be coming to the hospital. I was never so relieved to see them. I greeted them and explained the severity of the situation concerning Carol and the baby. They were upset when they saw Carol suffering. The doctor quickly went to the nurses' station and identified himself as an MD. He told the senior nurse that he wanted Carol's primary physician either to get to the hospital as quickly as possible, or if unable to do, to quickly call another one. The wheels of activity began moving remarkably with speed. The OBGYN and the backup physician arrived in a very short time.

After what Carol had gone through, I would have deferred to any assistance, as long as it ended the pain she was undergoing. Finally, Carol's doctors, her relative, a pediatrician, an anesthesiologist, and I decided that a caesarean was necessary. However, I was the one who told her about the decision. She agreed to it. Carol had been in labor for fifty-six hours! What Carol went through should never have happened.

Carol was prepped for the operation. Her two doctors, an anesthesiologist and a pediatrician comprised the operating team, with attendant surgical nurses. I kissed Carol; held her hand, and told her how much I loved her. In turn, she told me that everything would be all right. She was very brave. Though I had become an emotional jerk, I did my best not to have her see me falling apart. Carol's family and I went into the surgical visitor's waiting area. Sunday, January 16, 1972 was the day that Carol's and my life would be changed forever.

About an hour after Carol had been wheeled into the OR, an announcement came over the PA system asking me to come up to nursery. Her relatives and I quickly went to the nursery and were met by the pediatrician, who shook our hands and then asked me, "Would you like to see your son?"

The pediatrician took all of us to the nursery whereupon we looked in and saw the most darling sight I could have ever seen—other than if I had seen you being born. There was your brother Mark in a bassinette! As I looked at him, tears began streaming down my cheeks. He was so beautiful, even as he lay there crying. I wanted so much to hold Mark, as I wanted to hold you eight years earlier. I was so choked up that I could hardly talk. The pediatrician said the operation had gone well for Carol, and that upon being taken out of her, the baby was thoroughly examined and everything was fine, and that his crying was normal for a new-born baby.

The obstetrician and his partner came down the hall, congratulated me and told me that Carol was fine and that I could go in to see her. Carol was tired but relieved. She had been so brave through her ordeal. Carol needed to recover from the C-section, and would be in the hospital for six days.

We both agreed to the name of Mark, since he was a boy. Pilgrim, guess what? Your brother Mark was born at 9:03, the morning of January 16, 1972, and 21 inches long. He weighed eight pounds, six ounces. Carol needed to get some sleep, so I told her I would be back in the afternoon after she had awakened, and had gotten refreshed. I kissed Carol goodbye, and then went down to the nursery to see Mark before I went home. The nurse indicated to me the crib in which he was sleeping. He looked wonderful sleeping. What a difficult experience for darling Carol to have undergone. She was so great.

I tearfully blew Mark a kiss and waved goodbye to my newly born son—as I would have done with you under the identical circumstances. I could not stop crying. I think you understand, Pilgrim. Yes, fathers do cry when seeing their first born. Darling Pilgrim, I wish you could have been able to see Mark and hold him shortly after he was born. The two of you would have immediately bonded. Pilgrim, I could not thank our Heavenly Father enough for delivering Carol from imminent danger, for the timely intervention of Carol's family, and for the safe delivery of little Mark.

My darling Pilgrim, how does it feel to have a younger brother? Mark is Carol's first child and my second one. You, of course, are my first-born and only daughter. I still remind myself that though your body was aborted, your spirit and love will always be with me. Someday, in the future, I will tell Mark about the wonderful older sister he has in Heaven, who our Heavenly Father has lent me to spend time as a spirit with me. He will also know that you love him as you would were you living here on earth. Our Heavenly Father loves you so much that he has taken away the pain of your abortion, and instead, has replaced the pain with redeeming love for all of us who were responsible for the events leading to your tragic death.

I know that I have been caught up with Carol's pregnancy and the birth of Mark, thus I have seemingly ignored you. Nothing could be further from the truth. While Carol and I prepared the requisite necessities for Mark's birth, I often thought about you and wished that you had been with us in life. It would have been wonderful to have your input, and enthusiasm present in laying the framework for Mark's "homecoming" into the world. Pilgrim, as I close this specific letter, once again, I thank our Lord for the triple blessings of Carol, you, and Mark. I love all of you so very much. I thank you specifically, my darling daughter, for being Mark's sister. It is time for another letter, darling daughter. Pilgrim, what a rough and bizarre four days for Carol and Mark! Whew, I will never forget what I refer to as the "tyranny of time" regarding the difficulties that Carol and Mark endured. I can smile now.

I love you always,
Dad

"AND BABY MAKES THREE"

Pilgrim, I finally got home after Mark's birth and the end of Carol's terrible ordeal. Upon arriving home, I took a 5X8 note card, and wrote a note to all of our neighbors telling them that we just had a baby boy named Mark. I pinned the note on the mailbox. Speaking of Mark, he was born on Super Bowl Sunday, January 16, 1972, and so when I got home, I thought that I would watch the game—which was between the Dallas Cowboys and the Miami Dolphins. The Cowboys won 24-3. I fell asleep on an intermittent basis while watching the game. However, I stayed awake to watch the end of the game and the post-game highlights. Pilgrim, it was then time to become reacquainted with both Carol and our newborn son. Carol slept for several hours, then phoned me from her private room, and mentioned that she had taken a shower, did her hair, and put on a fresh gown. Carol told me the nurse had brought Mark into her. She then nursed him and that he went to sleep in her arms. I have an idea that my new darling son had been as traumatized by the birth experience as Carol had been.

After talking with Carol, I showered, changed clothes, and drove back to the hospital with a couple of nightgowns and a bathrobe for her. Carol looked great after what she had endured. I hugged and kissed her carefully because of the C-section. I filled out some forms, such as the birth certificate, and some other related paperwork. Carol and I then walked down to the nursery holding hands. I brought our camera so I could take pictures of Carol and Mark. When the nurse saw us coming, she gently lifted Mark from his bassinette, brought him over the nursery window, and showed him to us. Mark was a bit cranky; however, he was as beautiful as he had been when I had previously seen him, earlier in the day. I took some great pictures of your brother. I also took one in Carol's room of Carol holding Mark, as she was getting ready to nurse him. I also found out the hospital had already taken some pictures of him.

I am now segueing into a new paragraph. Pilgrim, I would have taken many photos of you—had you been allowed to come to term. . My comment is not meant to be whimsical, but based upon the reality of a father seeing his child born—which might have happened if circumstances had been different.

God is merciful and provident to us. It, however, as earlier alluded to, took me a long time to accept the obvious fact that you had not been granted the right to life. Pilgrim, you have a younger brother—possibly your first sibling—yet I have loved you and Mark equally. Mark's birth has reinforced my realization that our Heavenly Father gives us human beings an opportunity to get things right—the second time. Pilgrim, the birth of Mark has brought about a complete sense of peace and gratitude, because as January 16, 1972. I became the father of two of the most wonderful children a man could have—you and Mark.

Pilgrim, Carol's and my gift to you is your brother Mark. He is the redemption for what happened to you in 1963. The Lord blessed us with a little boy, but simultaneously, he charged us to safeguard Mark's life and to love him with all our heart—as I love you with all my heart. Yet, God has remarkably given me the peace to know that while Mark is my earthly child, you, however, are now my heavenly daughter, and the older sister of your brother. You are not a fanciful entity that just exists as a figment of my imagination; you are now a spirit in Heaven who though no longer having human components, still is my daughter and Mark's sister. Please remember that. Let me now take you back to Mark's leaving the hospital so you can catch up.

Carol and I brought Mark home from the hospital the following Saturday. I had the opportunity to hold and carry Mark to the car, as we got ready to drive home. Carol laughingly showed me how to hold your brother. I had to realize—as most new fathers—that the baby was delicate, but durable. Carol indicated that I had to rest Mark's head in one hand, while simultaneous holding him against my chest or shoulder with the other hand. Whew, that was easier said than done!

Pilgrim, I knew that Willow married and began a family sometime in the 1970s and I am happy for her and extend to her only my best wishes. Your mother and I have to thank the Lord that He saw fit to bless us with your younger siblings—all of whom are now adults. .

Back to Mark, we got him in the car that Saturday morning, and Carol held him while I slowly drove to our apartment. I drove slower than I did ten days before when I was trying to get Carol to the hospital in a snowstorm. We got Mark home and he actually went to sleep in his crib.

We were home but a short while when we heard soft knocks on the door. Guess what? It was the beginning of a parade of our wonderful neighbors coming to see our new addition. They all brought food and/or gifts for him, and we took our neighbors into his bedroom to show him to them. I remember that everyone tiptoed softly into look at him. The neighbors cooed at him. They came back several times later in the week to either hold him or just smile at him. Pilgrim darling, I know that if you were with us, you of course, would be the doting, protective sister. I would bet on that. Darling Pilgrim, I always regretted that your mother and I never were able to proudly show you to family and friends.

Being a father meant that I had to learn to contribute to raising our child. This meant washing diapers, learning how to change his diapers, without sticking him or having to deal with sudden accidents. It also meant sleeping lightly enough during the night to wake up when Mark would begin to whimper, and then bringing him to Carol to nurse. After changing him, I would put him on his back between us for a while with the two of us facing him. Then after awhile, I would pick Mark up and carry him back to his crib, change him if necessary, and gently put him down, at which time he would go back to sleep—or at least hopefully so. Though this comment might sound unusual, I only wish that Willow could have had the ultimate joy of holding you.

It was not long before Carol and I noticed how Mark was beginning to change, as he began to slowly acquire abilities, such as hearing and seeing. Mark would smile when he heard our voices, and as he began being able to see, he would look into the direction where either of us was standing. He enjoyed the physical contact that we gave him, and I enjoyed holding him in my arms as he snuggled against my neck. .

Do you remember one of my earlier letters, Pilgrim, in which I described how, when I was living in New York City, I reacted with sadness to seeing a young couple arm in arm pushing a baby carriage and talking happily with one another? The reason for my sense of melancholy was that when the above incident took place, it was when you would have been born in 1964. Carol and I had a covered carriage/stroller in 1972 that we put Mark in and would take him for walks, arm-in-arm. As proud parents, we took countless pictures of Mark, such as when his first tooth came in, when he sat up, and when he began crawling, which *was* a sight in itself. Mark would crawl with his little rear end sticking up, and as fast as he could toward one or the both of us. Carol and I found it humorous to watch him doing his thing. I enjoyed fatherhood, Pilgrim, because I was so blessed to have the chance to connect with a human being that I helped conceive Sadly,. your mother and I never connected with you—which itself was depressing to think about.

You would have spoiled Mark—as so many big sisters do. Little one, I am sorry that your mother and I did not have the occasions to indulge you. Maybe, by later having children from our marriages, your mother and I might have finally learned that selfishness, immaturity, and acrimony are sins in themselves—just as abortion is a sin.

Pilgrim, Mark certainly changed Carol's and my lives—especially mine. I enjoyed learning how to take care of him, as I certainly would have enjoyed taking care of you. Changing Mark, giving him baths, feeding him, and shoulder-walking him until he fell asleep were not chores to me. I looked at these activities as being wonderful experiences. On second thought, Pilgrim, I would share the above responsibilities with you, because you probably could do as well, if not better, than me—and it would give you and Mark time to bond with one another.

Nine years had passed since the tragic events of 1963 that saw the taking of an innocent life of a little unborn baby girl in Southern California. For many years, the pain regarding what happened to you, my daughter Pilgrim, was overwhelming. However, my pain diminished when Mark was born. It was not long before the cold winter chill in Utah began to give way to spring in Utah County in 1972. Mark started making his impact on his apartment neighbors, and on the staff and patients of the Utah State Hospital, where his mother took him to show him to everyone. I also showed him to my graduate school colleagues, and to my professors, one of who said he thought fatherhood was good for me. Mark has the biggest blue-green eyes, blonde hair, and the most infectious smile that his parents ever saw on a baby—their obvious bias notwithstanding! Carol and I proudly exhibited him as one might a prized painting. We were caught up with our pride regarding Mark. All parents are that way. Carol and I believed Mark to be the most important thing in our lives. Ironically, Pilgrim, there might have been a time that your mother would have believed you to be the most precious possession she could have ever had—if you had been brought to term.

Pilgrim, I went back to working on my dissertation while doing such inventive things such as having your brother in his carrier seat on the table while I alternated between writing, feeding him, and, oh yes, changing his diapers.

I found that I could be either multi-faceted or multi-tasked when it came to the above. What I did was attempt to write my material on my legal pad, while doing the following: feeding Mark a bit of canned baby food, giving him a drink from his bottle, talking to him, letting him play with my finger, nuzzling him, and changing his diapers. Were you here, I would let you do your sister thing by doing some, if not all, of the above. After all, Mark is your brother. Actually, when I got Mark to sleep is when I could begin on the dissertation.

What has come to mind is my imagery of you being eight years old. I perceived you to have long hair like your mother, with somewhat angular facial features, and her smile. You possibly would have had my blond hair and blue eyes—hopefully that would be all. However, I believe you would have had my cynical sense of humor—though let us hope that at eight years old that would not be too apparent.

. Pilgrim, as an aside, I wonder what might have happened had you been granted the right to be born and whether or not Willow would have kept you. Had Willow kept you I would have been able to have an active part of your life because I would be paying child support and other related expenses, and no matter where I lived, I would have been able to get visitation rights or time allotted with you during the summer. No doubt by the time you were eight years old, you could have traveled unaccompanied on a plane to come to see me. It would have been a fantastic emotional experience meeting you at an airport as you got off the plane. I am certain I would be tearful as I gathered you in my arms, hugged, and kissed you.

Had your mother given you up for adoption, the decision certainly would not have been an easy one for me to accept, but that would have been a choice that your mother made, yet one far better than an abortion. I would have been devastated, but nevertheless, at least I would have known that our Heavenly Father would have been protecting you and putting you in the arms of wonderful parents. I would have felt secure knowing you were alive and well taken care of by your adoptive parents. Though we may have never actually been together after your birth, the three of us—Willow, you, and I—would have still been irrevocably linked for life, and the fact that the Lord would have been watching over you, would have brought peace to your mother and me.

Speaking of making choices, we traded in Blue Baby in 1972 for a Ford Gran Torino four-door sedan, because we needed a larger vehicle for Mark. It was sad to trade in Blue Baby; "she" had been a super automobile the years we owned her. The VW had taken Carol and I to many a great place throughout the country and it brought a wonderful baby home from the hospital. When we purchased the Ford, we bought a baby-seat for the front seat—since the car had bench seats—and a baby bed for the back where we could put Mark when he would be taking a nap on a trip. Guess what Pilgrim? When Mark was almost seven months old we took him on a trip to Las Vegas. It was about a seven-hour trip, but he did quite well traveling. While we were in Las Vegas, Mark enjoyed himself, especially when Carol and I took him to the hotel pool. However, Mark was anything but pleased when, one evening, Carol and I got a babysitter for him while we went to a dinner show. I still remember that during the show, Carol and I were nervous about whether Mark was okay. When the show was over, we got back to the room as rapidly as possible only to find that Mark was still up and crying, and the poor babysitter frazzled! We paid her a bit more then the required rate; she deserved it. We held Mark and he went to sleep.

Darling daughter, I bet that you probably would be in second or third grade in 1972. I would have enjoyed you describing your favorite activities, such as who your best friends were, your favorite classroom subject(s) and the name of your teachers. I would have asked your mother if she would be kind enough to send me a copy of your semester grades, and a school picture of you. I know you would be tall for your age, but a beautiful little girl. As an aside, when Mark was older, I really enjoyed his school pictures. Seeing the photographs was enlightening because I got to see his schoolmates, teachers, and where his classroom was. Darling Pilgrim, I hope you would have been as excited to send me your report card and school photograph, as I would have been receiving them. I know I would be so proud of you—if for no other reason than the fact you are my daughter.

Well, Mark's first year went by so fast, which meant Carol and I had to baby-proof the apartment because your brother was like a water bug! He was everywhere at once. He was becoming more delightful as he was approaching his first birthday. Mark was beginning to walk; actually, what he did was to stand up, then propel himself from one point to another, whereby he could grab something to arrest his progress. He thought it was so funny, and it was. In fact, Carol and I laughed so hard at his endeavors. He would follow this game plan from one side a room to another. He also did a lot of talking and would either have a spirited conversation with his parents or with himself. By the time Mark was a year old—or shortly thereafter—he was able to walk. Speaking of first birthdays, I wish you could have been with us darling Pilgrim, for Mark's birthday. We had a number of pictures taken of Mark—many that I still have. We had a birthday cake for him, and attempted to get him to blow out the candle on the cake. However, he was more interested in trying to obliterate the cake! Nevertheless, Mark's first birthday was a memorable one.

Pilgrim, how I wished you too would have had a first birthday with its attendant wonderful memories. Willow and I never were given the opportunity to be with you for such a joyous occasion. My darling I am sad when I am confronted with the fact you would never have any actual birthdays. In fact, it is painful to think about that.

I have wiped my eyes and will go on with the narrative. The year 1973 was a pivotal one: Mark was now a year old and ever-changing, and was he ever growing. He now had his own personality, and he and I were becoming ever closer. We had this wonderful bonding as father and son. It was always wonderful to hold him or to put him on my shoulders and take him places. He enjoyed taking walks with me and I would often take him to a stable that was about two blocks away, where he would have a great time petting two horses named Prince and Jeb—who, in turn, looked forward to seeing Mark. And Mark and I would bring carrots and apples for Prince and Jeb. The two horses enjoyed being doted on by Mark. Prince and Jeb looked upon Mark as their friend. The three of them were inseparable

By the way Pilgrim, I know that Prince and Jeb would have liked you as much as they did Mark. In the meantime, Carol had gone back to work after a few months home with Mark. She worked the second shift, so she got a babysitter to stay with him until I got home after driving the afternoon bus routes. The babysitter was a young high school student named Jill. She and Mark had this mutual admiration society when it came time to each other. Jill was a very sweet young lady who just seemed to bring out the best in him. Mark felt very much at ease with her. Jill told me a number of times that when Mark heard me coming up the walkway, he would either crawl or get up and run to the edge of the sofa, holding on to it until I opened the door—ever carefully—and I would pick him up as he squealed with delight. I would hug him and kiss him and he would kiss and hug me back.

Reunions with Mark—though daily—were always wonderful. By the way, Pilgrim, your younger brother was fascinated with trains—maybe I should admit I was just as attracted to trains as he was. I would take him to the Provo railroad station to watch the freight and passenger trains go by. We would wave at the train engineers; many of them would wave back and blow their train whistle. Mark thought that watching trains was a great event. He even made friends with other railroad aficionados who were also down at the station watching the trains. Pilgrim, guess what? When I was a small boy, I used to be hooked on trains. You in your youthful maturity—what a clever oxymoron—would probably have thought it was passé to spend time watching trains, maybe not. By the way, one Sunday, when Mark was two years old, I took him on a train ride from Provo to Price, Utah. He loved it! He and I then returned to Provo by a Trailways bus. The two of us had a wonderful time, and of course, I would have sent you copies of the photos I took of Mark on that trip. I know you would have enjoyed seeing them!

May I digress and reflect for several paragraphs? Do you remember that it was back in the summer of 1963 when you were aborted? I had no idea, back on that hot September day in 1963, when my plane to New York lifted off the runway at Los Angeles International Airport that my life would markedly change. Indeed, as I left Los Angeles that day, I had already bought into the belief that there was little that could be redeemed by staying in Southern California. I had gone as low in life as I possibly could. Therefore, it was time to move elsewhere. I have to admit though that I felt like a complete failure when my flight from Los Angles to New York became airborne. Do you recall, Pilgrim, when I told you in an earlier letter about how I spent most of the time weeping during the flight to New York? One reason for my tears was that I was actually frightened of what the future might hold. I had lost you and Willow, and along with the loss of the two of you, I thought I had relinquished whatever dignity a human being could have. During that flight, when I was not thinking of you and your mother, I was attempting to steel myself for an uncertain future.

Pilgrim, I could not believe that during that flight my mind could race as it did. As I described in an earlier letter, that while on that flight, I had so many emotions with which to deal that I was almost physically exhausted.

Yet, surprisingly, during the flight, I began to acquire some backbone by telling myself that I was not ever going to allow anyone to ever embarrass me again, or hurt those who I loved—and that included you darling Pilgrim. I can remember that Friday evening as the jet was making its final approach to the airport in New York, I became determined to make something out of my life—no matter how long it took me. I promised myself that I would no longer have a "spaghetti spine." Having said that, I knew I had my work cut out for me. So what if making these changes took a long time, I was going to achieve whatever goals I set out to accomplish.

As you know, change came slowly to my life; there was no magical transformation. However, the Lord began in late 1963 to assist me in making the necessary changes that I had to in life. By the time the summer of 1973 came about, Carol and I were parents of a beautiful baby boy. You had a baby brother. And I received my Ph.D. Gosh, Pilgrim. Who would have thought, back on that hot, steamy day in September 1963, as my flight took of from Los Angeles, that I would eventually be so blessed? Darling daughter, I certainly had no such expectations back in 1963...

Regarding my Ph.D., thanks to the Lord and His gifts, along with the help of Carol, my professors, and colleagues, I successfully completed and defended my doctoral dissertation one afternoon in the summer of 1973—less than five years after I had begun my graduate studies at BYU. The dissertation defense was two hours in length, and covered all aspects of what I had studied while in the history graduate program—including my language exams. When my dissertation defense was finally over, I was asked to leave the room. I was out in the hallway for what I perceived to be an interminable amount of time—actually it was for a very few minutes. The door opened and the Department Chairman beckoned me into the room. As I entered, he said, "Congratulations Doctor LePore and a job well done!"

Wow, Pilgrim, I was speechless, but, of course, very much elated. I just had to make a few small corrections to the dissertation, which I did the next day. When my chairman and I were alone, he congratulated me. He told me how much he had enjoyed being my chairman, and that he expected great things from me. I cannot recall anyone earlier in my life making such a statement. I then went home feeling blessed and full of gratitude. I could not thank the Lord enough for what had transpired over ten years. I owed the Lord everything!

However, I got home, Pilgrim, and found poor Mark had a fever of close to 104! He had roseola. Carol and I quickly took him to the emergency room where he was placed into ice baths until his temperature came down. Carol and I were frightened. However, Mark's temperature came down to 98.6. He was then given an antibiotic, liquids, and some medicine. The ER doctor told us to keep him hydrated and on the medicine. We got him home, and we held him, and then he fell asleep in Carol's arms and we then put him in his crib. I know I said many prayers for Mark while he was in the ER. Our Lord not only answered our prayers, but also brought Mark back to health. I had earlier thanked our Heavenly Father that I passed my dissertation exams. More importantly, though, I subsequently thanked God again for watching over Mark and answering our prayers.

I received my Ph.D. in August 1973. There were about 2500 other students obtaining their degrees on that same day. The graduate dean invited me to lead the graduation procession into the field house. It was quite the honor. I evidently did a decent job leading the graduates into the field house; no one was lost, and everyone—including me—made it to their assigned seats. After the graduation ceremony was over, one of my favorite professors came up to congratulate me. He said how much he enjoyed being one of my major professors, and that he believed I had a lot of ability. As he shook my hand, I remember that he made two profound statements: first, he said: "Herb, now that you have studied your craft, you should go out and teach your students what you have learned." He continued, "Don't be a person seeking status; be an individual of substance."

I never forgot those admonitions. Sadly, that wonderful professor is deceased. However, I have kept his advice—or at least have attempted to do so—with varying degrees of success. Pilgrim, I wish you could have been with Carol and Mark and had seen me graduate. I would have been so proud to have the three of you in the stands that day. We all could have been in a photo together.

Early in my introduction to the letters, I referred to the 1973 pivotal Supreme Court decision that affected abortion: it was *Roe v Wade* (1973). Well, Pilgrim, it is now 1973, and the Court, in a unanimous vote, said that abortion throughout the United States was now legal. Women could legally have abortions and did not need the consent of anyone to have an abortion. The Court's decision meant that women now could go to doctors who were allowed to perform legal abortions anytime during the pregnancy. I can still remember that when the decision was rendered, it began generating a great deal of discussion as to the constitutionality and morality of it. Those two issues still are vehemently argued now. The decision, though ostensibly a legal one, is a tragic situation to be in. Nevertheless, it brings about serious contradictions for those of us who, while advocating the sanctity of life, acknowledge the rights of people to make legal choices regarding their own bodies—even if to do so entails a tragic and difficult decision.

Anyway, however a person may react to an abortion, there are presently no legal or philosophical codes denying women the right to an abortion. Yes, there is the spiritual equation and a commandment that forbid the killing of innocent people—particularly unborn babies. However, having said that, the Lord has given people absolute freedom to either obey or disobey His laws. Women and whoever else is involved in abortions must live with their own conscience. Pilgrim, I had the right to be angry and grief-stricken regarding what your mother and her parents did. I even had the right to judge them for taking your life. My condemnation of them, however, should have remained on the proverbial side of the road, and been left up to the Lord—Nevertheless, though no less a sinner than Willow and her parents, I chose to judge and condemn them—this, in spite of calling myself a Christian. Yet, my emotions illustrated too well that I was no better of a Christian than they were.

The above *Roe v. Wade* decision made me think of your mother. I wondered what her opinion was of *Roe v. Wade*. I also pondered if Willow would ever suggest to any daughters that she had that they should have abortions if beset by unwanted pregnancies. Pilgrim, I pray your mother would never entertain or sanction such a horrible and cruel suggestion. I would think that Willow suffered enough by aborting you. I only hope *abortion* is no longer an operative word in her vocabulary By the way, the *Roe v. Wade* decision has brought about the implementation of abortion in the United States as being a mostly white, middle to upper class endeavor—though purportedly available to almost all women regardless of their socio-economic backgrounds. Sadly, unborn babies have become a "disposable" item in our culture.

Having discussed the above, I am no less against abortion. First, I am against the arbitrary taking of an innocent life, and I believe that life and the soul begin at conception. Second, I abhor the killing of someone who is so tiny and defenseless, and who is created by God. Abortion is spiritually and morally wrong and emotionally distressing as well. Nonetheless, the Lord has not given anyone the right to be judge, jury, and executioner when it comes to the abortion of a baby. Yet, people assume those roles so easily. As previously stated, there are better spiritual and ethical options for the mother, father, and any cohort involved in the decision-making process to take, as opposed to resorting to abortion—as a quick-fix solution. Besides, in my opinion, abortion connotes "cruel and unusual punishment" for an innocent being. Perhaps, fewer women and men would sanction abortion if they recognized the barbaric nature of it, and its long-term effect on all involved. As I commented earlier in the missive, there are no winners concerning abortion. Unfortunately, whether legal or not, women in America are still having abortions, and will continue to do so.

Pilgrim, though I pleaded with Willow to not have an abortion, what I also attempted to do was to get her to understand that you had a right to live. Willow and I, however, fell prey to playing God, and that was as much of a sin as having the abortion itself. However, today, of course, whether your mother would have an abortion or had any abortions after 1973 would legally be a moot issue. Yet, the stigma, pain, and related emotions associated with an abortion have become conveniently cloaked in the political correctness of the American judicial system. Though a wrongful act, to most people, abortion is sanctioned by the legal system. What *Roe v Wade* indicates is that as a nation we have become a calloused society. Pilgrim, we are now inured to such things as violence, murder, abuse of any kind, and, of course, abortion.

It seems that remorse and compassion are no longer dominant restraints to either making bad choices or to healing the pain and grief—associated with an abortion. We have become imbued with an ethical relativism that someday may bring down our nation, and abortion is one of its tragic components. That day may be nearer than we know.

The tragedy of you being aborted has likely gotten into your mother's psyche. I know what *Roe v Wade* did for me: The decision made me patently aware there subsequently will be millions of new stories of legally-sanctioned heartbreak and pain regarding abortions—particularly in light of the fact that one in four women by the age of forty-five will have had at least one abortion. An abortion cannot be reversed—and those of us who contributed in any way to it have to live with that realization for the remainder of our lives—this includes your mother and I. If we as people are to markedly reduce abortions in this country, we must alter our attitudes and behavior concerning sexual activity, and simultaneously offer social, emotional, and spiritually viable choices to women and men who believe abortions are their only options.

Well, enough history on *Roe v. Wade*. Pilgrim. Back to your brother Mark, who was becoming a live wire, and a well traveled one at that. We took him to places such as Lake Tahoe, Seattle, Seaside, Oregon, and Jackson Hole, Wyoming. He enjoyed traveling and was delightful when he would point out the car window from his car seat and say, "see." Once in a while, he would come down with a cold or flu on a trip and we would have to stop at a town, take him to see a doctor, get a prescription filled, then after taking the medicine, he would sleep in his car seat, and would later feel fairly well. Mark and I were close. We enjoyed our father-son time together, and always looked forward to it. Darling daughter, you would have enjoyed these trips with Mark, Carol, and me. Of course, we would have looked forward to having you with us wherever we traveled.

Pilgrim, since it is 1973, I am now the proud father of a nine-year-old daughter. Had you lived, I would have been able to tell all my friends, professors, and family about you. As your dad, I would not be able to stop bragging about you. It is a given that you would likely look like your mother; however, I think that you would have my humor, my idealism, and my compassion for the less fortunate. I would hope that not only now, but in the future as well, that you and I could always have quality time alone for us to talk and share things; after all, you would be a very articulate nine-year-old. It would have been wonderful to hear you share those things in your life you believed to be important. As with sons, fathers need time with and for their daughters. Of course, as a girl, you would likely have things that you wanted to keep to yourself. I would certainly understand. Darling, fathers usually know when children need their space and privacy, and their confidences maintained. I would always honor your requirements.

As most little girls, you would have been a voracious reader—and you would get that trait from your mother. Yet, I certainly would have looked forward to discussing with you the books that you had read. I would buy you books and send them to you. When I was about your age, I had a stepfather with whom I could not get along. However, he did something that affirmed my life—that was to get me to read. He bought me many of the great literary classics, had me read them within a certain period, and then interrogated me about what I had read. However, it was a great way to retain what I read—and it enhanced my love of books. Later, I would do that with Mark—though with much more patience than my stepfather. I have always been an insatiable reader though, since I am a senior citizen (politically correct term for old man), I read a bit less, and do more writing and traveling.

Well in 1975, after postgraduate work, I was offered a teaching position at a university in New Mexico. We packed up to leave Utah after about seven years—which included five years of graduate work. Pilgrim, it was very sad leaving Provo. Carol and I had your little brother in Provo. We had made many friends—both on and off campus. The three of us had a wonderful life while living in Provo. And I received my Ph.D. in American History at a great university. It was not easy to leave without some regrets. To this day, Pilgrim, I rank the years that Carol and I spent in Utah to have been the very best ones that I ever spent in my entire life. Gosh, I have become a bit teary and nostalgic about the period.

It is time for another letter darling daughter.

I love you so much,

Dad

THE UNHAPPY SHADOWS

We left Utah for New Mexico in 1975. Our move required driving straight through over Labor Day Weekend. It was a most stressful endeavor moving to another state. Well, we arrived in New Mexico frazzled and tired, and I had to begin teaching the next day. We already had one of our two cars in New Mexico. We had bought a 1975 Volkswagen Rabbit that I had taken down the previous week, when I had gone down to look for a place for us. I left the car there, flew from Albuquerque to Salt Lake City, where Carol and Mark met me at the airport with our 1972 Ford. I was glad to see them. We then began driving to New Mexico.

The week did not begin very well. Again, I failed in the selection of a place for us to live. When Carol saw the house that I had chosen for us to rent, she was not reluctant to let me know her disdain for my choice—or lack thereof. Her rebuke hurt. Carol and I however, regained our composure. We eventually rented a very nice two-bedroom apartment in an apartment complex that had professional people and fellow college professors. There were a number of children Mark's age, so it was not long before Mark had his group of friends—some of who were children of fellow professors. There was also a very nice swimming pool that was well used by the tenants and their children during the summer.

I was an assistant professor teaching four classes—including an evening graduate course. I was busy, but teaching was stimulating to say the least. Pilgrim, I remembered what my professor had told me when I graduated about being a person of substance as opposed to being concerned with status. Our department chairman was a stickler for titles. He wanted his faculty to be referred to as either "professor" or "doctor." We were expected to answer the phone with either of the above two titles. It was not a problem unless Carol phoned me, and then she would sometimes make a silly or jokingly sarcastic comment. We would have a good laugh. Within time, I attempted to dispense with titles—or at least mitigate their use. Titles do not make an individual a better person. I would rather be known as a lovable, fallible, yet good person as opposed to a person with a title or status.

Carol and I decided it was about time that your little brother made the trek to nursery school. The university had such an institution within the university laboratory school. Guess what though, it took Mark a while to get used to it. We had to remember that before now Mark had never been separated from either of us at the same time.

Both Carol and I sensed the anxiety that Mark had to deal with, and we attempted to reassure him when we took him to school that everything would be all right. When Mark realized that we were leaving the lab school, he would begin to cry. The woman professor had us leave so that she could spend time getting Mark acclimated to the environment and the other children. Normally, he would stop crying and become involved in the activities. I must admit, Pilgrim, that Carol and I also suffered his pain. We would hide it to the best of our ability, but whichever one of us picked Mark up after his morning period was over, we were as greatly relieved to see him as he was to see us.

Well, back to the first year of university teaching; it was exciting. The mix of undergraduate and graduate students was interesting, and teaching large classes was challenging. The students included Anglos, Native Americans, Hispanics, and African Americans—a wonderful cultural, ethnic, and racial mix. I was teaching both day and evening classes—so I was busy. However, I had time to spend with Mark before I would have to return to the campus for my night classes. Meanwhile, Carol had gotten a job as a nurse at a nearby hospital and her shifts were in the afternoon. This meant that sometimes we would get a babysitter to take care of Mark while we both worked. Surprisingly, Mark got along well with babysitters.

Pilgrim, you would have been eleven or twelve by the mid 1970s. Had you been living with your mother, you would have been in junior high school or middle school. You, no doubt, would have been busy with school activities, and would be tall and a beautiful pre-teen. I want you to know that I would have been communicating with you on a weekly basis—either by letter or phone. On second thought, I would possibly have done both. I would have enjoyed receiving pictures of you. I realize that boys your age would be taking more than a passing interest in you.

Though you likely would have a stepfather, I want to assure you that I would have always been accessible to you. Darling daughter, please remember that. I know that my family would certainly have missed you, but I would have arranged with your mother that you fly to New Mexico to spend one or more weeks with us. New Mexico is a beautiful place and there is a lot to do there. You and Mark would have enjoyed exploring the flora and fauna of the state.

At the end of my first year of teaching, I received a very nice evaluation by my department chairman. He told me that I had great potential as a college teacher. I felt very good about the department chairman's assessment of my teaching. In fact, as I recall, I was unconsciously beginning not to heed my graduate professor's admonition regarding substance versus status. Pilgrim, I was starting to be full of myself. How obviously short my memory was about what I had been told by my professor the day I received my Ph.D. However, down the road, I eventually recovered from my self—indulgence and in time went back to being a low-keyed human being.

Carol and I were busy with our professions and seemingly did not have time for one another. I was working hard with my teaching and research, while Carol was as busy with her nursing profession. We emotionally were losing touch with one another, though unintentionally. What instead was taking place was that we both devoted our time and energy to Mark, which, though important, should not have been a replacement for the two of us spending time alone with one another. Tragically, Pilgrim, Carol and I faltered in our responsibility to one another—we ignored each other's feelings and needs.

What happened to our marriage was the insidious drift apart—that neither of us was aware of until it was too late. I found out the hard way that this is a common event in marriages and that unless quickly addressed and corrected, marriages will eventually fall into disarray and ultimately into divorce. Tragically, this would be a terrible time for Carol and me. Mark, however, was kept out of our difficulties until 1980.

What Carol and I did, Pilgrim, was to abort our marriage, almost as callously as you had been aborted. Though the following statement sounds somewhat exaggerated, it was accurate: the trauma of our marital difficulties and eventual divorce were no less horrific than had been the shock of your death.

However, Carol and I initially attempted to stave off the divorce. The two of us went to see a marriage counselor. He told us that both of us had taken each other for granted and that we had ceased to communicate our needs to one another and also failed to be perceptive of one another's vulnerabilities. The psychologist wanted the two of us to undergo therapy both together and as individuals. I agreed to it—as if I had any choice if I wanted to put the marriage back together. However, possibly startling was the fact that Carol said she did not need therapy. Thus, no therapy took place, but what came about instead was the implementation of a "cold war" of sorts—that sadly remained in place for four years. There was very little respite in the hostility.

Carol and I took turns threatening divorce throughout the next four years. We did not physically or emotionally intimidate one another. It was just that every so often the tension overwhelmed us. We did our best not to show our stress to Mark, and thus attempting to hide our issues the best that we could. Remember when I told you that your mother and I failed to end our relationship before it self-destructed, well the same could be said about Carol and me; we both realized that barring a miracle, our marriage was doomed. Carol and I hurt just as your mother and I had hurt many years before. We attempted to purge ourselves of our pain by directing our emotions and love on Mark.   In spite of all of our problems, we otherwise had a decent home life. We took trips throughout the Southwest, the Intermountain West, and the West Coast, places where I ran marathon races. We also went on a trip during the Christmas break of 1977 to Disneyland, then to Beverly Hills to visit my Aunt Dora, who had been to see us while we lived in Provo. Carol, Mark and I enjoyed our stay in Los Angeles. Two of Carol's family members flew down from Seattle, and we went to the Rose Bowl. We then stopped off to see Laura and Craig. We then continued to San Diego where we visited the San Diego Zoo. We all had a great time. Then we drove home to New Mexico.

Darling daughter, let me take a respite from the previously alluded to sadness to say that no matter what was going on between Carol and I, Carol, Mark, and I would have been excited to see you. The time I would have spent with you would not have been long enough. However, I know that I would have had the responsibility to get you back to your mother. Darling daughter, you would have been fourteen years old and, in all likelihood, a freshman in high school. You, no doubt, would have been a stunningly beautiful young woman. By the way, I mentioned that Carol and I took Mark to Disneyland. Did you know that Willow worked there during the summers she was in college? Likely, she would have told you. Anyway, we would have gotten you, and taken you to see my Aunt Dora. I know she would have liked you right away. I would have asked your mother if I could have taken you to the Rose Bowl game—because we had an extra ticket. I am certain that when it was time for my family and I to leave, you and I would be weepy saying goodbye to each other. Even to this day, I occasionally become teary-eyed thinking of you and your mother. It is difficult to acknowledge this, but in spite of all the bad things that happened between your mother and me, I still loved her.

Please allow me a recapitulation of my relationship with your mother. I am writing this because I believe you would now better understand why bad things happened to our relationship. Every so often, back in 1963, there had a glimmer of love and hope—that being whenever your two biological parents left the mist of deception that enveloped them. At that time, we would have flash points of happiness and love towards one another. Unfortunately, our lack of honesty and respect destroyed our connection. Darling Pilgrim, tragically, I must say that your mother and I had nothing really to give one another—though we often deluded ourselves into thinking that if only the other person would only be amenable to what we wanted, everything would be all right. This naiveté, along with the fact that Willow and I reveled in our selfishness, were two of the most significant components to the disaster that beset your mother and me in 1963. Pilgrim, it still hurts when I write this because of the trauma associated with that summer.

My heart is heavy, Pilgrim, as I share with you the pain that happens between men and women. Many of us are emotionally fragile creatures. We profess being strong, but are actually weak. We often fail at the rudiments of relationships because we sometimes only love in proportion to what love we receive—or we believe that is shown us. Many of us are reluctant to be ourselves, because to do so is to be vulnerable, and we do not want people to see our shortcomings—or the real us. Instead, we often require the other person to provide us the reason(s) to love them. Above all, we leave God out of our marriages and relationships. I know of what I speak because I am certain that I have been guilty of most, if not all of the above. I wish I could hold you in my arms and tell you that everything was all right and that Carol and I had worked out our differences. Sadly, that would not be the case.

One can write books on how and why marriages and relationships fail, and give them to couples to read. Yet, there would be little guarantee that having read such books, couples would have successful marriages or relationships. Darling Pilgrim, it would take some time before I really addressed my anguish over why our marriage failed. I know that I failed to hold up my end of the marriage. My failure as a marriage partner made me come to realize that I had apparent shortcomings/flaws as a person, and had to deal with them. Sadly my darling daughter, grownups attempt to deceive other, but only deceive themselves. Well, on with my third year of university teaching.

Earlier in September 1977, I began my third year at the university, and once again had a busy teaching schedule that combined both undergraduate and graduate courses. During the summer before the 1977 college year commenced, I had spent time back in Washington at the National Archives, The Library of Congress, the Bureau of Indian Affairs, then on to Yale University, and the Newberry Library in Chicago to do research on a book dealing with the Indian Reorganization Act of 1934. The faculty senate had given me a stipend of $2000 to do research on the book, and I was looking forward to begin collating my research and then start my writing. Darling daughter, there were no personal computers back in 1977, so I had to resort to the time-honored 8x17 legal pad on which to write my narrative. Let me put it mildly, writing an entire monograph on legal paper was a labor-intensive endeavor. However, I had practiced years earlier doing a dissertation.

As fall of 1977 came about, Carol and I were coexisting. We very seldom argued or actually made pejorative comments toward each other. We both hid our pain behind the mask of civility—which in itself was a cruel hoax. Both Carol and I lost weight, and we obsessively doted on Mark. I guess that what love we had to give, we gave to Mark—because obviously we had none left to give one another.

While Carol and I were struggling with our marriage in the fall of 1977, I was back to my teaching. Things were going well. I enjoyed my students and the classes, Mark enjoyed going to kindergarten with his friends, and I had begun working on my book. Then one morning, the department chairman asked me to stop into see him after one of my classes. I went to his office and he told me had had some information to tell me. The State of New Mexico had reduced its college and university funding and only had money to maintain the faculty numbers of all the institutions until the end of the spring semester—after which there would be a reduction in faculty. Our department was to lose faculty based upon a process of seniority. . Nevertheless, I listened as the chairman gave me the news. He told me that I had done a superior job teaching, but that he had to follow directives from "higher headquarters." Ironically, I had just received notification that I had an article from one of my dissertation chapters published in a prestigious West Coast historical journal. I am not certain if I even shared that information with the chairman. I remembered that I told him that I would continue to give him and the university my best—no matter what happened. In fact, I said to him that I would not divulge what he told me to anyone on campus, but instead would leave it to him to decide when to divulge what he had shared with me.

I knew one thing: I would have to share the disturbing news with Carol; Pilgrim that would be a difficult and painful task. I had no choice, however, but to do it. How does one share misfortune with someone who has little faith or admiration in you as a person or husband? I did tell Carol exactly what the department chairman had shared with me. I attempted to reassure her that I might be able to find a job elsewhere for the following school year. The two of us, however, had the sinking feeling that might be almost impossible to do. I suggested we just look at how best we might address this issue, as opposed to blindly reacting to it. She agreed. I kept up a positive front. I remember I went back on campus to teach my afternoon class when the Academic Dean came up to me, offered his condolence for the news, and said that he had drafted a Letter of Commendation and a Letter of Recommendation, and that he would keep them until I requested they be sent to another university or college. He was kind enough to give me personal copies of the letters. I thanked him, and met another member of the department who would also lose his position at the end of the spring semester. We commiserated with one another. He also had a family. Though being fallible, I could acknowledge my defects. At times, I corrected one or more parts of my life, only to deal with the realization that I had other elements of my existence with which I was constantly dealing. Pilgrim, after the summer of 1963, upon leaving California for New York, I began to slowly learn responsibility, and was successful with it until things went wrong in my marriage to Carol. Once again, I would have to go back to the drawing board as far as rebuilding my life. Darling daughter, it was painful. God had to drum things into me so I had to face myself. I got a little better. However, Pilgrim, I would be spending the majority of my life undergoing emotional and spiritual reconstruction of one kind or another.

Every day, though, I dealt with ambivalent thoughts, such as maybe I should go ahead and have Carol divorce me, so both of us could get on with our lives, or that possibly Carol and I could work things out so that Mark's life would not be disrupted. I believe that Carol had the same thoughts. Pilgrim, I must be honest in that my biggest fear was losing Mark as the result of a divorce. I loved him so much and we were truly inseparable. I knew that if Mark and I had to be apart, I would have to deal with the identical pangs of loss, depression, anger, grief, and denial as I earlier felt with your death. Mark, of course, would have the same emotions to deal with if he and I were apart.

However, I was immersed in my teaching and research, so the teaching year went by rapidly. Meanwhile, I sent many letters of application for college teaching positions, but got very few positive responses, of which I received no offers for interviews or jobsMeanwhile, Carol and I continued doing our best to hide our pain and to go on with our lives. We told Mark that we were leaving either at the end of the spring semester or after the completion of the summer term. The two of us explained to him that there was not enough money to pay all of the professors, and since I was one of the most recent hires, and that I would have to look elsewhere for work. However, both Carol and I reassured Mark that we would not be leaving until New Mexico until the end of the summer, and that he would still have his group of friends. Mark seemed to accept what we shared with him.

Carol and I concluded that it was time to move somewhere else. My chairman tried to be helpful. He said that he kept hoping there might be some fiscal permutations in the state legislature whereby some money would surface to keep faculty in our department. I appreciated his efforts, though knowing the opportunity for retention was almost nonexistent. The fact that Mark had so many friends his age in the apartment complex in which we lived, helped to deflect any apprehension he might have had. The kids were always busy swimming or going places with parents, so that kept everyone busy. My chairman asked me if I would be the acting department chair while he was gone, so I was busy doing that and teaching three classes over the two summer school sessions. I enjoyed the multifunction job, and though the time for Carol, Mark, and I to leave was almost upon us, in some ways it was difficult to say goodbye—especially to my colleagues, chairman, and our friends. We had no idea what the future held for us, but we had decided to move to El Paso, Texas.

Over a two-day period, we packed everything, including our two goldfish, Jimmy and Dave. We put them in a bucket of water, and put it on the floor of the U-Haul truck that we rented to drive to El Paso in the late summer of 1978. Pilgrim, in 1978, you would have been fourteen and a freshman in high school. Your pictures would indicate you are a lovely, energetic, young woman, who would do well in whatever you undertook, plus you would have had boys crowding around your school locker. I know that Willow would have been every bit as proud of you as I was. It is back to reality. Well, we are here in El Paso. Pilgrim, it is time for another letter for you. Will these letters ever become joyful? I certainly hope so.

I love you so much,

Dad

THE DIVORCE

Pilgrim, Carol and I found a rather nice apartment on the eastside of El Paso, and we enrolled Mark into first grade at an elementary school about a mile away from where we lived. Carol went to work in the psychiatric unit of one of the local hospitals, and I was fortunate enough to get a part-time job teaching at a local community college and at the United States Army Sergeant Majors Academy. I felt so much better now that we were in a different city. My classes were very enjoyable—both at the college and at the Sergeant Majors Academy. Pilgrim, I felt refreshed and things appeared to be somewhat better between Carol and me. My teaching schedule was such that I was able to pick up Mark after school. Mark enjoyed his classmates and his teacher, and Carol and I became involved in the school PTA. I looked forward to my time with Mark. I would go to the playground with him and the evenings that Carol was working, Mark and I often went out to dinner, and unless he had homework, I would take him to the main mall in El Paso, and the two of us would have a wonderful time hanging out. The two of us were inseparable from the time he was an infant until he and Carol left El Paso to live in Seattle. Pilgrim, Mark was a blessing to me—even when we were separated by the eventual divorce. Though, I possibly did not deserve such a wonderful son, I have always thanked the Lord for the gift of fatherhood. He blessed Carol and me immeasurably with Mark, regardless of what was taking place between us adults.

El Paso was a large border city on the American side, and its Mexican side of the border was Ciudad Juarez, a city of comparable size. El Paso at that time had about 400,000 people, and ironically, its Anglo-American citizens were in the minority. A large portion of its populace was comprised of military retirees and active military personnel who were stationed the two primary military installations: White Sands Missile Range, New Mexico, and Fort Bliss, Texas. The desert was on the east and north, and a mountain range to the west, surrounded the city.

I hoped that the move to El Paso would be a kind of "milieu therapy" for all of us. That having been said, it was imperative that Carol and I begin intensive marriage counseling to bring our marriage from the brink of disaster into a viable, loving relationship. That did not happen. We instead fell prey to "whistling in the dark." After the divorce in 1980, I realized that the two of us had been in complete denial about what had to be done to preserve our marriage, and whatever love we had for one another.

Pilgrim, do you remember when I told you that you had died at the hands of three civilized, rational, ethical human beings back in Southern California in 1963? Well, two people of similar backgrounds aborted a marriage and brought havoc to the life of a small boy—these people were Carol and I.

Back in 1963, your mother and I never faced our disappointments in each other. We did not look realistically at what we two individuals were all about. We instead conveniently heaped the blame for whatever went wrong on each other. Carol and I did the very same thing years later. Pilgrim, I believe I can be forthcoming with you. I know that you love me in spite of the seemingly never-ending number of flaws I have. In all likelihood, I have disappointed you. Please forgive me darling daughter. I obviously was no longer a person of substance. I had conveniently left our Heavenly Father out of my life, though He had enriched my life so very much with Carol and Mark, and countless other gifts. I had become mired in the regrettable abyss of false pride, and that had led to my problems. I would pay, in many ways, for being the fool I was. I, heretofore, had a sacrosanct attitude about many things that caused me immeasurable problems, for which I would eventually be held accountable. I was cognizant of the above, but did nothing to correct my attitudes and flaws until pressed to do so. I was a jerk.

Meanwhile, Carol and I decided to buy a condominium, which we did, in early 1979. It was the first house we ever had, and we moved into it the week that I flew back to Boston to run my first of three Boston Marathons. It was interesting living in a condominium—though in some ways it was similar to living an apartment complex. The residents of the condominium complex included one or two young married couples, a number of retired couples, government employees, and a divorced young woman and her adorable infant daughter. Mark made friends with a couple of brothers who lived in the complex and the three of them became fast friends. Mark was selected to play on an elementary school soccer team that went undefeated. I enjoyed watching all of the boys' play—this, before girls practically swept the boys' teams off the soccer field.

Pilgrim, had you lived, I know that you would have had a great deal of athleticism. You likely would have been a skilled tennis player, field hockey athlete, or softball or soccer player. I would have enjoyed watching you participate in sports.

Darling daughter, Carol and I continued co-existing in 1978 and 1979 as we had the previous two years. We never had discussions regarding therapy or how to improve or marriage. Ironically, what confrontational behavior we had toward one another took place after our divorce. In the meantime, we simply held our breaths and maintained our heretofore co-existence. What we were doing seemed to work, though deep down, both Carol and I were depressed. With school being over for the summer, Mark and I were busy doing such things as going swimming, to minor league baseball games, and to the movies.

Mark was seven years old, and was growing. It was wonderful seeing him becoming a little man. Darling Pilgrim, in turn, you would have been fifteen years old in 1979. You likely would be going into tenth grade in the fall. You could fly directly from Los Angeles to El Paso—in fact on some non-stop flights. For a fifteen-year-old young woman, you would have already flown many air miles. Carol, Mark and I would have come to get you at the airport, and I would have taken a picture of you coming off the plane. By now, I would have had many photos of you. You possibly would have one or more younger siblings by your mother and stepfather. This would have meant that you had somewhat of an extended family. By 1979, it would be time to plan for your college years—though it could wait until the beginning of your junior year in high school.

As I mentioned in an earlier letter, I remember thinking back in 1963 before Willow aborted you, that if she had placed you up for adoption, you would be given to a wonderful family, and that someday we possibly would become acquainted. Darling Pilgrim, of course it was dreaming on my part, but it kept me sane to a degree. Prior to you being aborted, your mother and I had even argued over the issue of adoption. She was also against that—possibly, because it would have been difficult for her to give you up—once you were born. I now understand Willow's possible emotional dilemma and I feel anguished about it.

After the beginning of the fall in 1979, it was apparent to both Carol and I that our marriage was not going to get any better. As many marriages, ours' had fallen into irrecoverable depression. Both Carol and I knew the only choice that was viable was to extricate us from being married to one another. However, we both denied the inevitable: that it was imperative that the marriage end and we both get on with our lives. That having been said, neither Carol nor I forgot that Mark was part of our equation concerning the impending divorce—and that acknowledgment made things more difficult.

However, Pilgrim, the divorce was ever looming in the future. And it would not be long before the curtain surrounding our marriage would fall. In the interim, Carol and I attempted to be impervious to the obvious: that being the fact that neither of us had done anything to save our marriage.

Pilgrim, though human beings are at the top of the intellectual chain, we are inclined to be without logic when it comes to affairs of the heart. I include the institution of marriage in my assessment. We are well intentioned as far as our interpersonal relationships, yet many of us invariably fall prey to our emotions, and either ruin or alter once-healthy relationships or marriages. Unfortunately, Carol, and I were cardinal examples of what I just discussed. That did not mean that we were bad people; as I said earlier, it simply meant that we had made bad choices—which people do. Yet, I was the one most accountable for the destruction of our marriage.

By the end of 1979, the embers of our marriage were almost out. I remember that Carol and I were noticeably depressed. Mark was becoming aware of our pain and it was bewildering him. Finally, in January 1980—a day or so after his birthday—Carol and I sat down with him and told him that I would be moving out of the house into an apartment. We attempted to soften the blow of our news to him by saying that we just needed to spend some time apart to "figure things out." I will never forget the look of pain on your brother's face. He wanted to know if he had done anything to cause my moving out. Carol and I attempted to reassure Mark that he had done nothing wrong. The three of us were in tears. I told Mark between my tears that I was just moving a mile away; that he could spend the weekends with me, and that I would still be with him every evening that his mother was working. Yet, after I had ostensibly reassured Mark, I had to realize that my time with my little son was becoming less and less, and that someday, in the not too distant future, he and Carol would be physically out of my life. Pilgrim, had you been here on earth during this time, I would have had a difficult time giving you the above news. I likely would have been distraught. I felt as if I was a failure—and I was.

I moved to a furnished apartment approximately a mile away from where we lived. I met Mark everyday after school on the days that Carol was working. I would either cook dinner for us or we would go out to eat, after which we might hang out at the mall. Then Mark and I would return to the condo, after which time I would put him to bed, and then wait for Carol to come home—then I would drive to my apartment—feeling depressed. Pilgrim, I am sure Carol had the identical feelings. I relished the weekends that Mark and I could spend together. He enjoyed spending the weekends at my apartment. I would pick Mark up either on Friday evening or Saturday morning. We would do such things as go to a movie and/or the mall or go for drives around the El Paso area. Sometimes, we might spend a quiet evening in my apartment watching television.   Darling daughter, if I may make an analogy: I am certain by now that you would know that being apart from your brother was difficult, yet, it would have been no less difficult being away from you. Darling daughter, people often do not stop to realize that parents dealing with divorce or separation from their children, deal constantly with the excruciating pain of not having access to them. The aborting of you was similar in that it was horrible in so many aspects. The abortion meant that physically you would not be in anyone's life—including mine—but emotionally and spiritually, you are always with me.

What was going on in early 1980 was that Carol and I were laying the groundwork for the divorce. Both of us had acquired lawyers. The two attorneys drew up legal strategy, and it was but a short time later, that litigation was implemented. Meantime, I took a job in another city. Carol and I then arranged for Mark to fly every so often to visit me on weekends. I would pay for his fare at the airport where I lived and Carol or a friend of ours would take Mark to the airport and put him on a plane. It was about a forty-five minute flight from El Paso to where I lived. I remember so well, Pilgrim, what it was like seeing Mark come off the airplane the first time after not seeing him for several weeks. Pilgrim, I was in tears when I saw my little guy; I just rushed up, grabbed him, hugged, and kissed him. Mark was even tearful. Even the flight attendant who brought him off the plane was a bit teary-eyed. Noteworthy was that on that same Friday evening there were other fathers, and even one or two mothers, meeting their children. In fact, I recall that on Friday evenings when Mark would be coming to spend the weekend, there was often the same group of parents waiting to meet their children's flight from El Paso.

On Sunday evening, sadly, the same group of parents was there to put their children on the plane to fly home El Paso. Pilgrim, sadly I never had the opportunity to see you cry; I was denied the wonderful opportunity of holding you in my arms, sharing your pain and comforting you. However, I would be able to do that with Mark. The first weekend he came to see me was great; we had a wonderful time doing things and meeting people, and in general, just hanging out. Mark was happy all weekend until we were getting ready to drive out to the airport on Sunday evening. Then, my eight-year-old son became weepy and asked me to hold him. I remember I held him as he cried, and I tearfully reassured him that I loved him so very much and that everything was going to be all right.

Even as I write these anecdotes twenty-five years later (2005), I can still feel both Mark's and my pain that night. We finally regained some semblance of composure and drove out to the airport. While waiting for the inbound turn-around flight from El Paso to arrive, we sat quietly in the waiting area with Mark lying on my shoulder. This would be repeated numerous times in the future. Finally, the flight from El Paso arrived, discharged its inbound passengers, and then prepared for boarding for the flight back to El Paso. The unaccompanied children boarded first, and Mark, along with the others, were escorted onto the plane. I gave him one last hug and a kiss, told him I love him, and said goodbye to him. It was a heart-wrenching experience. I could barely hold back the tears. They just came.

The other non-custodial parents and I silently watched our children get on the aircraft, then the remainder of the passengers boarded, and the door closed as the jet was slowly pushed from the jet way. I walked quickly to the car, but stopped where I could see the lights of the jet as it rose quickly into the night sky heading westward to El Paso. Once the plane was out of sight, I got into my car, at which time, I cried before I drove out of the airport terminal and on to my apartment.

Pilgrim, relative to the above anecdote, I regret that in reality I never had the opportunity to have met you at an airport or even to have tearfully said goodbye to you as you boarded the plane to return home. It pains me that you never experienced the life you deserved. I hope you understand my anguish. The grief I had when Mark and I were separated by the divorce was identical to that pain that I had years earlier when I was aware of your cruel and calloused death. I have gotten to say goodbye to Mark and see his plane lift into the sky numerous times; however, I remind myself that I never had the opportunity to say goodbye to you or to see you lifted to Heaven—figuratively or otherwise. Darling little girl, once again, I am reminded that there was not even any due process shown to you nor were your rights defended by one or more lawyers. No matter how many years have gone by (42), as I am actually writing this story, I am unable to forget or to put aside the memory of horrific choices made by certain individuals who gave you no consideration as far as life. That was tragic.

We are a society, Pilgrim, that has not yet bought into the acceptance of men crying. However, I am glad that I cried because I could not save you. I mentioned earlier that I unabashedly cried when you died. Many tears were predicated upon anger for you being aborted, and the remainder were tears of grief. As a man and as your father, I have often wept for you.

Back in El Paso, our respective lawyers jostled for position in court regarding who would get the best settlement for their client. I am not aware to what extent the attorneys pressed for specifics; however, Carol became the plaintiff and I was the defendant. It was of little consequence as to what label either of us were given. What was important was that Carol and Mark receive whatever they wanted and needed as they planned to return to the Seattle area. The only request I asked from my lawyer was that I wanted at least six weeks every summer for Mark to visit me wherever I was, and two weeks at Christmas on alternating years. The reason for this, Pilgrim, was that I knew that I would eventually be on one end of the continent while Mark and Carol were on the West Coast. This meant I would not be able to see him other than at the assigned vacation periods. Carol agreed to my requests. She was also very generous in granting me the opportunity to see Mark whenever I would be on the West Coast. I was able to see Mark one time, because I had to travel to Seattle on business—and we had a wonderful time together.

The time finally came when Mark would be on his first six-week visit. I met his flight from El Paso that Saturday morning and when the two of us saw one another, we once again ran into one another's arms, hugged, and kissed each other and became tearful. Since I would be working during the day, I was able to have him go to a daytime vacation camp. After work, I would pick him up. Every morning, I made a lunch for him, and made sure that he had his swimsuit, a couple of towels, and whatever else he needed. Mark made friends easily with his peers. One weekend, he and I drove to the amusement park known as Six Flags over Texas. It was a long trip, and when we got to Arlington, Texas, the weather was 115 degrees. The next day, it cooled to 109. We got to the amusement park early on Saturday morning; so we went on all the large rides while it was still relatively cool. Then in the afternoon, Mark and I rode the waterlog ride countless times because it kept us cool. Mark and some other little boy became acquainted, so they rode the waterlog ride by themselves while their parents and I visited. Wow, Pilgrim, imagine what it would be like being at an amusement park such as Six Flags over Texas in 109-degree weather. Fortunately, there was plenty of shade. Your brother would have been delighted to have you on the trip to Arlington, Texas. I have an idea that you two would have ridden rides the entire day and left me to my own designs.

Mark and I drove home on Sunday morning and got back home in the afternoon. We lounged around our pool with the other tenants. Pilgrim darling, it was not long before Mark called Carol and became angry with her over the phone. I noticed that insignificant things bothered him, and he would yell at her and tell her he did not want to ever see her. I would get him off the phone and hold him. Pilgrim, your little brother was in pain. All three of us were in great emotional distress. Mark would also get angry with me and tell me that he wanted to go home and never wanted to see me. He would settle down as I held him and just let him cry and express what he was dealing with. I was to find out later through therapy, that Mark's anger was based on his fear of losing one or both parents—not by death—but by separation or emotionally. Mark was frightened of the future, knowing that he and I were eventually to be separated for over a year before we would see one another again. Pilgrim, I was apprehensive as well, and certainly depressed. I hurt for Mark. He was my life, and it would not be long before we would become separated by distance and time. A parent can have no greater pain knowing that he is separated from his children by time, distance, or death. Pilgrim, it would not be very long until I exhibited the same type of depression when Mark flew to Seattle to live, as I did when I found out that your mother had aborted you. Both bouts of depression, understandably, were long and excruciating.

Pilgrim, I realized my life was so hollow and that I had emotionally and spiritually nowhere to go but back to God. Yes, I knew that the Lord would erase my sins, but I also realized I had to make restitution to those whom I had hurt—including Carol and Mark—in what way would be decided by our Heavenly Father. In essence, I had consequences to face. Speaking of our Heavenly Father, during the summer of 1980, I began going to a very large Southern Baptist Church, which I enjoyed very much. I needed a church and theology that kept my feet to the fire so to speak. I gave my life to Jesus in that church—though I would have to rededicate my life several times over the next decade. It was a very friendly church and had a wonderful singles group. It also had a Wednesday evening supper for its parishioners and Mark and I enjoyed going there on that night. The dinner and fellowship were great and served as a means to keep my mind off my depression, and instead on the Lord and on Mark. Pilgrim, I knew that I needed the Lord, and that I would always need Him, because without our Heavenly Father, I was a loser.

Finally, the six weeks were over and it was time to fly back to El Paso with Mark. Why was I flying back to El Paso as opposed to simply putting Mark on the plane and sending him home? Well, Carol had sold our condominium and I had to fly back to El Paso to sign the contract, because according to Texas law, we were to divide the money made from the sale. Carol picked us up at the airport and took us to the condominium where I said a lengthy goodbye to Mark—though I knew that I would get to see him, one more weekend before he and Carol left for Seattle. A friend watched Mark until Carol returned home after taking me to the airport after we signed the sales agreement. Carol and I did not have much to say to one another than comment about the transaction and that Mark would be up the following weekend for his final visit. We went to the realtor's office where we signed the sales title, and Carol then took me back to the airport where I left to return to where I lived.

During the hours that we were together, Carol's and my conversation was somewhat awkward; however, it was generally a friendly one. Future conversations would be more than awkward; some of them would be downright hostile. Darling daughter, if you had lived and been with Willow, I am certain that your mother and I at times would have been abrupt to one another. Divorced or disengaged parents have emotional and psychological turf they have to guard—or believe they have to. Though you are in your late teens, I hope your mother and I would never have attempted to negatively influence you against the other parent. I know I would not allow that to happen because your happiness and emotional equilibrium means too much to me.

Anyway, I flew back home and upon returning to the empty apartment, I began feeling depressed. I looked on the bed and saw one of Mark's t-shirts lying there. I remember I picked it up and put it to my cheek where my tears began falling on it. The night before Mark had left to go back to El Paso, I had done his laundry so that all his clothes would be clean. He had helped me pack his bag, and why the t-shirt had not been packed was initially an enigma. However, I received an epiphany of sorts: I realized that consciously or otherwise he had left the piece of clothing out of his bag as a remembrance of him. My darling Pilgrim, Mark would perform that ritual well into his late teens and early twenties when he came to visit me. A therapist told me years later that children of divorced parents often leave something at their non-custodial parent's house to serve as a reminder of their presence and love. Darling daughter, I am certain that had you been coming to visit me on summer vacations as a child and young woman, you also would have left me mementos—such as lockets, little notes, etc.

Well, Mark's final weekend with me came to fruition. I met his flight from El Paso on the Friday evening of our last weekend together before he would leave for El Paso for good to fly to Seattle. It was wonderful to see him come off the aircraft and to hug and kiss him; however, we both knew it would be our last time together for a year.

We spent the weekend just hanging out without any specific schedule, which gave us time to share our feelings with one another. Pilgrim, a little eight-year-old boy does not normally articulate as well as an adult. Yet, your brother was able to plainly share his pain with me. He did it by not saying very much. Mark's reticence, however, spoke volumes.

I attempted to help him deal with his issues regarding our impending separation, the divorce, and his moving to Seattle. I told him I had the same anxiety he did about his going to another part of the country. However, I told Mark that no matter how far we were apart geographically, he never had to worry about me not loving him, and that I would always miss him. Concerning the divorce, I told him that his mother and I did not want to divorce one another, but that we had grown apart, and that he had nothing to do with the divorce. He nodded to my comments.

The weekend went by too quickly, and then it was time to drive the ten miles to the airport. We drove to it in silence. I think we both were near tears as we parked the car and walked into the terminal. I remember as we checked Mark's bag in and had his ticket validated, the agent told us that that our flight would be late. After checking in, Mark wanted to go up to the waiting area. Not surprising, we saw some non-custodial parents there with their children waiting for the same flight to El Paso. We once again exchanged perfunctory greetings, Mark and I sat down, and eventually he lay down and rested his head on my lap. Neither of us said anything. About 45 minutes later, the flight to El Paso came and it was time for him to board. I just held him and told him I loved him. I then gave him a hug and a kiss as he joined the other unaccompanied children on to the plane. This time I stayed at the gate until the door on the jet was closed. I then walked quickly to the airport parking lot, where, once again, I was able to see for the last time the lights of Mark's plane as it took off from the runway and disappeared into the night sky. Pilgrim I was numb until I got home and saw one of Mark's socks on the bed. I then sat down and cried for a long time. Darling daughter do you remember earlier in the book when I describe how I sobbed when I sensed that you had already been aborted. My weeping that night after Mark left was a replication of how I had cried those many years earlier on that beach in Southern California.

The next day Mark flew to Seattle. He spent time with some of Carol's relatives until she got to Seattle, after which time they moved into an apartment. The enormity of Mark being gone, hit me as if I had been struck by lightening. I felt very much alone and disconsolate—as I had Pilgrim when you died. I obviously do not do well with separation. The loss of both you and Mark devastated me. Once again, I would become immersed with grief, anger, and pain.

Going on with my life was not easy. Being alone in a city where I really had not established close friendships compounded the sense of loneliness. As I mentioned earlier I tried turning to God, and this time, I was a bit more successful than I had been back in California when you had died Pilgrim. I was more honest with the Lord this time. I did not attempt to negotiate with the Lord; I knew better. Pilgrim darling, a divorce is a death. A couple loses the will or ability to love one another anymore.

Speaking of the Lord, though I was honest with Him as far as my sins, I at times hedged on acknowledging all of them. Our Heavenly Father had to often be tough in making me accountable for my role in the breakup of my marriage. I believe that one way he got my attention was to allow me to have a prolonged period of depression as the result of being separated from Mark. In essence, by being away from the one person who I loved unabashedly—that being Mark—I had to agonize often, if not constantly about not seeing him. To this day, though I believe in a loving and merciful Lord and Savior, who washes away our sins and pain, He is also holds us accountable for the results of our sins.

Pilgrim; remember your mother and I had to be held responsible for our part in your conception and abortion. Therefore, to be glib about the divorce would have been unconscionable on my part. When I married Carol, I believed our marriage would last for a lifetime. We had wonderful years together and were blessed by the birth of Mark. But what happened was that we did not stay vigilant and the marriage collapsed. My confidence regarding marriage was and still is a subject for discussion. I have not ever remarried after Carol's and my divorce—which is going on twenty-six years—because I wanted to be accessible to Mark. Frankly, I have not felt confident enough to try marriage again.

Darling Pilgrim it was rough keeping it together as far as dealing with separation from Mark. I would phone him one a week and we would have somewhat sad conversations—which were not meant to happen—but would often evolve during the course of our talking to one another.

Both of us were feeling the pain and the strain of the divorce and separation. However, we would somehow work our way through our conversations, and then say emotional goodbyes to one another. I used to enjoy getting Mark funny cards and sending them to him. By keeping in touch with Mark, I was able to keep myself together. What I had a very difficult time with was when some friend or well-intentioned person would ask how Mark was, and I would burst into tears. Do you remember Pilgrim that people used to tell me that when it came time to addressing your abortion, that I should just, "get on with your life" or "you'll get over it because everyone does", etc. These hackneyed comments—though genuinely expressed—often just made me more depressed and grief-stricken. There was no doubt, however, that I was losing it as I had with your abortion. Why not get unglued? Carol and I had undergone the death of our marriage, and I was separated from Mark.

Well Pilgrim, it was time to return to El Paso. There was nothing wrong where I had lived. It was simply the fact that I missed El Paso, and I had a job opportunity back with the federal government that I accepted. I had some very good friends back in the area, and surprisingly, Pilgrim, I felt a need to reconnect with the environs in which Carol, Mark and I had lived. The adage, "You can't go home again" was one that I chose to ignore. Darling Pilgrim, I believe the next letter will be a somewhat nicer letter for the two of us. Thanks for being here for me.

I love you so much,
Dad

TRANSITION AND REMEMBERING ANITA

Well, it was back on the Interstate to El Paso. In some ways, Pilgrim, I felt as if I was a reincarnation of one the characters out of John Steinbeck's classic novel, *The Grapes of Wrath*. I had everything I owned in a U-Haul trailer on the back of my car and began driving westward. The trip was spent thinking about what had transpired the past several months. I thought quite a lot about Mark as I drove across the desert onto high plateau area of western Texas. It was pleasant but cool as I drove during early December 1980 to El Paso. As a reminder my child, it would not be long before you would be seventeen years old. This could mean I would be flying out to California to see you graduate from high school in the following spring. I know I would be ecstatic about seeing you graduate. I would be taking tons of photos of you and would be so very proud of you. The best picture taken would be that of Willow and I standing proudly on either side of you after you received your diploma. Darling, no matter what your mother's and my feelings might have been toward each other, we would have been united in our love for you.

Anyway, I got into El Paso and drove to the apartment that a good friend of mine had gotten for me. It was not too far, from where Carol, Mark and I had lived. In fact, I drove by our condominium many times while back in El Paso, and as expected it brought back a myriad of memories. I got a job with the federal government at Fort Bliss and enjoyed my work.

Pilgrim, it had been almost a year since Mark and I last saw one another, and now he was coming back to El Paso to spend six weeks with me. Finally, the evening came that he arrived from Seattle to El Paso. When he got off the airplane what I saw was a tall Mark!

Gosh, I almost did not recognize him! His hair was longer and he was a tall, seemingly gangly nine-year-old. It was great to hug and kiss him and in fact, Mark appeared to be a happy boy. I felt he was glad to be back in El Paso because though it evoked some difficult memories, there was still a group of his friends and familiar places. There even were some friends at the condominium complex that we would visit. Darling Pilgrim, it seemed that both Mark and I were settling in as far as old memories and emotions.

Though things went well while Mark was with me, I noticed that as we got closer to the time for Mark to fly home, we became less spontaneous and once again lost in our own selves. I later realized that we were detaching from one another emotionally in order to be able to handle the eventual separation. Do you know what Pilgrim, Mark and I had this same type of behavior for most of his subsequent visits no matter where I lived. And oh yes, as he had done the previous year, he left an article of clothing. Of course, I cried. When I put Mark on the plane to make his long flight to Seattle, I was not as depressed as I was before because I knew I would be seeing him that Christmas. Saying goodbye was no easier, but Mark and I could look forward to Christmas and that was a wonderful feeling. Time to be with you daughter.

Darling Pilgrim, you no doubt would likely have been in your first year of college. That would have been wonderful. You would be in college during the first presidential administration of Republican Ronald Reagan—a Californian like yourself. He had been Governor of California back in the late 1960s and early 1970s.

Pilgrim, discussing California, I wonder if you would have gone to one of the California junior colleges or maybe you would have matriculated to a major university. In either instance, you would have been an excellent student. I mentioned earlier that your mother had taught for a number of years at one of the local colleges in Southern California. Pilgrim, with your intellect and passion for knowledge, I could have envisioned you being either a physician or a lawyer. You no doubt would have great people skills. I would have been so proud of you, and would have enjoyed phoning you at your dorm on weekends to find out how you are doing. I am certain you would have had a barn full of young men vying for your attention. As your dad, I would have gently admonished you to study—which I did not do much of as an undergraduate.

Well, the first of many Christmas visits of Mark's came and I met him at the airport. Wow, when Mark came of the plane, I almost did not recognize him. Here he was almost ten and was becoming tall. It was great to see him again. We of course embraced one another. Though I usually talked by phone with Mark once a week, we still had a lot to share. He was in fourth grade and was doing well. He brought a school photograph of his classmates and the teacher. Though our divorce was traumatic, Carol, however, was a super mom to Mark and apparently kept him in line. Mark seemed to have adjusted to the fact that his mother and I would be permanently apart. I had a small Christmas tree that I decorated and we put all our gifts under it.

The only thing that reduced the joy of Christmas was the news I had gotten that a former college student of mine and dear friend, by the name of Anita, had been diagnosed with liver cancer. She was a wonderful person who taught art back east, and who planned to move to Arizona to teach. She was a very attractive and artsy woman, who in many ways was a "soul mate" of mine. She was only forty-years old when she received the news of the incurable cancer. She had a daughter in college at the University of Texas at Austin, and had gone to school there as well. Though Anita hung heavy on my mind, Mark and I had a great time together during the Christmas that he spent with me, and even though I had to put him back on an airplane on New Year's Eve day to fly back to Seattle, I knew that I would be seeing him in about six months. Though a woman teacher of mine came along to see Mark off and to provide some emotional support, it was a sad moment. I was already feeling a void when I put him on the plane. I remember I hugged Mark, told him I loved him, and that I would see him in six months. I phoned Mark once a week, it, therefore, was a source of comfort to the both of us that we would still be in touch.) My woman friend and I stayed at the gate until his plane took off; we then left the terminal.

Once again, there had been an article of clothing left by Mark. Frankly, I anticipated a ritual—though it was a sad one. Speaking of clothing Pilgrim, if you came to visit me, I would have had a larger apartment with two bedrooms, so that you can have your privacy and closet space for clothes. Concerning Christmas, I would hope Willow would not have minded if I phoned you on Christmas day—after all I am your father. Frankly, I believe your mother would have been gracious; and, in fact, encouraged you and I to phone each other on Christmas. When I lived in Southern California I used to spend every Christmas with my dear friends Laura, Craig, and their extended family. Christmas was always a wonderful day at their home. However, when I moved to New York City in 1963, I remember Christmas day of that year because I was 3000 miles away from Craig, Laura and their children. Though I had the opportunity to phone them on Christmas day, it was very sad not being with them.

In late 1981, Pilgrim I was offered a position as a deputy chief historian for a major command for the Department of Air Force at Langley Air Force Base, Virginia. I would be getting a promotion. And I would be transferring from the Department of Army to the Department of Air force. Again, it was "On the Road Again." Since I was driving, I would be given five days to drive from El Paso to Hampton, Virginia—a distance of 2100 miles. As I was saying my goodbyes to my colleagues and friends, and was packing, I received word that Anita had died and that she had been cremated, and that her ashes had been scattered over the desert in Arizona. I was heartbroken. I felt remorse for not having flown down to Austin to see her before she died. I kept telling her that I would be down to spend time with her—but though well intentioned—I never did get to Austin while Anita was alive. I felt as if I had betrayed my wonderful friend. I had no excuse.

I left El Paso early the next morning and drove east on I-10. I was grieving for my great friend Anita. Pilgrim, you would have liked her. She was a blithe spirit who really loved people, and was very talented. Anita was eclectic in the way she looked at life, but at the same time, she was unpretentious while achieving great things. Young people adored her because she listened to them and genuinely cared for them. College-age youth were smitten by her charm and her vivaciousness. Anita, by her love of life, championed it until the day she died.

Darling daughter, I still remember years after you had been aborted, Anita and I were once discussing abortion, and during our conversation, I related the tragedy of your death. Anita commented that she believed women who had abortions had not lost the basic maternal ability to love a baby, once it had been born, but had emotionally misplaced their sense of responsibility to the child within them. Anita had only been able to have one child that being Cassie, and she cherished every moment of being a mother. I really missed this beautiful, amazing, compassionate woman.

Darling though I was excited about my new assignment and promotion, and the fact I was going to be working for a major Air Force command on the East Coast, I was miserable with grief over Anita's death. Several times as I drove east on I-10 I had to pull the car off onto the shoulder because I was crying so much and the tears were blotting my contacts. Anita had been a real friend. I had met her when I was teaching in Alaska. She was a student of mine and a woman of great intellect, but was very unobtrusive about it. Anita's husband Paul had been an engineer at the local paper plant. They were an unusual couple in that they enjoyed having people of different backgrounds in their lives. Anita and Paul invited my first wife Jessica and I for a drive one Sunday in their jeep station wagon. It was great because we went on the logging roads and up on the high points overlooking the island. By the way, we met their daughter, who was about four years old in 1966—which meant she would be two years older than you. Her name was Cassie, which was short for Cassandra. Jessica and I eventually became good friends with them. Her husband Paul was transferred back to the Lower 48 and Jessica and I lost contact with Anita and her family.

It was not until I was teaching in New Mexico that I received a letter from Anita. She had gotten my address from the Alumni Office at BYU, so she sent me a note. She was living back East and told me that she finished graduate school at the University of Pennsylvania several years before and was teaching. She said she had gotten divorced and that Cassie was in high school. When I gave a paper at a history conference in Pittsburgh one year, she came to hear me present my paper. It was great seeing her. Anita and I kept in touch and remained close friends up until her death. Pilgrim, there are people who are amazing, and Anita was one of them. She had more talent, intellect, and *savoir-faire* than ten people put together. Yet, Anita was sensitive and caring. She did not wear her accomplishments on her sleeves. In many ways, Anita was unusually unobtrusive. Above all, Pilgrim, she was a loving, loyal and fantastic friend. There are not many of those kinds of people. Anita was a unique person.

Pilgrim, it is now back to the trip that took me from one end of Texas to the other end of the state. It took twelve hours. Fortunately, I had a practically brand-new car, so it was an easy drive. I called Mark from Longview, Texas, which was near the Texas-Louisiana border, and let him know I was on my way to Virginia. He was excited, especially when I let him know that his plane ride from Seattle to Norfolk, Virginia would be a long one. He enjoyed flying. Just imagine darling daughter, flying from Los Angeles to Norfolk—it would be a long trip because you would have to change planes—either in Chicago or Atlanta. However, since you would be eighteen years old, you would handle it quite well. For one thing, you would not have to be escorted off the plane because of your age as your brother Mark was. He used to be embarrassed by the airline's requirement for unattended children. Thinking of that makes me laugh.

After traveling through some of the most beautiful country in the United States over a three and one-half day period, I arrived in Hampton, Virginia. It was situated across the bay from Norfolk, and the entire Tidewater Peninsula was vested in history. As the result of having been earlier to Langley Air Force Base for the job interview, I had already put a lease payment on a large studio apartment in Hampton, Virginia. So, upon my arrival in Hampton, I drove to my new abode. I reported to my new job the following Monday. Pilgrim, our nation was involved in the, "Cold War" so Langley Air Force Base was an extremely busy facility. The Air Force ran a, tight ship. One had to get used to identification requirement, limited access, classified material, etc. Thus Pilgrim, I always had to be alert as to where I went, whether or not I had access to certain files, or if I had closed and locked our security safes. It made the job more interesting. Well, darling daughter, the time came for Mark to make his first trip to the East to see me during the summer of 1982.

In June 1982, your brother got off the plane at the Norfolk Airport and I took a picture of him as he came into the waiting area. He was taller with longer hair, and after we hugged and kissed, he asked if he could play some video games. So of course, he played his games, and then we drove through the tunnel to Hampton and to the apartment. I had arranged that while I worked during the week, he would go to a YMCA summer day camp, and then after work, I would pick him up. The first day Mark was in Hampton, the two of us went to see the second Star Wars movie. We always enjoyed them and I believe you would have liked them as well The following week, Mark and I went to Washington, D.C. to see my sister Lorraine..

The remainder of Mark's stay was busy; we went to Williamsburg, Virginia, and to Busch Gardens and enjoyed ourselves immensely. However, once again, it came time for Mark to fly back to Seattle. As we approached his day of leaving Virginia, we both became somewhat quiet and pensive. I would not get to see Mark for another year and that would be painful. I think he had similar feelings as well.

I can remember when I took Mark to the airport Pilgrim. I was feeling depressed. And this time I was also dealing with separation anxiety, and I was thinking about Anita. As to be expected, I had dealt with similar feelings back as in the summer of 1963. However, I was feeling particularly anxious the day I was putting Mark on the plane. Possibly one reason for my trepidation was that once again, Mark and I would be on the opposite ends of the continent, and would be separated for a year. We got to the airport and Mark and I played the video games then went to the waiting area for the flight to Atlanta where Mark would then connect to his flight to Seattle. Finally, it was time for pre-boarding of unaccompanied children. I did something unusual: I asked if I could walk Mark to his seat. The agent said I could. I walked him to his seat, then tearfully hugged him and kissed him, and turn around and walked back to the waiting area. As the other passengers were boarding the plane, I just stood by the window of the boarding area and just stared at the aircraft. Simultaneously, I was attempting to hold back my tears. When the plane turned on the tarmac, I took a picture of it taxiing out to the runway. After I watched the aircraft take off, I went back to the apartment. It would be another year until I saw Mark—that would be 1983—and you would then be nineteen years old.

Pilgrim, I will never cease acknowledging you and loving you—though I write about Mark and other people. You deserve my affirmation, love, and respect, and that of others who were responsible for you being aborted. Hence, I enjoy in the incorporating of you into my life, and the lives of those who I love, or who are very important to me.

Remember that in 1983, had you lived, you would have been nineteen and approaching the threshold of life. Pilgrim, you possibly would have been thinking about whether or not you wanted to go to graduate school after you finished college or begin a career. Your brother Mark, your mother and I were given opportunities to make choices throughout our lives. You, however, did not have such an opportunity. Therefore, as you know, I have given you life by proxy darling daughter because you deserve being a part of both Mark's and my life—and always will.

I went down several days before Easter of 1983 to Austin, Texas to visit Anita's family and Cassie. I also was going to see another good friend of mine who lived in Austin. It was a dreadful time to visit Anita's family. The family members were still dealing with her death, yet they were so very kind to me, and I had the opportunity to see Cassie who I had not seen for several years. Anita's mother showed me a picture taken of Anita the last week she was alive and in the hospital. Anita was quite thin, with no hair, and had what I perceived to be a vacant look on her face. The photo upset me because the last time I had seen Anita she was healthy, beautiful, and full of life. Pilgrim I had seen death before, but what I observed in that picture was Anita not being able to have the dignity of a peaceful death. I felt such an immeasurable sadness for the loss of this beautiful, talented woman. It subsequently took a long time to work my way through it. I only wish that Anita had been in a hospice setting when she died because it would have been more loving and peaceful of an environment.

Yet, Pilgrim, what comes to mind is the fact that you were never granted the dignity of a peaceful and solemn death. No one attempted to make your last minutes or seconds free of pain. There were only the angels that tearfully took you quickly home to the Throne of the Lord after you died. There were no humans by your bedside mourning your death—not even Willow. Yet, your mother no doubt suffered inscrutable physical pain when she was aborting you.

I have thought about her pain, because much of her anguish was also my pain. I have often asked myself if Willow's physical and psychological pain, coupled with the ever present risks of infection or something possibly going terribly wrong during the abortion procedure, were acceptable options for her as opposed to carrying you full term. Your mother knew too well that she took inordinate risks to abort you Pilgrim. To this day I ask myself if your mother can rationalize your death. I do not believe that she can—and I believe she is only too cognizant of her inability to explain away what she and her family did to you.

On Easter Sunday of 1983, a friend and I were driving on a country road outside of Austin when we came upon a large patch of beautiful Bluebonnet flowers. We stopped and got out of the car. I then took several photos of the flowers. I bent down and pulled two of the bluebonnets out of the ground, later wrapped them, and brought them back to Hampton as a tribute to Anita. I silently cried one last time for Anita. I know she would have enjoyed the flowers.

I flew back to Norfolk the next day and returned to my job, and looked forward to Mark's return to Hampton. Several weeks passed and it was time for Mark to come east to be with me for six weeks. He got off the plane and we hugged and kissed one another. He was taller with blonde hair and seemed a bit more mature. Pilgrim, it was great to see your brother again.

We were both a bit more subdued this year than we had been back in 1982. Mark was eleven and going into sixth grade in the fall. We followed a similar schedule of events and travel in 1983 as we had the previous year.

Mark and I went to Washington again as we had in 1982 and did the sightseeing bit with gusto. We also went visited Williamsburg as we had in 1982, and then spent time at Yorktown, where the last and pivotal battle of the American Revolutionary War was fought. My daughter, it would have been great if you could have flown from Los Angeles to Washington to spend time with Mark and me, and to meet your Aunt Lorraine—my half-sister—and her family. I have to remember that you would no doubt have had a busy schedule back home in Southern California, which meant that I would try not to be selfish by monopolizing your summer. By the way Pilgrim would you by chance happen to have a particular young male friend who you would like to tell your brother and your dad about? We would enjoy seeing the delight in your expression as you tell us about him. Mark and I would really look forward to hear you describe this young man to us. However, darling daughter, please I would admonish you to go slow in your friendship.

I am certain that in all likelihood your mother would have already issued a similar admonition. You would be levelheaded so I believe you will would before you act. Pilgrim, I am so very proud of you and love you so much—as does Mark. A big sister is good for him.

Well, the six weeks went by rapidly and it was time to put Mark on the plane to fly home to Seattle. We were both comforted by the fact that we would be seeing each other at Christmas of 1983. We had less trouble saying goodbye to one another, though saying goodbye to Mark would never be easy.

Summer turned into fall and it was during this time Pilgrim that I began training to run my 20th marathon in November. It would be the Marine Corps Marathon in Washington, D.C. Since I had been in the Marines, it was only appropriate that I run it.

Guess what darling daughter, that same fall I was offered a position back with the Department of Army to be its first command historian at the US Army Aviation Branch and Center at Fort Rucker, Alabama. I was to be promoted to the next grade level—which was a command level grade—and I would be moved down to Fort Rucker in the middle of November. Pilgrim, I cannot tell you how excited I was! I attempted to be unobtrusive or at least maintain some humility. I say that tongue-in-cheek. I could not thank the Lord enough for this new professional opportunity. This new job opened up many new opportunities. I phoned your brother Mark and told him the news.

Pilgrim let me go back to the Marine Corps Marathon saga. I trained for the Marine Corps Marathon and ran it the weekend of November 10th, 1983 with about 15,000 other running fools. I ran a slower time than I usually did because I nursed a sore hamstring so I would not damage it any more than I previous had. However, I ran a decent time and got to see a lot of our Nation's Capital while running. I had a great experience running that race. However, little did I know that marathon would be the last one I ever ran because of subsequent injuries.

Pilgrim, even if before I had begun running marathons, somebody had told me that I would likely become injured if I ran, I would not ever have changed a thing. I would have kept on running as long as I could, and as long as I did. I ran twenty marathons, including three Boston Marathons, the New York Marathon, and the Pikes Peak Marathon—it being the most difficult marathon in the country. I was blessed to be able to run these marathons, and countless other races, and I enjoyed running.

By running marathons, I met wonderful people throughout the country. Darling Pilgrim, we should do what we enjoy and never apologize for trying to do our best. That was what marathon running was all about. I am certain that you would have had a zest for life and would have accomplished many wonderful things. I believe this is what the Lord has given us all—that being the opportunity to seek satisfaction and His grace. Enough of my pontificating about marathons and life. Time to wrap up this letter.

I love you.

Dad

" I NEVER PROMISED YOU A ROSE GARDEN, BUT I WAS ABLE TO GIVE YOU ONE"

I left Hampton, Virginia about the last week of November 1983. I had about a three-day drive down to Fort Rucker, Alabama. It was a comfortable trip, and I was feeling elated about my new career move to another part of the country—this time to the Deep South. The weather was very pleasant and I drove through the rolling hill country of the Carolinas, Georgia, and then on into Alabama. Darling Pilgrim, it would have been wonderful to have you and Mark drive down with me from Hampton, Virginia to the southern part of Alabama. By the way, in March 1984 you would have been twenty years old. Darling daughter, would you believe that by the time I had moved to Alabama from Virginia, I had already lived in eleven states during my life. My opinion is that time flies when everything is going well, and conversely, it stands still when we are suffering. The time was moving with great dispatch—which meant that all was well. I got to the Fort Rucker area the late afternoon of the third day, and stayed at a local motel. The next morning I went to the Headquarters Building and met my new supervisor, Colonel Monson. We exchanged greetings and then we went to the Civilian Personnel Office where I met the personnel specialist who handled my transfer. Her name was Gail and we had already become acquainted as the result of talking to one another a number of times on the phone. We hugged one another. Gail and I would become very good friends. Pilgrim, you will hear more about Gail. I then processed in to the post, and upon my completion of the paper work, Colonel Monson took me to the post library where I was assigned an office in the back of the library—where I would stay for the next year and a-half—before being moved to the Headquarters Building.

I was able to get a nice furnished apartment in Enterprise, Alabama. I found the people in Alabama to be friendly and casual. It was great to get a respite from the hectic way of life I had endured working at Langley Air Force Base. This was not to suggest that my work and responsibilities at Fort Rucker were laid back—not at all. Nevertheless, the contrast in life styles was appreciated. By the way, I had already made Mark's arrangements to come to Alabama for Christmas.

The Christmas vacation for Mark came none too soon. I was able to get his Christmas presents and a Christmas tree that I quickly decorated. Finally, the Sunday before Christmas of 1983 I drove to the Dothan, Alabama Airport to meet Mark. The jet from Atlanta came in with a full load of passengers; however, Mark was one of the first people off the aircraft and into the terminal. Wow Pilgrim, your little brother was not so little anymore. He was close to my height.

Pilgrim, I realize that you would have been spending Christmas Day with your immediate family in California in 1983, yet, I would have missed you terribly. Therefore, I would simply plan to phone you later in the evening. Think of it darling daughter, it would not be very long until you would be twenty-years old. March 1984 you would be twenty. The following March 1985, you would be twenty-one. Willow and I both would be very proud of you. During Mark's first vacation in Alabama, he and I had a good laugh about the fact that the federal government was moving me from place to place.

The day after Mark arrived, I took him on post at Fort Rucker to see a helicopter flyover by pilots who had just graduated, and their flight instructors. Approximately twenty-five or thirty helicopters flew over the parade field. Mark was very impressed by the flyover. I gave him a capsule history of how helicopters had played such a significant role in the Vietnam War. Pilgrim, you were too small to remember the Vietnam conflict, though I referred to it several times earlier in the book.

Mark and I had a wonderful Christmas in 1983. I had bought a new car so he and I looked forward to being able to go on trips in it. Finally, on the morning of December 31, 1983, I put him back on the plane at the Dothan Airport to begin his long flight home to Seattle. As expected, I was sad to see Mark leave, but Pilgrim, the goodbyes were not as difficult as they previously had been—though any goodbyes with Mark were rough. However, he and I discussed our plans to go to Disney World the following summer and that made the both of us feel better. Pilgrim, both Mark and I were becoming more adaptive to the divorce and the geographical distance between us. Mark was also become involved in school activities with his friends, and I was doing a lot of traveling throughout the country, and overseas while working for the Department of Army as a command historian. Therefore, both of us were busy to the extent that, though missing one another, we were no longer beset by the emotional pain that earlier had exacerbated our grief regarding our separation.

Darling Pilgrim, Happy Twentieth Birthday (March 1984)! I looked forward to when you would have turned twenty. Darling, I would have loved to have been able to celebrate that birthday with you. As I commented before, so many people believe that only the mother keeps an anthology or mythology of significant dates in regard to her aborted baby. That is so wrong, because many fathers—me included—remember and grieve, because we do not have our children. We keep important dates as well. I know that I will never have you in reality until we see one another in Heaven. However, Pilgrim, so many wonderful people throughout the years have assured me that I will see you someday. I know I will.

I can remember telling a friend about you. She being the compassionate person that she was really was touched by the fact that though I had no name for you then, that I carried you in my heart along with Mark. But, she and I agreed that you were with me in any capacity that I wanted you to be.

Speaking of 1984, your brother Mark flew to Alabama that summer to be with me for six weeks. It was wonderful to see him; he was so tall and gangly, but a very handsome young man.

I took Mark to Disney World in Orlando, Florida in the summer of 1984. We drove down in my little 1984 Ford Escort. We had a wonderful time—especially at Epcot Center. Pilgrim, darling, it would have been great to have you with us. I took so many pictures of Disney World and of Mark. Yet, had you been with us, I know I would have taken countless pictures of you and Mark together.

Darling, fathers sometimes have a difficult time letting go of their children as they grow up. To be honest, I had a difficult time letting Mark go. I finally realized I had to relinquish my reins. Were you living, it would have been somewhat difficult letting you go too—at least emotionally speaking. I think you understand what I am saying. After all, I never could let go of you when you were tragically aborted; no loving father could have done so.

I had to put Mark back on the plane to Seattle in early August. It was sad, but not as melancholy as before because, we kept in close communication with one another when he got back home.

Do you remember my friend Gail who I had talked about when I discussed first arriving at Fort Rucker? Gail and I became very good friends. However, we did not date one another. Gail was divorced, but had a boyfriend in a neighboring state. She had a son who was a couple of years old than Mark, and we both found out that we had been raised only fifty miles part when we were younger. She been raised in Maryland and I was raised in Pennsylvania. She had married her high school sweetheart who became a helicopter pilot in the Vietnam War, and she had seen him off to Vietnam while pregnant with their only child. He returned home safely from the war, but eventually the marriage fell apart. Yet, she told me that she always loved him. Mark met her—though briefly. But they seemed to be comfortable with each other.

Anyway, Pilgrim, it was but a few days after Mark had returned to Seattle that I found out that Gail had breast cancer. It was a terrible shock. It seemed that Gail had attempted not to let very many people know about it, because she was a private person. I found out about it after she had a double mastectomy. She took chemotherapy and radiation and was back to work in a short time. Pilgrim, here it is 21 years later (2005), and cancer treatments are so much better now than they were in 1984—though back then, the treatments were state-of-the-art. I remember that I finally was able to get in touch with her. We had a tearful telephone conversation, at which time I told her how special she was and that she was in not only my thoughts and prayers, but was also in those of many people. She appreciated that. She was able to come back to work, and we went out to lunch together. Gail and I always talked with one another, either by phone or by getting together.

Pilgrim, I was very fortunate to have wonderful women friends—two of whom, however, would tragically die young. After your abortion and the terrible emotional pain associated with it, I despaired of ever having close women friends. However, in reality, I was so blessed by our Heavenly Father to have some great women friends.

The tragedy of my relationship with your mother was that we became lovers, but never were real friends; nor did Willow and I ever truly respect one another. These were the principal shortcomings of our dysfunctional relationship. How very tragic. Life is too short to hurt one another, yet many people avail themselves of whatever time they have to be cruel to each other. Willow and I were no exception.

Since Mark was spending Christmas of 1984 in Seattle, I drove down to Palm Beach, Florida to see my sister Anne, who I described much earlier in my letters. I wanted to see her and her family, and we spent a wonderful vacation together. I had not seen Anne in about four years, and, unfortunately, I would not see her again after 1984.

Well, the year 1985 came about, and I was acutely aware of another birthday for you—that being your twenty-first birthday. At this time, I want to wish you a Wonderful Happy 21st Birthday, Pilgrim. This is a milestone, darling daughter. I only wish it would have been a reality. You would no longer be "Daddy's girl," but a mature, beautiful woman. I feel a pain thinking about that. Perhaps Mark and I would have put our heads together and bought you something unique—what I am not sure—but something you would hopefully have cherished.

Pilgrim, you would have been the equivalent of a breathtakingly beautiful rose, that was so unique that it would be left alone to be admired by all who observed it—including your mother and me. I would have done all that I could to have affirmed your beauty and goodness. Perhaps your mother and I would have been able to transcend the bitterness, denial, grief, and confusion of the past by planting a garden, whereby we memorialized you with the symbolic rose of love. I would like to believe that your mother and I, on your twenty-first birthday, would have been able to unite as your parents to tell you how much we loved you. That would have been a wonderful gift from us to you. Once again darling daughter, Happy 21st Birthday.

Darling daughter, may I share something with you? I remember that it was during 1985 that I thought of Willow more so than I had before. I am not certain as to why that was. It might have been because of your 21st birthday. Probably there were more subliminal reasons. I have to admit that I have thought of your mother when I least expected it, and occasionally I said a prayer for her.

As I said in an earlier letter, your mother and I are inextricably linked together by you and always will be. I am certain she is aware of that as well I am. After all, you were, and still are, our first child.

Pilgrim, I have to admit that I would not be able to forgive Willow and her parents until almost twenty years later. Darling daughter, please understand that my obvious reluctance was that I was still devastated by your brutal and unwarranted death—and the dynamics associated with it. If the Lord granted me sensitivity in one area of my life, it was to be capable of mourning for you no matter how long it had been since you were aborted. At twenty-one, I think you would have understood my anguish. Pilgrim, I was denied the opportunity and joy that a father can have seeing his daughter become a woman. Yet, in 1985, had you lived, you would have been graduating from college and planning your future. Of course, both Mark and I would have been at your graduation. We would not have missed that for anything in the world. However, your future was denied by your death, and as well, my anticipation of wonderful things to come for you.

Although Mark filled my life, I, still dealt with the anguish of tragically earlier having lost my first child—that being you. A second child does not replace the first child; it simply supplants it, and becomes its own personality.

Once again, no matter how many children Willow and I had with our spouses, we have to acknowledge that you were our first baby. Therefore, because of the pain of your cruel death, forgiveness would take time. I would forgive your mother in time, but I knew, then, back in 1985, I would never forget what happened that terrible summer of 1963 and why you died. Forgetting was not a viable option. The reader should know that the parents of an aborted baby do not forget it or the circumstances of its death. Willow and I have received the Lord's forgiving grace and pardon regarding the abortion, but we are on record in Heaven as being your parents—and always will be. To think otherwise is either naivety or insensitivity.

Well, back to the mortal world. In the spring of 1985, I had to have some surgery. However, I was blessed that while I was in the hospital Gail visited me. In fact, when I came out of the recovery room, and was wheeled back to my room, there was Gail sitting by the bed with a floral arrangement of flowers and two Get Well balloons. As to be expected, I was groggy, but I was awake enough to thank Gail as profusely as I could for her thoughtfulness—such a great friend. She came to visit me several times while I was recuperating. The year 1985 went by smoothly. I got well and returned to work. Mark came for the summer and we had a great time together. I moved from Enterprise, Alabama to Ozark, Alabama that summer. I rented a larger apartment, which meant Mark could have his own bedroom.

It was during 1985 that my dear friend Gail decided to transfer overseas to work for the federal government in Germany. She told me she thought she needed to get away—so to speak. A number of her friends and I asked her if that it would be better if she waited a couple of more years to be certain if the cancer was healed. Gail said she thought it had been in remission long enough for her to work overseas. We were concerned for her. Gail, however, was a real trouper and said she was going. We had a farewell luncheon for her, and I told her to keep in touch with me. She and her son then left for Germany. We all missed Gail. She was a wonderful friend. In fact, about six months later, in 1986, she phoned me from Germany telling me there was a vacant government historian position in the command in which she worked. I almost took it, but something told me not to take it—and I think I know what it was. Shortly after I talked with Gail, her cancer resurfaced and became virulent. She was sent home in late 1986 to spend her last days working at Fort Rucker and being with her son and her friends.

A number of close friends of Gail, including me, met her when she landed at the Dothan Airport. She was so weak from the flights from Frankfort to Atlanta, then on to Dothan, that she had to put into a wheel-chair. She looked so frail! We all ran up and hugged her. Pilgrim, cancer is such a ravaging disease. It is terrible. The year 1987 came, and Gail tragically was not becoming any better. She would go to work every day, and I would come over to see her—when I could.

Pilgrim, you would have adored Gail: she was vulnerable, fallible, lovable, and so considerate—just as you would have been. One day, as Gail and I were spending some time together, I felt moved to ask her if she had a church or a minister that she would want to be responsible for the service. She said that she had not been to church for a very long time.

We then began discussing religion, and I just asked her if she was at peace with the Lord, because to do so would have given her some comfort. She said no. However, something told me to not go any further at that time, because there would be a more judicious time to minister to her.

Several weeks later, Gail became sick and was taken to a hospital in Dothan that had oncology facilities. I asked the minister of my church if he would mind coming down to Dothan to witness to Gail. First, I phoned Gail and asked her if I could invite the minister to come to see her. She enthusiastically agreed. The pastor of my church and I drove down the next evening to see her in the hospital. Gail had a couple of women friends there when we arrived. However, she was glad to see us. The pastor, whose first name was Frank, initially engaged in small talk with her, and then slowly began sharing with her the significance of being forgiven of her sins by the blood of Jesus. He further told her that Jesus loved her and died for her, and that death was the door into Heaven. It brought tears to everyone in the room. Frank then invited Gail to accept Jesus as her Savior—and she did! Pilgrim, Frank led us in a prayer for Gail. It was a wonderful evening, and Gail even began feeling better. As a parallel thought, Pilgrim, you have already been with Jesus, so you would have been able to reassure Gail that Jesus will be there for her when she leaves this world for Heaven. Gosh, you could be there waiting to greet her when she arrived in Heaven. Pilgrim, all of us in Gail's room all felt the spirit of the Lord with us in that evening.

Gail was wonderful friend to many people and lived life with gusto. Gail was an only child who lost her parents at a young age, and who was raised by a grandmother. If anyone knew loneliness and heartache, it was Gail. Pilgrim, I remember that I at times in 1987 I was thinking that Gail deserved to be healed and live a long life.

Pilgrim, in the month of March 1987—when you would have been twenty-two—Gail had to go back into the hospital because of a relapse. A friend of Gail's phoned me and told about her setback. I drove down to the hospital in Dothan on a cold, windy night. I drove down a practically deserted US Highway 231 from Ozark to Dothan. When I got into hospital and up to Gail's room, the oncologist was just coming out.

I asked him, "How is she?"

He responded, "She's not well."

I quickly went into the room. Gail was sitting on the side of her bed looking pale and tearful. She saw me, and we hugged one another. I sat on the side of the bed with her, and we held hands.

Gail in a tired voice said, "The doctor said I have maybe only a couple of months to live."

I remember Pilgrim that I felt weak. These were the same feelings that I had when Willow's father intimated your death in 1963.

I also remember telling Gail that I did not want her to die and maybe the prognosis was wrong. Darling daughter, I was doing what Willow and her parents had done twenty-three years earlier when they aborted you—I was playing God. Back in 1963, I attempted to tell our Lord that you could not die because I did not want you to! As many desperate people who struggle with seeing loved ones and dear friends die, I wanted to bargain with God. I had no business doing that. Though she was aware that it would only be a matter of time before she would die, Gail reached out to comfort me by saying, "Herb, no matter when I die, I will always be with you!"

What a wonderful expression of friendship and Christian love. I finally gained some composure and held her hands and told her how very special she was to me. I believe that possibly there were angels in the room that night that cried—as they very well might have for you—when they took you to Heaven.

Gail and I talked for a brief time, and then I hugged her, said goodbye, and told her that I would see her back in Enterprise, where she lived. Pilgrim, I went down the elevator, got out into the parking lot, and got into my car, and sat there, cried, and banged my fists on the steering wheel. Gosh, Pilgrim, I remember so well that I kept saying out loud, "Lord, you can't let Gail die. You just can't." I did this repeatedly for a couple of minutes, then turned on the engine and drove back to my apartment in Ozark. I was wrung out.

Gail eventually left the hospital. A number of her friends from the office in which she worked, and I took turns sitting with her the last couple of weeks of her life. I came over to her apartment two consecutive Saturday mornings to sit with her. While I was there, the first weekend, Gail was lucid, and asked about Mark, and even told me that she knew that the Lord was blessing Mark. She told me about her life and her love for her son's father, and, of course, for her son. We shared other things, and I felt that Gail was slowly preparing for the inevitable. Pilgrim, I knew the presence of the Holy Spirit was with us. Pilgrim, I will share with you something that heretofore I have not shared with many people: I believe that cancer is one of many satanic diseases that are meant to destroy the body, will, and spirit of people. However, I know that Jesus has triumphed over it—by His crucifixion. Pilgrim, life is so precious, yet people seem to take it for granted.

Gail became so ill the following Monday morning—after the second weekend that I had visited her—that she was taken to Humana Hospital in Enterprise, Alabama. I called her at the hospital; there were several friends, who were with her. I told them and her that since she was not alone, I would come right after work.

In the meantime, Gail told me that she had signed a living will that her lawyer had made up for her. He would be the executor. The end of the workday could not come fast enough. I got down to Humana Hospital a little after four-o'clock. When I got to the room, there was one of Gail's co-workers there with her. Gail looked as if she was in a coma. She had the back of her bed up, and it appeared she was sitting up. Her eyes were closed—but I am certain she heard whoever was in the room. I went up to her bed and held her hand, and said something to her. I believe I felt a squeeze as a means of response. It was not long before quite a number of people came to visit her. Yes, they knew Gail was dying, but at the same time, they all did such things as hold her hand, touch her face, and brush her hair back. People sat on her bed and talked to her. Pilgrim, it was beautiful! So many friends were with that evening, and even several doctors, came to be with her, and to check on her. Gail had decreed in her living will that she be allowed to die. People prayed over her. Wow, Pilgrim, the Holy Spirit was truly there in that room. And I know that her guardian angels were waiting to take her home—as were your angels also waiting in 1963.

People even stood in the hall outside of Gail's room waiting to get in to see her. I am almost crying as I am trying to type this. About 8:00 p.m., Gail's breathing became somewhat labored, but she did not seem in distress. A doctor came into Gail's room and with tenderness checked Gail's vital signs; he said that he was unable to pinpoint when Gail would die. Gail died around 9:00 p.m. I kissed her on the forehead, signed the death certificate, and along with a number of her other friends, made the funeral arrangements. Gail had died with peace and dignity. She was now home with the Lord. My close woman friend arrived shortly after I got to the hospital, and so I took her in to see Gail. She said a tearful goodbye to Gail. I quickly called the funeral home and told them about Gail's death. The funeral director said he would come and get Gail; meanwhile, a friend of Gail's went to Gail's apartment, and got some burial clothes and gave them to my friend who took them to the funeral home. Gail wanted a closed casket. We honored her request.

Pilgrim, The funeral home was so kind to us. It even gave us a nice casket for Gail's funeral. We asked if we could hold the service at the funeral home's chapel. We were told that we could. The funeral home personnel were very solicitous to us, and to this day, I will always remember their kindness. And, of course, I had to thank so many of Gail's friends for their support in arrangements for Gail's funeral.

Gail's funeral took place on a Friday morning. My pastor officiated over it, and I gave a short, but, hopefully, significant eulogy. Gail's funeral was well attended. Pilgrim, why I have been so descriptive of my dear friend Gail, her life, her illness, and her death, was because she was Willow's age. Gail was a most noble, loving human being, who blessed everyone's life that she touched by her generosity of spirit. She had wonderful friends—and with humility— I would like to think she thought of me as a significant friend. Darling daughter, next to being blessed with Mark and you, the Lord blessed me by granting me the opportunity to have Gail as a great and loyal friend.

Darling daughter, I shared with you from the depths of my heart about how real love can conquer death. My dear friend Gail epitomized that. She was loved by many and loved people in return. She would never have sanctioned the taking of a life. Gail respected the sanctity of life—no matter what its form. She did not leave this earth with titles, letters, material riches or publications. Gail went gently, but swiftly, to Heaven to be with her Lord. He welcomed her with opened arms, and likely said, "Well done, good and loving daughter. Welcome home."

Gail's death was a celebration because people who knew her and loved her—and there were many—celebrated her life. She was fortunate in that she died peacefully with her friends and some of the hospital staff around her bed.

After Gail's death and funeral, winter turned into spring, and with it the birth of new life throughout the flora and fauna of Lower Alabama. Mark was getting ready to come to Ozark for the summer. He was now fifteen, and could travel by himself—which he began doing. I had told him about Gail's death, and he offered his sympathy and concern.

I visited Gail's grave on Memorial Day, 1987, and left a bouquet of flowers—including a couple of roses on her grave. Someone else had brought a vase full of flowers for her as well. Gail now also had her own rose garden, just like you would have had on your 21st birthday. I cleaned up around her grave, and stood silently for a while just thinking about her. I left with the intention of coming back to visit Gail's grave. Unfortunately, Pilgrim, I never returned, because in a few months I was transferred from Fort Rucker for a new assignment. However, I did memorialize her by having a block for the new Army Aviation Museum, at Fort Rucker, inscribed with her name on it. Today, a visitor to the museum can see the block with her name on it. Maybe, someday, in the not too distant future, I can take a quick flight down to Fort Rucker and visit Gail's grave. Pilgrim, I miss her. She was a wonderful friend.

Before I forget, Pilgrim, a Happy Birthday on your twenty-third birthday. You could be very likely in graduate school pursuing either a Masters Degree or a Ph.D. in some field. I am sorry that I did not spend more time with you in this letter as I have in previous ones. I know that you realize that there were very significant people and circumstances that I believed necessary to have shared with you, and will continue to do so. I could not be selfish and spend time "self-actualizing" while there were other people who were just as important as me—if not more so. You and Mark, of course, are the two most important people in my life.

Speaking of Mark, he came to Lower Alabama in the summer of 1987. Mark and I took trips to Busch Gardens in Tampa. He and a group of teenagers from the church went down to Panama Beach, Florida for several days and had a great time. Then Mark and I went on a bus trip to Atlanta for an extended weekend and had a wonderful time. Mark was now fifteen and becoming taller; his voice was almost as deep as that of an adult. He even told me that he had a girlfriend in high school. Love blooms rapidly for adolescents, but often and unfortunately fades as fast. I was planning to see Mark at Christmas time, so everything was going smoothly. I put him back on the plane for Seattle, and then returned to being the Aviation Center's Command Historian. I was thoroughly enjoying my job. It entailed research, writing, and teaching, traveling to interesting places, meeting and interviewing prominent Americans, and giving papers.
In 1987, life was good Pilgrim. The only area in which I was having problems was concerning a relatively long relationship I had with a woman. We had to back off from each other for a while—which I think was good. In fact, what I did was to take a week off work when everyone was returning home from summer vacation, and go down alone to one of the beaches along the Gulf of Mexico and spend a week at a friend's condominium.

Pilgrim, the beaches along the Gulf had whiter sand than those of the West Coast or South Florida. The Gulf beaches were also cleaner. But what I enjoyed about the Gulf beaches were that they were accessible. The week I spent at the condominium was restful with wonderful weather, and not too many people on the beach. Gosh, Pilgrim, you would have been twenty-three in 1987.

Hey darling daughter, before I forget, might you have a "special friend" that you would have wanted to introduce me to so I could scrutinize him. You and I would have to sit down and you would have to share everything about him. Yes, your father would be intrusive—because I love you very much—and would not want to see you disappointed. Keep me posted.

The week's vacation at the beach ended; but I extended it by driving up to Auburn University and seeing the Auburn Tigers beat the University of Texas in their football home opener. I had season tickets to the Auburn home games in 1987 and Auburn had a great year—particularly when it beat the University of Alabama 10-0. Auburn fans were in a league by themselves. They were raucous, but delightful. Auburn had a 10-1 season in 1987. I enjoyed being with 80,000 other fans each Saturday. As an aside, if you lived with Willow, you might have gone to local college games in Southern California.

The fall of 1987 went by fast. I was busy with my job, and really feeling the Lord's blessings upon me. I believe I was using what talents he gave me. I could not ask for anything more. Sometimes, I would reminisce about the past, and think about the year 1963—which was 24 years removed. What I thought about, Pilgrim, was what had transpired with you and I the years after we left Southern California. Darling, to use a Frank Sinatra song, you and I had some, "Very Good Years." Do your realize all the states that you and I and others in our lives—particularly Mark—have lived? At that time, we had lived in twelve states—thanks in some measure to my government job, and to university teaching jobs. Darling Pilgrim, we have been richly blessed.

Fort Rucker was a great place to work. The civilians and the military worked well together. People were professionally motivated, and the US Army Aviation Branch and Center for whom I worked was a great place with a wonderful and rich history. I looked forward to working there until probably being transferred up to Washington, D.C. to work at the Army Center of Military History. However, there was going to be another change in our lives, Pilgrim. It would eventually be another move—and one to a place that I knew little about. I would be transferring to the Midwest, to an Army post known as Rock Island Arsenal located on the Mississippi River. Goodbye South, hello Midwest—I think.

I love you Pilgrim,

Dad

THE 'ROCK ON THE MISSISSIPPI

In Late September 1987, I was invited to apply for a recently vacant position as the command historian at Rock Island Arsenal, Rock Island, Illinois. This facility is the largest arsenal of its kind, and has served significant roles during all of America's wars since the Spanish American War to the present operations in Afghanistan and Iraq. From 1987-1991, it had 14,000 employees—most of whom were civilians. The "arsenal" as it is known, is situated on the Mississippi River between Davenport, Iowa and Moline/Rock Island, Illinois. The island is about three miles long and about one and one-half miles wide. So just, imagine the population density, if you will, darling Pilgrim. The Center of Military History asked me to apply for the opening, and told me that were I to obtain the position, it would be an important promotion to a high-grade level. At first, I was reluctant to apply, because I enjoyed working for the Army Aviation Branch, and had the privilege of being its first incumbent historian. During the five years I was at the Aviation Center, the command and staff were instrumental in getting the history program into high gear. During my five years at Fort Rucker, I received exemplary support from the Commanding Generals and the Chiefs of Staff—particularly one. He was the finest officer I had ever worked for—during my entire military and civilian government service.

Pilgrim, I really had to weigh the pros and cons of leaving a wonderful position. However, I finally decided to apply for the job, though not being certain if I would be considered for an interview. Finally, on my way home from travel abroad I found out I was invited to fly to the Quad Cities—as the region is known—for an interview. So, I was quickly given plane tickets, money for travel, and orders, and away I went. I got to Chicago without any problems, and then got on a small commuter puddle-jumper that could have passed for one of the Wright Brothers' early models. My destination was Moline, Illinois. The flight was the last one to the Quad Cities for the day. It was filled with disgruntled and tired passengers. Pilgrim, I sat next to a man who was employed by a major farm implement company, who kept telling me that the Quad Cities were falling apart, and the future of the area was uncertain. In fact, he told me to get the next plane out—which would have been early the next morning. Wow, what an encouraging welcome, and I was not even hired yet! I interviewed the next morning for the position—and six weeks later, I was offered it.

It would not be easy leaving Fort Rucker, Alabama. I had enjoyed the people, the post, my colleagues, the area, and my job. I, of course, would have bittersweet memories of Fort Rucker. I would be leaving my lady friend—who wanted to stay in the South—and sadly, I would not see the grave of my dear friend, Gail. Nevertheless, her spirit would always be with me. The people and command group gave me a very nice farewell luncheon, with well over 100 people in attendance; and much to my surprise, and gratitude, I was awarded the federal government's third highest civilian award. I attempted to give a going-away speech, but I kept being choked up. However, I got through it.

Pilgrim, we are on the move again. Guess what though, we will be doing our last ten years of government service at Rock Island Arsenal. This means that we will become Midwesterners. The year 1988 will be approaching, and you will be twenty-four. I notice that you have a rather starry-eyed look. Does that mean that you are in love? I think it does. Darling, I am so happy for you; I just ask that you please be careful with your feelings. Sometimes we confuse infatuation with love. I speak tragically from experience with your mother—though I can unequivocally say that I had loved her. Pilgrim, you would be at the age where the world would be at your doorstep. A long time ago, after the angels took you to be with Jesus, I knew that you would not only be my wonderful spirit child, but a star in the universe as well. As I get ready to go to a new area of the country, new experiences, and friends, I just look toward Heaven and know you are the brightest star in the universe—as your mother once was!

Pilgrim, I remember I finally got to the Quad Cities on a cold, snowy day in January 1988. I had driven two and a half days from Alabama to Illinois. I would be living in another state, and therefore, another notch in my belt. The Midwest was so different than the South, in areas such as population, topography, urbanization, infrastructure, quality of education, etc. People who worked on Rock Island Arsenal lived on both sides of the river though the island was considered part of Illinois. As I had at previous posts or bases, I checked into the Civilian Personnel Office—which by now was nothing out of the ordinary. I processed in; reported to the Chief of Staff of the incumbent command; then went down the major avenue to my office. I walked into the history office and met my colleagues. They were an interesting and mostly energetic group of individuals. The total number of historians under my supervision numbered eleven, including historians in other parts of the country.

Well, Pilgrim, unbeknownst at this time was that this is where I would live from 1988 up to the present. Possibly the Lord was telling that my peripatetic living style was over. However, at the time I first came to the Quad Cities and Rock Island Arsenal, I believed it would be but a few years before you and I would be moving elsewhere. Rock Island Arsenal was difficult to describe. It was a defense facility where the civilian work force—at least in my opinion—prevailed. I already mentioned that the island had 14,000 people representing several major units, such as Production, Resource Management, Maintenance, Ammunition, Logistics, etc. There were other smaller units on the island. Each of these major branches had a high-ranking civilian director. Sometimes these branches worked harmoniously with each other; other times there was internecine strife between these organizations. Conflict on the arsenal sometimes reared its ugly head, mostly between organizations attempting to get the ear of the incumbent commanding general or chief of staff. Most of the time, though, the respective directors, their subordinates, and work force worked hard and with great professionalism to perform the required missions—and performed them well.

However, it was but a short time until I began to enjoy the Quad City Area (QCA). It numbered about 400,000 people, with a diversity of industry, management, retail, agriculture, and a strong educational base. The area was also known for its work ethic, its overall job satisfaction, morality, and the friendliness, loyalty and kindness of its citizens. The QCA was religiously composed primarily of Christian-Judaic values. The demographics were mostly white, middle class, and Protestant and Catholic. The people in the QCA were and are amazing people.

I lived in a nice town known as Silvis, Illinois for twelve years until my landlord sold the house I was renting because he was getting too old to maintain it. In 2000, I moved to East Moline, Illinois where I still live. Pilgrim, though I have traveled extensively throughout the world while living in the Quad Cities, I always return home to the QCA.

Mark began coming to visit me in the summers and at Christmas in the QCA beginning in the summer of 1988—which was the summer of a long drought. He was not impressed with the heat Pilgrim, but we did get to go to Wrigley Field in Chicago to see my beloved Cubs play. It rained while we were up there. However, we came back to the QCA, where it was dry as a bone. The year 1988 was a drought year, but conversely, in the summer of 1993, the Mississippi River flooded over its banks on both sides of the river from around Dubuque, Iowa south to Quincy, Illinois. The smaller rivers in both states flooded. Rock Island Arsenal, however, was saved from flooding because of the extensive sand bagging. I would have taken you to see the flooding. I think you would have been in awe. Midwest weather can be precarious.

In fact, darling daughter, I was down jogging along the Mississippi River in Moline, when the river began spilling over its banks one Saturday afternoon in the early summer of 1993. I had to sprint across the lawns of houses to get back to my car, and barely got out of the parking lot when the water began flooding the parking lot. Whew! Oops, forgive me for not mentioning that you would have been twenty-six in 1990. It would have been likely that that there would be talk of a probable wedding soon.

Darling Pilgrim, had you been able to have a wedding, I would have been the proudest father in the world! I would have put money away for your wedding. Nevertheless, I probably would have worried myself into a state of frenzy that your fiancé was not good enough for you. Fathers tend to do that, though sometimes they can be irrational. Though I likely would not have been you custodial father/parent, the fact I was your biological father would have been sufficient enough reason for me to be concerned as to whom you married. You would likely have had a stepfather, who would have been the custodial father figure. Nevertheless, I would have never relinquished my love or my paternity of you. Were you to get married, I would hope that your mother and I would be able to transcend our differences so as to have a united front regarding your wedding. I would have wanted to pay for the wedding—or at least assisted in paying for it. Pilgrim, I would understand if you wanted your stepfather to give you away. Pilgrim, that is the way it should be. Though, in a somewhat selfish way, had you wanted me to give you away, I would have been ecstatic to do so.

The biological parents often escort the bride down the aisle. Darling daughter, I would have been more than happy to acquiesce to your wishes to have your mother and I take you down the aisle. I believe your mother and I would have been able to put aside our likely animus toward one another to be civil toward each other. I would only ask as you return up the aisle with your new husband that you reach over and give me hug, so I can whisper, " I love you" and shake my son-in-law's hand. If fortune would swing my way, I would be happy if I was invited to be in the receiving line. I am sure that Mark would also want to have been at the wedding. Pilgrim, I enjoy keeping your memory alive during these many years since your death, by planting into my psyche dates, anniversaries, perceptions of events, and associations you would have had with live people.

Well, I hypothetically got you married, and things were relatively well until 1992, when I hit an emotional speed bump. My mother—your paternal grandmother—was dying of cancer. She lived in Los Angeles, but had come east to Washington, D.C. to see my half-sister Lorraine, during the Christmas season of 1991, at which time she was diagnosed with pancreatic cancer. She was eighty-one at the time the medical diagnosis and prognosis were given. Pilgrim, would you like to hear about your paternal grandmother?

Pilgrim, heretofore, I have not yet talked with you about my mother. Over the years, I had other more important issues to discuss with you as well as dealing with very strong emotions regarding your mother and the abortion. However, I knew that that it was imperative that I eventually divulge and discuss certain aspects of my family of origin—which included Tillie.

Pilgrim, your grandmother Tillie was the driving catalyst in my life during my formative years. Yet, she and I had a relationship unlike that of most mothers and sons. Darling daughter, I hope what I share with you will not be too disturbing. Moreover, I hope you will have a better understanding of my family and its influence upon my life.

I love you very much,

Dad

TILLIE

Darling daughter, your paternal grandmother's name was Tillie. She was a first generation American, being of Russian-Jewish parentage. Her parents had come to the United States in 1905, and as thousands of other Russian Jews, they settled in the tenements of Brooklyn, the Bronx, and Lower Manhattan, New York. My grandparents lived in Brooklyn. My grandfather worked in the garment district in New York City. He and my grandmother raised four children. There were two boys and two girls. My mother was the second or third child.

The Jews suffered immeasurable anti-Semitism no matter where they lived in the United States throughout the early 20th Century—Brooklyn, New York was no exception. The Jews who immigrated to the United States from Eastern Europe from 1900 to 1920 found they were maybe a bit less victimized and persecuted than they had been in Europe—where most of them lived in abject terror. Russian Jews, along with Catholic and Jewish Poles, the Irish, and Italians suffered the ignominy of usually being thought of and treated as non-persons. Darling Pilgrim, my Russian grandparents—along with other Russians who emigrated from Russia—were, according to many White Anglo-Saxon Protestants (WASP), guilty of two apparent faults: they were not (WASP), and they were Jews. Therefore, they were believed to warrant only menial jobs, second-class citizenship, and the convenience of being discriminated against because they were Jews.

Since my mother was a Jew, I was born and raised a Jew. As a little boy, during World War II—at the height of the Holocaust—I had to deal every day with prejudice and discrimination, while going to school in of all places Washington, D.C—our nation's capital. Eventually, I learned that fighting was the only way I would get a measure of respect—even occasionally when I was in the Marines, I had to fight some ignorant clowns, who made an aspersion against my heritage.

No matter what Tillie's family had to suffer, her parents were imbued with the determination to see their children become part of the American Dream. My grandfather worked extraordinarily long and arduous hours in the sweaty garment shops that permeated the lower West Side of New York City. My grandmother—who had the most beautiful handwriting that I have ever seen—raised her four children in a small inner apartment with no inside toilet facilities. She sent her children to school where they learned to speak English, and then upon returning home in the late afternoon, they, in turn, would teach my grandparents rudimentary English. My grandparents also went to night school to learn English in order to gain their citizenship. My mother and her siblings were natural born citizens.

Your grandmother Tillie was a beautiful woman—even up until the time she died. When young, Tillie had been lithe, with reddish-blond hair and very blue eyes. She had a narrow thin nose, and a cleft chin. Tillie had a beautiful face and long neck. Pilgrim, when I was a little boy, I was so enamored with my mother, that if men whistled at her, I became very protective of her. Your great aunt—my Aunt Dora—who lived in Beverly Hills during the 1970s and early 1980s, looked like my mother. They were both extraordinarily beautiful women.

Your grandmother Tillie and my Aunt Dora—probably from the time they were born—competed with one another—no matter what the venue. Because of their striking looks, they were quite often assumed to be of a Central or Northern European Protestant background. Though markedly resembling one another, Tillie and Dora were contrasts in many ways. They could love and hate each other simultaneously, and until the day each of them died, this type of filial relationship still existed. They both suffered tragedy and disappointment in their lives.

Darling daughter, do you mind if hereafter I refer to your grandmother by her first name? I think she would not mind at all if you called her "Tillie." Tillie and I unfortunately had been estranged for many years. Prior to the period of her dying, I had not seen my mother since 1983, and prior to that time, not for thirty years. I had made numerous efforts to contact her, only to be rebuffed by her. One reason that Tillie became angry with me was that I gave my military life insurance policy to Anne while I was in the Marines. Tillie then wrote a mean-spirited letter telling me that she wanted nothing more to do with me. I guess it was time to disown me, Pilgrim. Tillie could be a bully—particularly when she actually knew she was wrong. She was loath to admit her wrongdoings or any pain that she might have inflicted upon people. My grandparents used intimidation as a means of getting their children to kowtow to them. My mother and her siblings followed suit regarding the threat to "disown" someone. When Tillie married the man who was to be my father—a Sicilian-Catholic immigrant—my grandmother threatened to say the *Kaddish* over Tillie—thereby declaring her dead. My mother's siblings came to her defense, and told my grandmother that she would have to say the *Kaddish* over them as well. Granny backed down, but never forgave my mother for the purported embarrassment of marrying a Gentile" (aka "goyem"). Pilgrim, your paternal side of the family could be lovable, but at the same time were self-destructive. You will shortly know why.

My younger sister, Lorraine, called me from Washington in December 1991 to tell me about Tillie's illness. Though Tillie and I had no communication with one another, she was my mother and I still loved her dearly. Pilgrim, since you would have been in your late twenties, I know that you would have wanted to meet your grandmother. Tillie may have had little use for me; however, I know that after she would have met you, the two of you would have been close friends. Pilgrim, if you had started a family by 1992, Tillie would have been a great-grandmother. That would have been great.

In early January 1992, Tillie was out of the hospital and living with Lorraine and her family. The doctors had told Tillie that she might live between six months and a year. Pilgrim, I felt helpless. My eighty-one year-old mother's life would likely end soon. I decided that I would come to see her as often as possible before she died. I hoped that we could make amends to one another. I loved your grandmother regardless of her feelings for me. Lorraine said that it would be a good idea to visit Tillie.

My first trip came about near the end of January 1992. I was excited to see her. I flew to Washington, and then took the Metro to Virginia where Lorraine and her family lived. Lorraine's *au pair* met me and took me to the house. Tillie was upstairs in the drawing room when I got to Lorraine's home. I opened the door and there seated on the divan was this beautiful woman—your grandmother, Pilgrim. Tillie still had the gorgeous facial features that had made her the great beauty she was as a young woman. She had not encumbered herself with glitzy Hollywood-type face-lifts or any other plastic surgery. I kissed her on the cheek and held her hands in mine. She was happy to see me. We talked about a myriad of subjects, including Mark who was a sophomore in college, our family, my work, and about Carol.

Pilgrim, there are some women who are blessed with wonderful features that remain with them until they die. Your great-Aunt Dora and your grandmother were two such women. Though ill, your grandmother Tillie was lucid, articulate, and completely aware of what was going on around her. I forgot the earlier pain and disappointment we had tragically caused one another. Darling daughter, during our conversation, Tillie suddenly began in a soft voice telling me about how she was alone in a room in labor with me at Brooklyn Jewish Hospital, the evening before Yom Kippur. The date was October 5, 1935. Either next door, or across the street was a synagogue, in which Yom Kippur services were taking place that evening—or maybe the services were being held in the hospital. Tillie told me that she began having contractions, and yelled for help. A nurse came, checked her, and went to the synagogue to get her doctor. During this time, the opening prayer, the *Kol Nidre* was being chanted, and Tillie could hear it. The nurse returned with the doctor who checked your grandmother and found her contractions had ceased. Tillie apologized for getting the doctor away from the service.

Your grandmother said something that almost floored me. She told me the doctor said to her not to worry, that God would decide when this baby (me) would be born, and that it was His will that I would be born on Yom Kippur. Guess what, darling Pilgrim? I was born the next evening on Yom Kippur! Tillie's eyes were wet when she told me all this. Pilgrim, I wish you could have been with me when your grandmother said what she did. I had never seen such a loving, almost nostalgic look as she told me this. I was teary-eyed as well. I think Tillie was attempting to make amends—and I was doing the same. It would be a slow process if it would succeed at all. In fact, nine years earlier, in early 1983, I phoned Tillie to ask forgiveness for whatever I had done to bring hurt into her life. Surprisingly, she accepted my pleas for forgiveness.

Tillie and I spent an enjoyable two hours together conversing about many things. Since it was the Sabbath evening, Lorraine, her family, and Tillie and I shared the Sabbath bread. In fact, Tillie blessed the bread. It was a wonderful evening with Tillie and Lorraine's family. Tillie and I spent the next afternoon talking alone. I let your grandmother direct where she wanted the conversation to go—and it went many places. However, she and I gingerly skirted any commentary about our past. My mother and I had a wonderful weekend together. I left the next afternoon to fly back to the Quad Cities.

Before I left, I gave Tillie a hug and said, "I love you."

She replied, "Thank you."

Knowing my family only too well, Pilgrim, I took my mother's reply to mean it would be as good as it would get. As an aside, I remember that I began to think that I had seen certain traits and mannerism in Tillie, which I had seen before in someone else, but I could not remember then who that other person might be. Later, however, I realized the other person was Willow. Well, Pilgrim, I spent the time on the flight home thinking of Tillie. During the next several weeks, I was able to make another trip to see your grandmother Tillie. I noticed the second weekend with Tillie that she appeared tired at times—that alarmed me.

Pilgrim, I worried about Tillie's health; however, she seemed perky when I was with her. We were starting to relate with one another, and I enjoyed sharing things with her. She once asked me why I was a practicing Christian as opposed to no longer adhering to the Jewish faith. I explained that I believed in Jesus and His offer of salvation. I did tell her that my Jewish heritage was still uniquely mine—and that I would never renounce it. She seemed a bit disgruntled when I stated my reason, but said nothing. Nevertheless, I could sense the pain of disappointment in her face. Yet, I was not going to let that discord stop me from loving and caring for your grandmother Tillie.

My darling daughter, your grandmother from the time she was a young woman until she died, was wrapped in tragedy, cruelty, despair, grief, and anger. Here is another letter. However, it deals with Tillie and me, and the dynamics of our relationship.

I love darling you Pilgrim,

Dad

THE TRAGIC EPIPHANY

Tillie and Lorraine flew to Los Angeles in early February 1992, so to be able to close out Tillie's estate, and to sort things out that Lorraine might want. My younger half-brother, Joseph, also flew out from Florida to assist his mother and his sister. I am sure that Tillie was dealing with a great deal of emotion. Though I never had been to my mother's place, I am certain it held a lot of meaning for her. I believe that Lorraine's husband, Scott, a government attorney, flew out to Los Angeles to assist with any legal issues. I had offered to fly out as well, but Lorraine said I was not needed. Valentine's Day was a few days away, so I arranged for a small floral arrangement to be sent to Tillie for Valentine's Day. This was to be a means to tell her that I love her and to wish her Happy Valentine's Day.

I received a surprise phone call from Tillie on Valentine's Day evening. She phoned to thank me for the flowers. Tillie sounded happy to have received them, and told me how lovely they were. Tillie sounded great. I told her that they were a small tribute to her for being my mother—this from her fifty-six year-old son. She seemed moved by my comment. We talked a few minutes then I talked with Lorraine and wished her a Happy Valentine' Day, as well, and asked her how things were going. She said everything was going well. However, it would not be very long until I found out that everything was not normal. Things had taken place in Tillie's home that would have an eventual, tragic influence on Tillie and me. That aside, your grandmother and I had a wonderful talk, and I told her that I would see her after she returned to Virginia.

I looked forward to seeing Tillie on the Mother's Day weekend. Pilgrim, had you been alive, it would have been wonderful to have you, your husband, and any children, to come along with me to see your grandmother. I am selfish when I say that, because I know that Willow would have expected you to see her that weekend, so please forgive my presumption. Well, I arrived in Washington that Friday afternoon with a special gift for Tillie. It was a music box that when open chimed the Stevie Wonder song, *"I just called to say I love you."* These were my feelings toward your grandmother—even those many times in the past when I phoned her, and she had either been curt, or refused to talk with me. I also bought her roses for Mother's Day.

I was excited to see Tillie. I gave her a hug, handed her the roses then, asked her not to open my gift until Mother's Day. I never had a Mother's Day with Tillie. Lorraine got home that evening from work, and things became somewhat tense. Lorraine and Tillie began arguing. I believe Lorraine initiated the argument as a means of controlling what was going on in her house. I frankly began to think that Lorraine did not want me to be visiting Tillie. There was an almost unannounced, but perceptible resentment by Lorraine toward me, because Tillie was cordial to me. I felt that I was an interloper, particularly since Tillie had ostensibly welcomed me back into her life. However, Lorraine did not like that happening. Pilgrim, I knew my family of origin too well. It lacked the ability to be a cohesive family unit for very long. Something obviously caused my sister to attack Tillie the way that she did. There had been periodic difficulties between the two women; however, I would have thought that Lorraine would have been more considerate of Tillie.

The tension between your grandmother and aunt continued throughout the weekend. I attempted to diffuse it by taking Tillie into another room and just the two of us having a conversation about whatever came up. Tillie seemed depressed—and I could understand why. Pilgrim, I was depressed as well. I did not want Tillie to die. I loved her, and I actually believed the two of us might partially repair our long-damaged relationship. Your grandmother and I talked about many things—mostly superfluous. However, Tillie mentioned that my father had been an alcoholic, and that comment would come back to haunt me soon.

We all stumbled through Friday evening and the following Saturday. Tillie was becoming irritable, but I believe it was because of the constant bickering between her and Lorraine. I tried to get your Aunt Lorraine to be more amenable with your grandmother. I attempted to tell Lorraine that our mother was ill and dying. That, however, did not make Lorraine stop. These two women were involved in some agenda; they both stubbornly believed they individually were right, and the other person was wrong.

Fortunately, Mother's Day arrived. Everyone seemed to be on their best behavior—no easy chore in my family. Tillie came down the steps with the music box I gave her. She opened it and played the song. She smiled and thanked me profusely for the music box. The two of us gave one another a hug and a kiss on the cheek as I wished her a Happy Mother's Day. As it came time for me to eventually leave, Tillie began to become depressed again, and mentioned that she did not mind dying, and that her only regret was that she would not live long enough to see her grandson Kyle grow up.

I thought what she said was touching and sad. Lorraine told me she was going to drive me to the Washington National Airport. Lorraine normally would have taken me to the Metro station—where I would get the train to the airport. I thought nothing of her offer and thought only that it was a very nice gesture. I said my goodbyes.

Pilgrim, Tillie thanked me for her Mothers Day gifts. I held her hand and kissed her lightly on the cheek, and said, "I love you."

Tillie said, "Thank you." Though we saw one another one more time, the above farewell would be our last.

Lorraine and I drove toward the airport; I told her that I was concerned for Tillie, and that I thought she needed more rest. Lorraine made some appropriate response. She continued driving when she asked me the following: "Do you know the circumstances of your conception?"

I was taken by surprise! I actually for a second thought I might say, "By the missionary position?" I had no idea what your aunt was talking about.

She looked over at me and asked me, "Do you know that you were the result of a rape!"

I was stunned. Before I responded to Lorraine, I asked myself, "What is she talking about?"

I finally said, with a note of circumspection, "I have no idea what you are talking about."

Lorraine said, "Mother told Scott and me while we were in Los Angeles that your father raped her and she became pregnant with you."

I almost sank into my seat. I remember staring straight ahead. Lorraine continued with her commentary. According to her, while Scott and she were helping her clean out some closets, Tillie suddenly became upset and began crying. Scott and Lorraine asked her what was wrong, and she told them the following: She had been officially separated from her husband and was living alone in an apartment, when one night, he drunkenly forced his way in, beat her, and raped her! (My brother Scott corroborated these remarks). By now, my eyes were becoming glazed, and I was having a difficult time comprehending the enormity of Lorraine's comments. Lorraine then said that Tillie went on to tell them that she had never told me because she was not certain how I would respond. I say this with love: how did my mother expect me to react? However, I later realized that likely in order to protect me, my mother never told me what happened to her. If I remember correctly, Lorraine said that Tillie told them that after she was assaulted, she called Dora to come and take her to an emergency room. I wondered why Lorraine told me all this on Mother's Day. Nevertheless, I let that issue fade into oblivion.

Though initially somewhat numb, I recovered enough, to become angry because of what happened to Tillie. I was also upset at Lorraine for telling me what she did. This epiphany now opened a Pandora's box of memories and answers. We drove the remainder of the trip to the airport in silence. Pilgrim, my eyes, however, began tearing—for my mother. I was now the little boy who many years before adored the beautiful Tillie from always afar.

My mother had never allowed me as a child to be held by her. Nor, had I ever been able to physically protect her. Yet, Tillie had been violated. I wanted to kill the man who did that! For a second, I hated the name "LePore." I thought it to be ugly and dirty. Who or what else was there to hate? Pilgrim, I hated Willow's parents for what they did to you—but never like the way I despised my father. Ironically, I never knew the man. Lorraine and I finally arrived at the airport; I got out with my suitcase; gave Lorraine a kiss, and asked her to give my love to Tillie. I then walked into the airport; checked in my luggage; then walked to the waiting area for the flight. I remember that I stopped at a concession stand and bought a cellophane-wrapped brownie—with the intention of eating it. I got to the waiting area and sat in one seat not doing anything but thinking, or sometimes, attempting to think. Pilgrim, my mind went blank occasionally that Sunday evening, as it had on that afternoon back in 1963, when I had sat on the beach in California, and had been distressed about you and Willow.

Anyway, it was time to board the flight to St. Louis. I boarded rather numbly, found my assigned seat—a window seat—and just stared out the window. I had undergone a similar scenario in September 1963. Well, the aircraft got airborne, and I just stared—either out the window—or straight ahead during the entire flight. We finally landed in St. Louis two hours later; I then made the connection to the Quad Cities. Thirty minutes later, we landed in the QCA, at which time I went to the baggage carrousel to get my luggage. I looked in my left hand—where I found the brownie I had bought back in Washington. It was intact as opposed to my confused emotions.

I found my car in the parking lot, drove home, sat on the sofa for a while, not knowing what to think. I believed I a called a friend of mine about what happened. She commiserated with me, and just listened to my pain. I did not sleep well that night. My pain and anguish was for my mother—not for me. I sensed that she was emotionally very lonely, and had been so for a very long time. Tillie did an extraordinary job keeping her secrets and concomitant pain to herself all these years. Pilgrim, your grandmother must have suffered so much in so many ways because of what happened—her sufferings were to become my sufferings as well. I will explain later.

I normally would have called Tillie on a Monday morning to say hello and to wish her a great day—particularly after I returned from spending time with Tillie, I always thanked her for the opportunity of having been with her. Tillie seemed to enjoy the calls. However, I decided the Monday after my return from Washington, to forego my perfunctory call to her. I needed time to allow what feelings I had to settle in my psyche. When I got to work on Monday, I kept myself busy with a degree of frenzied activity. Finally, my secretary came into my office and told me that I seemed obsessed with something. At first, I was going to deny it. However, I asked her into the office. I told Marnie, my secretary, the news that I had gotten back east.

Marnie told me that she would honor my confidences—which she did. She was taken aback about what Tillie had gone through all these years. Pilgrim, I can remember once again becoming angry at Willow and her family, after hearing what my mother had gone through to give birth to me. I commented to myself that if anyone had a right to have had an abortion, it was Tillie, who had been savagely beaten and raped; yet, she chose to not abort me. Tillie instead decided to give me life—which eventually would have devastating consequences for the two of us. Conversely, your mother and I were mutually responsible for her pregnancy by our thoughtlessness, arrogance, and immaturity. Willow, however, was not raped, threatened, cajoled, etc. Yet, your mother had you killed because you likely were an impediment to the social well being of both her and her parents, and because Willow never believed your life was worth saving. Willow and Tillie ironically treated unwanted and unwarranted pregnancies differently. One baby lived, the other died.

Monday evening, I got a phone call from Lorraine. Without missing a beat, she told me not to call Tillie anymore because the phone calls were depressing Tillie. I listened to what Lorraine said. This was too much of a coincidence. When I phoned Tillie—which was only once a week—as I mentioned before, our phone conversations never exceeded two minutes! There was an unhealthy, and somewhat malevolent agenda going on, and I think I knew what it was. Someone was possibly fearful that if I got back into Tillie's good graces, she might leave me some money, and thus reduce their inheritance. I would have never accepted any money from my mother, because all I would have wanted was the two of us reconciling. Pilgrim, like many families, my family of origin believed status, opulence and money were the three primary signatures of success and happiness. There seemed to be very little else important in life. Even love itself seemed to be based upon status, and love was looked upon as being a peripheral commodity.

Rather than respond with what could be an unpleasant dialogue between my sister and me, I just asked her to give my love to Tillie, and to tell my mother I was thinking of her. Pilgrim, the idiocy of what had transpired over Mother's Day indicated how shallow people could be. I was ashamed to even be part of my family.

Pilgrim, I am not saying I was of a sterling character—not at all. However, I learned throughout life to have enough remorse to regret when I hurt someone. Remorse obviously was not a genetic trait of my family. Pilgrim, I know that you would have felt pain for your grandmother. Tillie did not warrant being treated the way she was by some of her family members. It will be but a brief time before you will come to know more about Tillie and me. I did what Lorraine asked of me, but with a sense of confusion.

It was during the summer of 1992 that my nephew Kyle was going to have his Bar Mitzvah. Everyone looked forward to coming to Virginia for it. There would be family members and friends from throughout the country. Pilgrim, I must honestly say that I had some sense of trepidation, as to whether I should fly East for the Bar Mitzvah. It was not long after my arrival for the Bar Mitzvah that my anxiety was affirmed. Though I had not contacted Tillie per my sister's request—I believed that Lorraine's request to be specious. Yet, I was looking forward to seeing Tillie. I was staying at a hotel with my brother Joseph and his family, who I had not seen for quite some time. We drove over to Lorraine's house the evening before the Bar Mitzvah to break bread. We walked into the house and Tillie was sitting on the stairs in sweats, hardly acknowledging anyone. She barely smiled at me—but said nothing. Something was very wrong. I asked Lorraine about Tillie, and found out that she had fallen a couple of times, and had to be taken to an emergency room for examination and treatment for bruises. Tillie fortunately had no broken bones. I remember that I asked Tillie if she was all right. She answered yes. I was hurting for my mother, but she was not aware of it or she simply ignored me.

We all had dinner together; afterwards Tillie went back upstairs to the drawing room. I asked Lorraine's husband if Tillie would be able to go to Kyle's Bar Mitzvah. I offered to stay at home with her if she was unable to go. However, Lorraine's husband said Tillie would be able to go. During the evening, your grandmother said but a few words to Joseph, his family, or to me.

The morning of the Bar Mitzvah, we got dressed, and drove over to the synagogue where it was going to be held. Upon entering the synagogue, Joseph and I happened to see Tillie standing with a woman friend of hers. Tillie acknowledged us with a nod, so we walked over to where she and her companion were. She stiffly said hello to us, and introduced us to her friend. Tillie introduced Joseph as her son. I was simply introduced as "Herb LePore." Well, there should have been no surprises. That type of scenario had happened before.

Tillie and I had played this non-recognition game before—only it had been about forty years—and done as well with my sister Anne. I said hello to my mother and her friend. Joseph and I then walked away. Tillie's actions corroborated the ready existence of our family's dysfunctional behavior.

Pilgrim, I believe, however, that your grandmother would have felt reassured by your presence. She would have believed that you were not there to hurt her or to take anything away from her—be it her money or her goods. I sensed that Saturday of the Bar Mitzvah that the only person Tillie really believed loved her unconditionally was her grandson Kyle.

Speaking of Kyle, his Bar Mitzvah was a wonderful event—full of tradition and symbolism. I was very proud of my nephew. Tillie was as delighted as any grandmother would be at a Bar Mitzvah—she was crying with pride. I believe she read from the Torah—or excerpts from it. Pilgrim, it was amazing to see something that brightened Tillie's life. Joseph, his wife Bonnie, their children Shauna and Rob, and I went back to our hotel after the Bar Mitzvah luncheon, and Bonnie remarked how during the luncheon, Tillie stayed away from the rest of us.

Though Tillie was so happy for Kyle—as we all were—she looked tired. After the Bar Mitzvah, Bonnie and I made a comment to Lorraine's husband Scott that Tillie needed a rest. He appeared annoyed by our remarks—but I did not care. Tillie was now eighty-two years old and dying. She needed all the rest that she wanted.

I had an idea that I would not be seeing my mother after that evening. Though there was to be a Bar Mitzvah breakfast in the morning, I had enough emotional trauma. I was not going to stay in Virginia after Saturday night. I was to take an early flight home on Sunday morning. I am certain that Tillie was beyond caring if I stayed or left. However, if possible, Tillie and I needed to say our goodbyes. There were many people at the dinner. But Tillie and I seemed to give each other a wide berth.

When we got close enough to speak with one another, Tillie noticed that I was wearing a wrist brace and asked what was wrong. I said that I overused my one wrist on the computer. She solicitously told me to not strain it. That was primarily the extent of the conversation between mother and son. We tragically never talked with one another again!

The following morning, I said goodbye to Joseph and his family, and to Scott, and took the Metro to the airport and flew home. Joseph called me later that evening and said that Tillie asked where I was, and he told her that I had flown home. He said she shrugged her shoulders and said nothing. I knew that my mother and I would not ever have contact with one another. Unfortunately, Tillie was once more being victimized. She was fighting pain, grief, and anger with reciprocal behavior—as she had done all her life.

Pilgrim, the months went by without any communication between my mother and me. I think that Tillie was getting near the end, when in September 1992, my brother flew up from Florida to see her. He told me that Tillie was weak and seemed to let her mind wonder. Joseph also said that during the course of a conversation with Tillie and Lorraine, Tillie suddenly asked, "What should I do about Herb?" Joseph said no one offered any suggestions. Tillie was likely looking for some validation to contact me. She received none.

Tillie died in October 1992 shortly after Lorraine had phoned me to tell me that our mother had only a short time to live. Lorraine asked me if I wanted to talk with Tillie; since it was late and Tillie was possibly asleep, I said no. I then asked Loraine that I not be notified about Tillie's death because of the emotional politics being played out in our family. Joseph, however, phoned me a couple of days later and told me that Tillie had died. I later phoned Lorraine who told me that Tillie died after being in some cardiac distress. However, Tillie did not die until Lorraine had driven home from her office to be by her bedside. According to Jewish law, Tillie was buried two days later. I did not attend the funeral. Tillie was buried next to her second husband, Carl. When she died, the little music box was still on her dresser. My sister asked me if my nephew could have Tillie's music box. I said yes.

Approximately a year after Tillie's death, I went to Washington for a history conference, at which time Lorraine took me to see Tillie's grave. Lorraine and I spent a few minutes there at our mother's gravesite without saying much of anything. We then left. I have not visited Tillie's grave since that summer of 1993.

I love you darling daughter,
Dad

THE PHONE CALL AND REMEMBRANCES FROM A PAST FORGOTTEN

I decided after my mother's death that I would search out as much information as I could relative to the two of us. After many phone calls, I finally contacted the Jewish Social Service Office in New York City which requested that I send a letter with the request for information and why I needed the data. I sent the letter, but I did not hear anything, so I thought there might not have been any written records on either of us. Much to my surprise, I was wrong. I received a phone call from a woman social worker from the above office on December 24, 1992. Pilgrim, I want to share this information with you, because it will hopefully provide insight to my mother and myself.

I was getting ready to leave my office on Rock Island Arsenal at about noon on December 24, 1992. The rest of the staff had left so I was turning appliances and lights off and making certain the office was secure at Christmas. The large building in which I worked was almost deserted. I was just about out the door when my phone rang from my inner office. I quickly answered it. A woman on the other end of the line asked me if I was Herbert LePore. I said yes.

She introduced herself as a social work administrator from Jewish Social Services in New York City. She had received my request for information, and was able to retrieve documents relative to Tillie and me—even after many years. Pilgrim, I was excited, yet apprehensive, as she began reading from her back reports: The social worker read from a hospital log from the Jewish Hospital in Brooklyn, in which it was mentioned that on October 5, 1935, Tillie checked herself into the hospital to have me. The administrator noted that according to the entry sheet your grandmother Tillie was physically ill and emotionally distressed. She continued to read to me that it appeared that Tillie seemed to be possibly under nourished and confused. I was also told that during the Depression period that included the 1930s, pregnant women were often undernourished because of the lack of prenatal care, or eating the wrong foods.

As I aptly listened over the phone, the social worker continued to tell me that Tillie had a difficult time with her labor and delivery, but that eventually I was born—with the help of forceps. I was mesmerized just listening to the social worker's narrative about Tillie. The lady proceeded to tell me more. Because of Tillie's physical and emotional conditions, she was unable to nurse me. The doctors thought it best for Tillie and me that I be placed in a pediatric section of the hospital for further evaluation and care. I can imagine how frightened my mother was. She and I were both ill.

Tillie and I were physically and emotionally apart; therefore, we were deprived of any bonding. Being a Jewish male baby, I was, however, accorded the Bris (circumcision) eight days after I was born, at which time Tillie was allowed to see me. Pilgrim, as I sat at my desk, I was becoming affected by what I was hearing. As the social worker continued on, I noticed a break in her voice as well as she described how Tillie tearfully pleaded with the doctors that she be allowed to have me with her; Tillie was told firmly, but compassionately, that she was not in good enough health to be able to take care of me. It seemed that my mother was dealing with heartache after heartache. Tillie was just too physically and emotionally ill to do anything but just try to get well. Darling Pilgrim, as I respond to what I have just written, I find myself becoming incensed at the man who was my father. I am ashamed that he was my father—especially after what he did to my mother. I grieved as I listened to the comments about Tillie.

From day one, my mother and I underwent a prolonged separation that no child or mother should ever have to undergo. We would be apart for six years—though Tillie, my grandmother, and my older sister Anne— were able to see me intermittently during that period. Anne would be with me in my last stint spent in a foster home. Shortly after my birth, the New York's Children's Court decided, after consultation with the requisite medical staff, that because my mother was physically and emotionally ill, with an unsettling home life, I should be put in the New York City Jewish Foundling Home. Obviously, everyone—including Tillie—was notified of the court's decision. The social worker told me that Tillie was likely allowed to hold me and say goodbye to me before I was taken away. I would spend three and one-half years in the foundling home. After that period spent at the home, the Children's Court transferred me to two foster homes—where I stayed until I was six years old. I found out by conversation with the social worker that there were boys and girls who were at the Jewish Foundling Home from the time they were infants to the time they were sixteen years old. That revelation is so sad.

Pilgrim, I remember asking the social worker whether it was a case-worker or a nurse who took me to the foundling home. She thought it might have been a social worker, and in fact, said that I was probably wrapped up in swaddling cloth and taken by cab from the hospital to the home in Manhattan. I was shocked to find out that I was in an institution at such an early age. The lady said about three weeks after I was born, the court enjoined the hospital to prepare me for transfer to the foundling home. The administrator read something to the effect that Tillie became further depressed upon having to relinquish me. Pilgrim, listening to what I just described made me appreciate and love my mother more. Having said that though, in future years, my love for her will be tested by her cruelty and indifference. The social worker shared some personal observations: she said that though the foundling home setting was as warm and loving as it possibly could be, with the broad age range of the boys and girls that it had to serve, it was difficult to give prolonged care to any one child. In all likelihood, I never received the close bonding with a real mother figure that I warranted. Therefore, it should have been of no surprise of my inability as I was growing up, to relate to women because of the feeling of abandonment.

I recall asking the social work administrator if Tillie had contemplated giving me up for adoption or attempted to do so. Pilgrim, the administrator said succinctly that Tillie did not entertain such a possibility. I was surprised that Tillie wanted to keep me. She had every reason to have given me up for adoption. However, Tillie did not do so. She was willing to attempt to love me—though no doubt her effort to do so would be difficult—and eventually unsuccessful.

Pilgrim, meanwhile, my mother was attempting to put her body and mind back together. She finally physically recovered; however, she would never fully transcend the horror of being beaten and raped by my father.

Tillie never received the extended psychotherapy she needed. Her mother also had physically and emotionally abused Tillie when she was a young girl. I am not a clinician; however, I knew enough about my mother to sense she could not fully love anyone—particularly herself. I would emulate this proclivity.

Pilgrim, it was bizarre that on Christmas Eve afternoon, 1992, the holiest of holidays, I was at my desk in my office of an almost empty very large office building, talking with a social worker in New York about what had transpired fifty-seven years earlier. We talked easily for an hour. She kindly offered to send a corroborative letter concerning the earlier disseminated information. Though I believe the administrator was Jewish, I wished her "Happy Holidays." She responded in kind. Pilgrim, what a rough afternoon—but one that I was glad that took place.

I got off the phone and I was emotionally worn out. I sat at my desk until about 3:00 p.m. and then I drove off the practically deserted island, went home, and wept for your grandmother—and possibly even for myself. I wept for the beautiful, but ill, mother who gave me life—though at a cost of great suffering. I cried for myself because I was taken away from Tillie, almost as traumatically as you had been ripped from Willow's womb. Tillie held me only for a very short time. We had very little time to ever bond. No matter what, my mother had been a brave, but frightened young woman who made the choice to have me—when she had every reason to have aborted me. Had I no other reason to love my mother other than the fact that she gave me life; that itself would have been worth my complete love for her.

It was about the second week into 1993 when I received a letter from the woman with whom I corresponded on Christmas Eve. The letter presented a chronology of pertinent events relating to my early life. Guess what, Pilgrim? There was a list of significant baby dates, such as when I sat up; had my first tooth; also the day that I first began to walk. The commentary said that I was a "darling, affectionate baby." That remark was enough to make me become teary-eyed. The letter said I had blue eyes and curly blond hair with an infectious smile. Wow, Pilgrim, someone obviously believed that I was a cute baby. A few years before Tillie died, she gave Lorraine some baby pictures of me. I am not certain if I ever saw them; Lorraine, however, said they were taken when I was a year old. Evidently, during the time I was at the foundling home, Tillie and my grandmother often came to visit me. Later on, as an adult, I saw a picture that my Aunt Dora had of Tillie and I together when I was about fifteen months old. I had a hoop in my right hand and was holding Tillie's hand with my other hand, and we were looking at each other and smiling. I remember Tillie looked beautiful in the photo..

Your grandmother was described as a "tall, very attractive blonde lady." The letter also mentioned that Tillie had gone to school at Adelphi College on Long Island, where she had majored in English and Theater.

Your great Aunt Dora told me that Tillie and a famous—now deceased—actor by the name of Danny Kaye had gone to high school together, had been in plays with one another, and had been good friends. After reading about my mother's background, I asked myself, "Just how could my mother have gotten together with such a jerk as my father?" Pilgrim, I think that my father, a Sicilian, was barely educated. Darling daughter, my mother had few equals when it came time to selecting bad marriage mates.

The letter contained in its narrative a disturbing revelation that heretofore I had repressed: it alluded to when I was ten years old and taken by the District of Columbia Juvenile Court from Tillie and my stepfather for "child neglect." Much to my surprise, the letter also stated the fact that subsequent to my removal from Tillie, I had been sent to a school for emotionally disturbed children, and then on to a boy's school in Pennsylvania. I was not embarrassed about what the letter said, only the fact it brought back the memories it did.

Pilgrim, regardless of the feelings about my childhood, I love you too much not to be honest with you. Therefore, in the following letter, I will share that part of my life when I was a small child, and the fact that much of it was in disarray and pain. I do this darling Pilgrim to illustrate the painful, symbiotic relationship that two emotionally ill people—Tillie and I—had with one another, and how it destroyed us as mother and son.

I am glad you are forever my daughter.

I love you,

Dad

THE SUN SORROWFULLY SETS

Tillie, my older sister Anne, and I were reunited in 1941. Anne and I had been in a dysfunctional foster home—the memory of which is still harshly embedded in my psyche. "Our gorgeous mother" obviously came to save us. We were so happy because we believed that we had Tillie to ourselves, and as most small children, we fancied a perfect life with our mother. However, much to our dismay, and to our eventual horror, there was a man with her. She introduced him as "Daddy!" Pilgrim, "Daddy" was neither an attractive or pleasant man—nor did he exhibit paternal instincts. Anne and I, years later, would reminisce how from the onset of our contact with him, "Carl" as I will call him, was very controlling and cruel. It was not very long before, "Daddy" was replaced with ""father," and "mommy" became ""mother." Anne and I were to "know our place." "Father" had an ominous presence about him. Tillie seemed somewhat afraid to say very much. I learned that Carl was a brilliant lawyer who met Tillie while she was working in New York City in 1939. Theirs was a whirlwind romance. Tillie and Carl got married after a short time, and I guess Tillie became pregnant, but sadly, her baby died in childbirth. All of this took place before Tillie and Carl came to get Anne and me. Anne and I were told that we would have Carl's last name—which possibly denoted he had adopted us. Both Anne and I would come to abhor hearing that name—even years later.

The four of us drove from New York to Washington, D.C. to stay in an apartment while Carl found work. From the onset, Carl seemed resentful of Anne and me. Years later, I found out why: Tillie did not let him know that she had children until after Carl and she were married. Why the deception, Pilgrim, I have no idea—unless Tillie believed Carl would not marry her had he found out that she had children. Tillie might have been accurate in her assessment of Carl. Yet, he might have annulled the marriage based on Tillie's subterfuge—but Carl evidently decided to stay married to Tillie. .

From the time that we were in Washington, Carl used both Anne and me as battering rams. Tillie—possibly out of fear—did nothing. Two neurotic adults and two traumatized children played the ever-sickening game of destruction. Anne and I would act out because of our hatred of Carl; in turn, Carl would become incensed and beat the both us. It was not very long that to an objective outsider, the four of us were crazy as loons. Meanwhile, Tillie began to take part in the beatings and attendant cruel punishment. Occasionally, she would simply stand with her arms folded looking impassively and smoking a cigarette, as Carl beat us with his fists or with a paddle. Another extreme measure of punishment inflicted upon Anne and me by Tillie and Carl was to make Anne and I stand against a wall with our arms outstretched, or putting us in a room without food for at least two days. Pilgrim, what I just said is no fabrication of the truth nor is it exaggerated It actually happened..

It was not long before Anne and I found it difficult to even respect our own mother. In the 1940s, there was no such thing as group rates for psychotherapy. Had such an opportunity existed, the four of us would have kept a psychiatrist busy and wealthy. Anne finally went away to a boarding school for a while. She unfortunately was returned to the parental control of Carl and Tillie. Upon Anne's return, Carl took up where he left off regarding the beatings and neglect. Anne, with the help of Tillie's sister Dora, was eventually taken away for good. I, however, remained to become the moving target for both Carl's and Tillie's malicious and calculated mistreatment.

I can still remember as a small seven and eight-year-old boy, that I wanted my mother to be happy and to love me. I did not want her sick or afraid. Tragically, the mother that I loved was disappearing from my eyes. Pilgrim Darling, Tillie was becoming a shell of a woman. Carl was murdering her spirit. He controlled her completely. Carl was as cruel as he was brilliant. Several times, Carl beat Tillie, and I could do nothing. I felt so ashamed of myself. Pilgrim, I had the same emotions the night I gave your mother the $500 to abort you!

I could deal with Carl's beatings of me. When he beat me with either a belt or a makeshift paddle, he would have me count slowly as he hit me. However, at the tender age of eight, I became psychologically the "artful dodger." As I was counting for Carl, I realized that every stroke was one less, and also by simply tuning him out. I stayed emotionally alive.

It was about when I was eight, that Tillie began beating of me as well. Tillie had become Carl's "trusty" when it came time to beating me.

Corporal punishment was always by beatings, punches, slaps or shakings. I remember one time that I had done something that maybe merited me being punished. Tillie began beating me with a frenzy. She seemed unable to stop. I finally ran out of the house, frightened to death, but more afraid of what was happening to my mother. I finally came in expecting the worse; however, Pilgrim, Tillie was sitting at the kitchen table smoking a cigarette and crying. I started going over toward her, but she simply waved me away and continued crying. I went up to my room and cried as well. Pilgrim, I can remember wanting your grandmother and I to run away. She did not deserve what was happening to her. Carl cruelly and deliberately turned my mother against me. I was afraid of Carl, but I hated him so much that I wanted to kill him!

I just wanted him dead. I was becoming as psychologically ill as my mother and Carl. Actually, there was the likelihood, that I was already emotionally ill. I was often not being fed, but was many times beaten. Therefore, I developed a bizarre technique of survival. I began begging for money from strangers; I stole money and food—occasionally, the latter—even from garbage cans. I would skip school, take a bus to downtown Washington, and spend an afternoon in a movie taking a nap. In school, I attempted to bully smaller or weaker children, to compensate for my inferiority complex.

My survival also included my tuning out reality, and whenever possible, living in a fantasy world—one in which my mother loved me and was my friend. I believe this would be known as "compensating." To this day, however, I think Carl was crazy as a fox, and cruel as a wolverine. He had little, if any remorse, the years I spent with him—which fortunately were only four. Besides being cruel to me, he was unimaginably mean to Tillie.

Pilgrim, Tillie and I were as traumatized as we had been, when nine years earlier, in 1935, she checked into a hospital to have a baby that ultimately she could not love. Over the years, Tillie began to acquire a hard look. However, she was no less beautiful, but just looked sad and depressed. Pilgrim, meanwhile, I began not trusting anyone—particularly women. I did not want to risk being abandoned as Tillie had essentially deserted me. When I was nine years old (during World War II), I remember that I thought that maybe I could join the Marines, go to war, and die a hero. My teacher, however, told me that I had to be older, and by that time, World War II was fortunately winding down. How was I to be a hero if my own mother did not love me? I felt that if I died a hero, Tillie would love me. This was a seemingly bizarre fantasy by an emotionally ill and lost child. Pilgrim, I had no other way to deal with my pain.

Because both Tillie and Carl were Jewish, I was sent to Hebrew School during the week, and on Saturdays I attended services at a local synagogue. As could be expected, I equated the authoritarianism and symbolism of Judaism with Carl. He professed that he was a good, practicing Jew. Therefore, I thought that God loved only those who were good Jews. Though Carl was cruel, the fact that he was a "good, practicing Jew" meant that I had to be a bad Jew, otherwise why would he beat me? In all likelihood, Carl's God was a good God, while I merited no deity to call my own. This undoubtedly meant I was not even good enough to be a Jew.

After all, God would not want to love a bad Jew—and I obviously was a bad Jew—even at eight years old! This was my syllogistic take on Judaism as a small child. Nevertheless, I enjoyed going to the synagogue because it got me out of the house, and it entailed a pleasant bus ride. Upon arriving at the synagogue, I would sit in the back of the synagogue, either daydream or watch what was going on around me. Unfortunately, I did not understand much of the service and ritual until years later. Because I often went without meals, Pilgrim, I looked forward to the luncheon after the morning service. After all, what I had at lunch might have been the only meal I had that day. After eating, I would summarily take the bus home—savoring every moment of freedom. In spite of being ambivalent about Judaism because of my confusion about it, eventually at thirteen, I took a Bar Mitzvah. Nevertheless, I became a Christian later in life.

By the time I was ten, the beatings had become more intense; in fact, earlier, when I was nine, Carl broke my nose with a paddle when I turned around and he hit me in the face. Tillie stopped the bleeding. Pilgrim, I went to school the next day with a note that said I had fallen down the stairs.

I was almost suicidal, because there seemed to be no way out of my pain. In desperation, I began running away. I had nothing to lose—except possibly my life. Suicide was a way to get rid of the pain. In actuality, I made no overt efforts to kill myself; I just thought I would be better off dead. Every time I was brought back from running away, Carl, and often Tillie as well, beat me. I then would be locked up in the attic until it was time to go to school. At school, I would summarily plan my next getaway.

Pilgrim, I ran away to places such as, Baltimore, Maryland, and Richmond, Virginia, and to Arlington, Virginia, and Rockville, Maryland. One of the times I ran away, I did a stint of walking around downtown Washington, D.C. all night long. I later slept in the bushes by the Lincoln Memorial that night. In essence, I had my brush with history. I would be gone on the average of three days before I turned myself into the authorities. I was like an animal. I would do anything to get away from Carl and Tillie. Begging and stealing were the two primary traits I used to survive. Pilgrim, desperate people do desperate things. Yet, I know that our Heavenly Father protected me during the time I ran away—why I was not certain.

May I give you an example of the Lord's protection? The first time I ran away, it was to Rockville, Maryland. It was in the month of January, and the temperature got down to zero or below. It was so cold. All I was wearing were my clothes, a sweater and a mackinaw. I had no gloves, but I did have a cap.

Pilgrim, I remember I walked into a residential area of Rockville; I skulked in the alleys until I saw a house with a sofa on the back porch. Pilgrim, I lay down on the sofa, curled up, and was not certain whether or not I should attempt to sleep in the bitter cold. However, I did fall asleep, and slept fitfully. I believe I slept for about two hours. Pilgrim, the Lord had His angels protecting me from possibly freezing to death. Eventually, I got up, walked around until it was almost morning, when three young men in a car picked me up, took me to a White Tower Diner, and gave me some money. I was famished. But, I had enough money to buy several of the small, square hamburgers and a hot chocolate. The night manager was compassionate enough to give me a couple additional hamburgers and some more hot chocolate. Dear Pilgrim, in my opinion, that diner manager was the quintessential "Good Samaritan." Upon morning's light, I had several bus tokens, so I took a bus back downtown to Washington. I spent the day there, begging money in order to eat. Later that afternoon, I got the bus back to Rockville. That night, a couple noticed I was walking the streets, fed me, gave me a bath, put me to sleep, and called Carl the next day. Carl brought clean clothes, and came and got me. There was a short respite from the beatings. However, Carl decided to renew the "unrestricted" beatings. Darling Pilgrim, I was tired of being crazy, and the only way for me to escape my insanity was to once more run away. Tillie and Carl had indeed become my enemies.

I loved my weak and confused mother; however, I had to get away from Carl and her. I was determined to do what I had to so I could get away. However, I wanted Tillie to worry about me. In my mind, running away was the only means by which I could get any attention from her. The fifth time I ran away would the last time. Tillie locked me in the attic after the fourth time I had run away—this time to Baltimore,—however, not until after both she and Carl beat me. Early the following afternoon, Tillie took my half-brother and infant half-sister out for a walk. I watched them leave and go up the street, at which time I simply got on my mackinaw and cap and went out the other attic window, dropped to the garage roof, then on to the street, and I was gone. I headed into downtown Washington, where I begged for money; then took a Greyhound Bus to Richmond, Virginia; later that night I was caught by juvenile authorities and put into a receiving home. I told the social worker that I ran away because of the beatings I was undergoing. Three days later, Carl came down on the train to get me. He told me I would not be living with him and Tillie any more, and that I would have the name, "LePore" for my last name. I was being given back my biological father's name. I had mixed feelings. I was glad to be leaving Carl, and have a new surname, but I wanted Tillie to leave with me.

When we got to Washington's Union Station, two police officers were waiting for us. They took Carl into a side room, and handed him orders to have me at the Washington Juvenile Receiving Home no later than 7:30 a.m.

When we finally got home, Tillie looked sadly at me and told me to go to sleep. We both had lost the battle for control of one another. The next morning, I took a bath and put on clean clothes to go to the receiving home.

The cab was waiting. Pilgrim, Tillie was nowhere in sight as I departed the house in which I had so many horrific memories. Carl and I got into the cab. I remember I became anxious. I thought I would never see Tillie again. The only person who I ever had truly loved symbolically deserted me. Ergo, this meant that she did not love me—or, at least, that premise seemed logical to me. My craziness notwithstanding, I believed I was not capable of being loved. Regardless of my anxiety, Carl and I proceeded to the receiving home.

I would spend six weeks at the receiving home while my future was being determined. The facility was actually a large detention center. Its walls were stark, and we children had institutional aluminum bowls, trays, etc. The "inmates" all wore institutional garb—which we changed every couple of days. We were controlled in a perfunctory manner, twenty-four hours a day. For example, we were not to talk while we ate. We were to keep our eyes on our food while eating. We could be physically punished if we did not do what we were told. As an aside, it reminded me of my first few days at Parris Island, South Carolina years later as a Marine recruit. Back to the receiving home; the children were segregated by gender, and the boys and girls were kept apart all of the time. I remember the boys slept in a large cell in which we were locked at bedtime.

Darling daughter, as most of the other children, I was frightened. The regimentation was unsettling. However, it was a more appealing alternative to where I had been. In fact, it was great to have three meals a day. Pilgrim, I had been in the receiving home for several days when Tillie came to see me. To this day, I remember I ran up and hugged her. She seemed surprised I did that. Tillie responded somewhat in kind. Tillie and I discussed many things. I asked her to pay some of my former classmates for having stole things from them. Pilgrim, I was a kleptomaniac. I am ashamed that is what had happened to my life while living with Carl and Tillie. However, Pilgrim, when I left the craziness of Carl and Tillie, I no longer stole, begged or bullied anyone. I thank the Lord for that.

I had to undergo a week of physical and psychological examinations and interviews by the Federal Juvenile System in Washington, D.C. The results verified what I already knew—I was a mess. The Juvenile Court decided to remove me from the venue in which I was living. Its reason: child neglect. I was to be sent to a school for emotional disturbed children. Pilgrim, just how does any psychologically and physically beaten young-ster—otherwise known as an emotionally disturbed child—ever get well? Darling daughter, unfortunately, such confused children never become well—your father included.

Darling daughter, children who are emotionally ill, do not ever be-come completely well; likely, at best they get somewhat better. Most psy-chologically ill children learn to put up walls for self-preservation. I was no exception. Such children fear the rejection and vilification that have beset their lives. Therefore, those of us who are psychologically ill, protect ourselves by simply not becoming involved in interpersonal relationships, or continually looking over our shoulders for an escape route when things go wrong. However, Pilgrim, in regards to relationships with the opposite sex, we often attract the same type of individuals that we are, or if they are better emotionally assembled than us, they eventually reject our sickness and us.

Pilgrim, after my six-week evaluation and stay at the receiving home, I was told I would be leaving the next day for New York and the Children's Village, a school for disturbed boys in Dobbs ferry, New York. Tillie got me and took me home. I can remember the day she and I left the house and took a cab to Union Station. It was a cold, wintry Friday when Tillie and I entrained from Washington's Union Station to New York City. The trip from Washington to New York City took four hours. Tillie and I hardly talked with one another while on the train. We were lost in our own thoughts. However, we occasionally smiled at one another. Upon arriving at Pennsylvania Station in New York City, Tillie and I took the subway over to Grand Central Station where we boarded another train for Dobbs Ferry, New York. We got up to the school in the afternoon, at which time I was quickly enrolled. The two of us were then taken to the boys' cottage where I was to live. Other boys were also there with emotional problems. I cried as Tillie and I got ready to part. Tillie hugged and kissed me, and then said words, which to this day, I have etched in the marble of my memory. She said, "I love you." I told her that I loved her too. Her words of spoken love would be the last time she ever said them to me. She then left. Nevertheless, her words sufficed in that they got me through a difficult time.

The school was good for me. I got rid of many bad habits, such as stealing, begging, being a bully, and falling into prolonged bouts of fantasy. Before I went to the Children's Village, my disturbed behavior actually kept me alive. A psychologist at the school told me that what I had done to extract myself from the insane venue, in which I existed, though not appropriate, was a measure of expected behavior.

Pilgrim, I never looked at the ethics of my previous behavior because I was simply too busy attempting to stay alive any way that I could. I got somewhat better as I became older. However, I was unable to maintain few, if any, close relationships with people. I was not unlike a dog that is afraid to let anyone pet or handle it for fear of being mistreated. As any emotionally ill or distressed person, I learned to cope within the boundaries set either by others in authority or myself. That is the way I have gone through life, Pilgrim. Until, your mother came into my life, I trusted no one—particularly women. For a short time, however, I let my barriers down and unabashedly trusted your mother. Both of us know what happened to cause Willow's and my relationship to end so bitterly. Subsequently, and unfortunately, the barriers have gone back up—with the exception of my love for Mark and for you.

Pilgrim, let us return to your grandmother, Tillie. She came to visit me intermittently, but never said those words again or hugged me as she did the evening I arrived at the school. I was always happy to see her, however, and there seemed to be a lessening of tensions between us. I actually became better, did well in school, and then I went to a boy's school in Pennsylvania for five years, and then into the Marine Corps for four years. During the time I was at the farm school, Carl was dying from diabetes, and came up to see me—possibly to make amends. Pilgrim, as I look retrospectively, I must admit that I was very sarcastic. I had no kind feelings toward him, and refused to call him anything but "Carl." I could not forgive him for what he did to Tillie and me. Ironically, when he returned home, he told my mother of my reaction to him. She wrote a pungent letter telling me how unappreciative I was of Carl. I was taken aback that Tillie defended the man who was so cruel to her!

Carl died shortly thereafter, and Tillie sent me another chastising note. I did not bother to respond. Tillie and I continued to drift apart. As an aside, Tillie had been held hostage emotionally, physically, and psychologically by two men who were cruel and sadistic. She had not ever been able to escape from the yoke of their tyranny other then by the divorce of my father, and by Carl's death. By the time Carl died, it was too late for Tillie to ever recover from the tragedies that had beset her adult years. She had become both a victim and a victimizer, because she had no marker in life other than to just exist on a daily basis. Even when she died, Tillie left behind her a family divided and angry. Yet, in spite of what took place between us, I always loved your paternal grandmother.

Within two years, the sun sorrowfully set on our relationship. Pilgrim, as I mentioned earlier, it would be thirty years before your grandmother and I reengaged in any communication. However, I still loved Tillie all the years we were apart. Tillie's terminal illness reopened the story of Tillie and me—which I discussed earlier.

Ironically, the two women in my life who I loved unabashedly—Tillie and Willow—were so much alike as far as demeanor and personality, that it was uncanny. Their birthdays were even very close to one another in the same month. What I just shared with you might be the reasons that I wanted to love women who had the same problems and fears regarding abandonment, rejection, abuse, anger, and grief as I had. Pilgrim, Tillie and your mother perfectly matched my psychological requirements. I wanted to make both of them well—foolishly hoping that if they were healed, or better adjusted, that they would love me and in turn I would also be better. I might have addressed this before: how could I make others well, when I was not in the best emotional and psychological condition myself?

Darling Pilgrim, I have written about your paternal grandmother's life as it applied to me, because what she was, I was also. We were linked together from my conception to her death. Tragically, circumstances—many out of our control—destroyed our relationship. The two of us were emotionally, physically, psychologically, and spiritually ill throughout much of our time together. We were, however, fortunate in that we both acquired an ability to survive; we could not, however, trust or love very many other people. Yet, darling daughter, your grandmother gave me life, which she could have ended by abortion. Sadly, she gave little more than life, because she had nothing else to give. Nevertheless, Pilgrim, she was an integral part of me, and in an oblique manner, a part of you as well. I hope someday you will better understand her.

I was reluctant to write about Tillie, but you needed to know about her. I hope I have not cause you distress discussing her. If I have, please forgive me.

I love you always.

Dad

THE LIGHT AT THE END OF THE TUNNEL

The decade of the 90s seemed to move with great speed—possibly because I would be retiring from government service fairly soon. The year 1997 was when I would be retiring from the federal government after 23 years of government service. So, in 1995, I was looking forward to retirement, and then on to new experiences, such as teaching, writing, and traveling. It was, however, early in 1995 that, one day, I noticed in my mailbox a letter with no return address, and an unfamiliar California postmark. The card that was in the envelope was handwritten. I knew I had seen the handwriting before. However, I was not certain as to where or when. Anyway, darling daughter, I read the card. It was a rather amorphously written note, in that it appeared to be hastily scrawled with no definitive narrative or message. The card simply said something to the effect that it hoped all was well with me. Pilgrim, what happened to get my attention, was where the signature block would have been, was the initial "W."

At first, Pilgrim, I thought that initial belonged to your mother. But, then I could not believe that Willow would have ever written me. The note illustrated that whoever wrote it was not motivated by compassion, or need to ask for forgiveness, or to initiate reconciliation of sorts. I perceived the reason for the card was to give me a simple heads-up that the person knew where I was, and was able to contact me. I realized that the individual who penned the note went to great length to find where I lived. They, no doubt, knew that I was divorced, so to use the initial "W" was not done in order to prevent a spouse or significant other from knowing about the dynamics of the card. The absence of a return address, and a postmark unlikely to be known by me indicated the author of the card did not want me able to make a response. The letter "W" puzzled me for long time until nine years later, at which time I believe I found the answer.

I would like to have heard from your mother—so I could ask her why she aborted you—and to find out if she was well. After I read and reread the card, I thought that if your mother had written it, she would have been a bit more informative and courteous. I pondered as to whether Willow had written the card, and if so, had there been a reason for her to have done so? I could not perceive your mother being kindly disposed to have written to me. I believed the card to be condescending at best. I did not expect your mother to ever be conciliatory toward me, let alone ask my forgiveness for what she and her parents did to you. Nevertheless, surprises do happen, but I did not anticipate any from Willow. In 2004, the initial "W" would resurface and have significant meaning. Pilgrim, it is time to get back to you.

Pilgrim, forgive me darling, for forgetting to acknowledge that had you been alive, you probably would have made me a grandfather—maybe once or twice over. I would be so happy to be the grandfather of your children. I could not think of a better blessing from the Lord than to have given me grandchildren by you and your spouse. Being older, but maybe no more wiser, I would have hoped that I served as a loving, caring guide for you as you would have been grown up. Your mother and I never were blessed with the opportunity to have seen God's handiwork through you. Therefore, I believe that the Lord granted me the privilege and opportunity of vicariously incorporating you into my psyche and life. As a thirty-some-year-old mother and wife, you, no doubt, would have given your mother and I beautiful grandchildren. What I would have missed, Pilgrim, was the opportunity to have been able to sit across the table from you and talk about anything that came to mind, or walked with you, my son-in-law, grandchildren, and their dog as we enjoyed the environment around us.

Speaking of children, your brother Mark (aka "Markie"), went to the University of Idaho for his undergraduate work in math and business. He then went to the University of Arizona where he received his MA in Economics—and studied with a Nobel Prize winner. After that, he went to the University of Rochester to work on his Ph.D. He now lives and works in Washington, D.C.

I retired from the Department of Army as a senior command historian in 1997, after which time I taught as an adjunct professor on the community college level. I already had been teaching as an adjunct faculty member at one local community college for seven years. I began teaching at the second one beginning in September 1997. Retirement from federal service was what I needed. I had enough of the bureaucracy and politics. Teaching now became a source of satisfaction for me. I was now getting out of the tunnel and into the light. I have enjoyed the stimulation of teaching,

Pilgrim. And I completed my research in 1999 for a book that I eventually began writing in 2000, and which I finished 13 months later in 2001. I got it published in 2003. Years earlier, I had co-authored a book on the Gulf War.

Since retiring from federal service, you and I would have done quite a lot of traveling to places such as Britain, France, Germany, Ireland, Austria, Denmark, and to Hawaii several times. I would have enjoyed sending cards and photos from these places, and showing my friends and loved ones where we had gone on our travels. Pilgrim, in 2004, I began turning my doctoral dissertation into a book. I was working diligently on it when something happened.

In early January 2004, I suddenly found myself thinking about your mother. I had no idea what might have precipitated my brooding about her. I attempted not to think of Willow by keeping extremely busy. However, the more I strove to not think of your mother, the more it seemed she was on my mind. One evening, Pilgrim, I found myself getting on the computer, going to a search engine, typing in Willow's maiden name, and waiting for something to happen. It was but a very short time that suddenly a plethora of information surfaced. Pilgrim, I can remember that I had hoped I would find nothing about Willow on the Internet, and by doing so, I would be obligated to put her out of my mind—and get on with my life.

However, what happened, darling Pilgrim, was that I uncovered a goodly amount about Willow's life—including a copy of a hand-written letter that Willow had written to someone. As I remember, I gave the letter a cursory read, then continued looking at the information that was unfolding in front of my eyes on the computer screen. I examined the data that transpired as I read the relative material. Your mother had married well; had taught for a number of years at a local college; was a community leader; had very attractive children, including a married daughter, who was the image of Willow, and Willow, herself was a handsome woman. I also found out that Willow's father had died near the end of 1994. Pilgrim, I refer to the above information, because later in the narrative, it will play an important role in some other revelations.

As might be expected, what I saw about Willow and her life, served as an oblique reminder of an earlier time with Willow, and memories that were not at all pleasant. I was a bit agitated, because I believed I had become compulsive, and if that was that the case, it bothered me. However,

Pilgrim, I began to get the distinct feeling that the Lord had His hand in what I was going through.

I kept asking aloud, "Why Lord, why now after all these years?"

Pilgrim, I was asking to be lifted from dealing with Willow. However, our Heavenly Father impressed upon me that I would eventually have to put closure on her—but not before I had to do certain things. One of which was to formally acknowledge your name—which I did in 2004.

I can still remember trying to understand why you had to be formally named, and was Pilgrim the name I should give you. The Lord did not take long to respond to my query. He impressed upon me that you should be named as a means to honor His glory, and to remind your mother and me that you were our child—and always will be. The name, "Pilgrim" was one I really believed was endowed by our Heavenly Father. As I had mentioned at the beginning of the book, *Pilgrim* denoted a holy voyage or trip taken for some spiritual purpose. As alluded to earlier in the missive, Pilgrim, you were initially taken to Heaven after your heinous death by two powerful angels. These angels then brought you into God's bosom—where he comforted you. However, as I mentioned before, our Heavenly Father granted me the gift of your spirit to accompany me throughout life for a period of years. I will refer again to these two angels and two other angels near the end of the book.

Another thing I had to do was to examine whether or not I was ready to actually forgive Willow and her family for what happened to you. Nevertheless, over the years, I had processed much of what I had to deal with concerning your mother, and her abortion of you. But, I remembered one scenario that was important to me: that scenario being that I could not condone what your mother and her family did regarding your death. To do so would have been a betrayal of you.

Indeed, had I forced Willow, physically or otherwise to have aborted you, if she wanted to have kept you, I hardly believe she would have been in any hurry to be compliant and forgiving of me—if ever. Pilgrim, I stand on my right to look at every aspect of your death before I forgive Willow. People have no right telling me when I should forgive the individuals responsible for killing you. After all, three adults spent little time weighing the severity or ethics of their decision to abort you, Pilgrim. As far as I am concerned, forgiveness still means accountability of consequences for the act of murder. However, I would eventually forgive Willow and her parents for your death, and, in turn, would ask their forgiveness of me. I will not, however, forget what happened to you, Pilgrim. May I repeat the comment I made earlier in one of the letters when I said, "Forgive everything, forget nothing." That axiom is still applicable.

I still loved Willow, but simultaneously, I did not like or respect her for what she and her parents did regarding your horrible death. I was trying not to condemn her or her family; however, as I said earlier, I could and would not condone what they did. In turn, I would expect no less from them. I would forgive when it was time to, not when people, many of whom had never dealt with the loss of a daughter by abortion, thought that I should. The time would come when I was ready to make such a decision.

Pilgrim, I was sitting in the Presbyterian Church to which I belonged a few Sundays after having read the Internet material about Willow. I was actually listening to the pastor giving his sermon. Suddenly, the letter "W" appeared on my mind. Remember, nine years earlier, Pilgrim, when Willow had likely written to me. I continued envisioning the letter "W". However, nothing seemed to tweak my psyche until as I was driving home, when something told me to look again on the computer at the letter that Willow had written to someone in 2003. I got on the computer, and went down to the signature block; suddenly I was having an epiphany of sorts. The first letter of Willow's name was written the identical way the initial "W" had been written on the card that I had received nine years before!

I could never have forgotten that initial "W." I believed Willow wrote that card to me after her father had died—but for what reason, I am not certain. I remember thinking that Sunday, that possibly Willow had confronted her father before he died, and either he asked Willow for forgiveness for what happened to you and her, or Willow decided that after his death, it was "safe" to write me. She, no doubt, thought I would not ever come across any significant information about her. However, I believe that nine years later (2004), the Lord granted me the information necessary to bring closure to Willow and her family. The above being said, until Willow and I forgive one another, and asked each other for forgiveness, we will be victimized by our pride, that in itself is a sin. But Pilgrim, I would hazard a guess that your mother is less likely to be in a hurry to forgive me. However, that will be her issue, not mine.

Darling Pilgrim, I earlier alluded to the fact your mother and I professed being Christians. If that was truly the case, why have we not been compassionate and loving enough to forgive and ask for forgiveness? Willow and I must do the above if we are to honor your memory, spirit, and unconditional love for us. There is a saying, "Pride belongs to the Devil." Neither your mother nor I can hide behind our palliatives, such as titles, degrees, reputations, community status, materialism, publications, or professional and personal accomplishments—when it comes time to dealing with the need for the two of us to forgive one another.

Darling daughter, I am being blunt regarding your mother's and my requirements of forgiveness. We both have to forgive one another and ask for forgiveness from the other. Up until now, I conveniently equivocated regarding forgiveness. I made forgiveness a touchy subject, when, in actuality, it should be the objective of my healing process.

No matter what Willow does or does not do, the first thing the Lord expects me to do is to forgive her and ask her to forgive me. This was a dilemma until the last weekend in April 2004, when I went to the healing retreat that I described at the beginning of this series of letters. The wonderful thing about the retreat, Pilgrim, was acknowledging you in a religious setting, giving you your birth name, having a public record made of it, and forgiving your mother. Having done that, I still had some individual things to do. One includes writing the following letter to your mother. Yet, until I read I Corinthians: 13, which admonished all of us to love, I was unable to write to Willow. Finally, after reading the above, I have written a letter to Willow.

I love you so much,
Dad

A LETTER TO WILLOW

Dear Willow,

Writing this letter to you was not an easy endeavor for many reasons. It was not until 2004 that I was actually able to forgive you. As opposed to just writing a simplistic comment of, "I forgive you," it is imperative that I let you know why I have forgiven you. You have that right to know. As I said earlier in the manuscript, forgiveness has to be nurtured, watered with the tears, anger, denial, pain and grief associated with it, reflected upon as well, and implemented when to do so is right. Because of the above emotions associated with what happened to Pilgrim, forgiveness of you was slow in coming, however:

1. I forgive you Willow because our Heavenly Father wants me to, and because I know, it is the right thing to do. I also forgive you, because to do so, gives me the right to relinquish my pain, grief, anger, denial, and any other negative emotions.
2. I forgive you Willow, because to do so grants me peace, self re spect and healing—and hopefully you as well.
3. I forgive you because not to do so after all this time makes no sense, and because we are too old to not reach out to one another in reconciliation and Agape love.
4. I forgive you because if I am the Christian I claim to be Willow, I must truly forgive you—no matter your role in the aborting of Pilgrim—and whether or not you will tell me honestly why you aborted Pilgrim.
5. I forgive your parents Willow, though it is not easy to do so, but if I am to forgive you, I must forgive them as well.
6. I forgive you because I believe we have both suffered inextricably for the unwarranted death of our precious baby—Pilgrim.
7. I forgive you because I still love you—because you are the mother of our child.
8. I forgive you because Pilgrim wants me to forgive you.
9. I finally forgive you Willow, because once you were the brightest star in my universe, and I will never forget that.

Willow, in turn, I ask your forgiveness for the following reasons:

1. Please forgive me for the pain that I caused you.
2. Please forgive me for not being the individual you wanted me to be.
3. I ask your forgiveness, Willow, for my lack of courage to do what was right for the two of us.
4. Please forgive me for not being enough of a positive reason for you to have wanted to bring Pilgrim to term.
5. Please forgive me, Willow, for being a confused, indecisive individual when confronted with your pregnancy.
6. I ask your forgiveness for not putting definitive and healthy boundaries on our relationship—by not doing so, I failed the both of us.
7. I ask that you forgive me for not ever really knowing you.
8. Please forgive me, Willow, for not validating your worth.
9. Finally, please forgive me for having gotten you pregnant.

God Bless you and Goodbye Willow,

Herb

GOING HOME

Well, darling Pilgrim, I am glad the above is over. It was difficult putting the reasons down as to why I should forgive you mother. I became emotional as I both forgave Willow and then asked her forgiveness. However, I now feel the "peace that passes understanding." I am now able to forgive Willow and her parents for their part in your death. I also rid myself of the mantle of pride and anger that influenced my asking your mother for forgiveness. Willow and I had both sinned, and as the result of our sin, you, our unborn baby died. So, why should I not forgive her? Willow and I were, and still are, your parents. Maybe by forgiving one another, your mother and I can be a source of comfort, understanding, and compassion to each other. Darling Pilgrim, I know this is what you would want for your mother and me. I see that you are getting a bit teary-eyed, but you are smiling. Thanks for the hug. I love you too.

Darling one, you and I have been through so much since we began our pilgrimage home forty years ago. Pilgrim, you reached for me shortly after you died, when I was heart-broken, angry, and confused. You took my hand when I was not worthy of anyone taking my hand. Our Heavenly Father wanted you to be my guide. Together, you and I have traveled the length and width of our country and to other parts of the world. We have been blessed with wonderful people in our lives who we will never forget, such as the children that I taught both at the country school in Northern Kansas, and the adolescent boys and girls at the state hospital in Topeka. These young people showed me the beauty of compassion , the love of teaching, and the joy of service to others. You were the spirit that comforted me when I failed at marriage; you wiped my tears when loved ones—including dear friends—died. Pilgrim, you knew Carol's and my joy when Mark was born. You had a brother, and we had a son.

Thank you for being patient with me when I was dealing with my lengthy confusion and distress regarding your mother. You loved us both, and, no doubt, cried because Willow and I were so irresponsible and full of anger and pride that you brutally died. Yet, you have unconditionally forgiven us. Darling daughter, you and I traveled the road of life—that was sometimes bumpy, and "less traveled." However, you were always there to encourage me, take my hand, and to reassure me of your love. An example of that love was the fact you suffered with me when I had address the anguish and pain of separation from Mark, after his mother and I divorced.

You remembered very well that same anguish and pain of separation after you left your mother's womb—yet you still loved your two parents—and continue to do so. Darling Pilgrim, you have made me realize that death is a transfiguration into eternal life, and into a far better place than we can imagine. Your tragic death was a reassuring epiphany of sorts. However, our odyssey together also has reassured me there is a Heaven.

When you were aborted, our Heavenly Father had his angels quickly bring you home to Heaven. It was during the years following your death that I realized how much the Lord grieves when we take the lives of innocent beings. He weeps because abortion is inimical to His plan of life for each of us. Yet, our Father in Heaven continues to love us who transgress from His laws regarding life. Through your death, I was able to comprehend the fragility of life, and the importance of living one day at a time. Our Lord was with me when I was lost and disconsolate after you died. However, the following took place on September 13, 1963.

When you, in spirit, boarded the plane, with me, on September 13, 1963, which took us away from Los Angeles to New York, little did I know it would be the beginning of a wonderful life together. There would be significant gifts from God, such as amazing experiences, fantastic people, including dear friends and loved ones, particularly, Mark and you. Pilgrim darling, I certainly was not worthy of the blessings bestowed upon me. Nevertheless, I thank the Lord that he let you accompany me through the valleys and mountains of life. Together, darling daughter, you and I—hand-in-hand—have seen the Lord's array of beauty and joy. Pilgrim, we began this odyssey when I was a young man and you were a new spirit. Now, as I am getting near the end of my life—though not just yet—I reflect on the greatness of life. Though there has been heartache, sadness, and the loss of beloved friends and family members, the Lord has been so generous with his gifts of love, joy, and allowing me the privilege of knowing and serving others. Pilgrim, I realize with so much clarity that the accomplishments that I had and presently have do not belong to me. They belong to others and our Heavenly Father. I left California in 1963, devoid of spirit and full of sorrow. Forty-some years later, I realized I learned a great deal from the tragedy of the summer of 1963. I learned how to love, share, be vulnerable, grieve, serve, be angry, yet eventually forgive.

Pilgrim, you were also with me when Carol and I found out that we were going to be parents. The Lord gave us the best gift possible—that being Mark. My love for Mark knows no boundaries because his birth, as yours, would have done—made me a more loving, fallible, and sensitive person.

Darling daughter, you and I have gotten to know one another so very well. You have been willing to share the odyssey with me the last forty years. What have the two of us not seen or done since we have been to-gether? We have done it all it—thanks to our Heavenly Father. I said ear-lier that I was not afraid of death. It is because I know that love transcends death. When the Lord asked you if you would be willing to travel through-out four decades with me; the fact you answered "yes" gave me great joy. I knew then that you loved me—though I was not worthy of it.

I alone could not have been as blessed as I have been without knowing that you were with me. When you died, forty-two years ago, I knew the angels took you to be in the arms of Jesus, but at the same time, I did not want to relinquish you—after all, I never saw you, held you in my arms, and never had a chance to love you as an earthly father would. The Lord knew of my pain, grief, and confusion. He made up His mind to do some-thing about it.

He decided that you should take a sabbatical of sorts from Heaven to help me travel whatever roads I was to take. I was initially embarrassed for you to see how weak of a person I was; yet, from the onset, you loved me and accepted me as I was. You also knew that I never wanted you to have been aborted. As unattractive as I seemed to your mother and her parents, I still had hoped and prayed they would have gone ahead and allowed you to be born. My shortcomings should have never factored into any deci-sion regarding you being born or not. That being said, I was privy to your death. Sitting on the beach that day in the summer of 1963, having been emotionally impaled by the dark arrow of abortion—I really felt that I had very little reason to live—so I believed. But, our Heavenly Father decided to take matters into His own hands and get me back on my feet—no mat-ter how wobbly I was.

My darling daughter, at times, I ostensibly took it for granted that you would always be with me here on earth. I possibly had fallen prey to becoming selfish, and not realizing that the Lord also wanted you to be back in His arms. I did not want to face that reality. However, I believe the Lord understands why I felt the way I did. Pilgrim, I could spend an entire lifetime thanking you and telling you how much I love you, and still, it would not be enough time. Of course, I feel the same way about Mark. And I as well could have spent an entire lifetime asking those I hurt in any way to forgive me—and, yet, that too might not be enough time. However, I have learned to make amends and ask forgiveness. The forty years since we have been together, I have learned so much about life, people, and even how often I have fallen short of God's glory. I have realized that I often sin, and have to get back up on my feet, and ask Jesus to forgive me, and hope I do better. Pilgrim, the frailties of being a human being are always apparent.

My darling little one, I have noticed you gazing intermittently and somewhat expectantly toward Heaven. I know that you did not have the opportunity to get to know many other unborn babies in Heaven because of being with me. I feel a bit guilty about keeping you with me as long as I have. I think you understand though. But because of *Roe v. Wade*, there are at least close to fifty million more aborted American babies with the Lord. Pilgrim, our Heavenly Father has many aborted children to grieve over. Will people ever learn not to be selfish with lives of innocent unborn babies? I wonder.

I cannot tell you enough how much I love you,
Dad

GOODBYE MY DARLING PILGRIM

Pilgrim, look, do you see what I see? There are two angels hovering over you. I believe we both know why they are here. They are here to escort you home to Heaven! I believe these angels have just arrived. Though their wings are large, I can barely hear them whirring. I believe these angels are different than the ones who took you to Heaven in 1963. These two angels look very young. Both are truly beautiful with gorgeous wings and have a heavenly countenance. Gosh, I can barely see them, because of the bright light encompassing them. They are smiling, and their smiles are beautiful and full of love! And they both of them are gently motioning for you to take their hands! You look so happy. Do you know what all this means? Darling daughter, it signifies that as your name, "Pilgrim" denotes, you are going home to that "better place" that you previously looked for and found—that being Heaven! The Lord chose that name for you. He also decided that it is time for you to fly back to His arms. I am so happy for you, little one. But, I cannot begin to tell you how much I will miss you. For these forty-plus years, you were my "alter ego" and my best friend. I did not get to see you go to Heaven that tragic day in the summer of 1963; for one thing, there were too many tears in my eyes; but I know now that I will have the opportunity to see you go back "Home."

Before, you go, I want to tell you again, my darling daughter, how much I love you. It is an infinite love, as it is for Mark. There is no greater love than between a parent and his children. The two of you have blessed me so much. Speaking of blessings, I know that I must have said this a dozen times: "The Lord has greatly blessed me." And He certainly did when it came time to you, darling daughter. Gosh, for four decades, you and I made a wonderful pair going down life's road. I will never forget our odyssey. Thank you so much for being with me, and for being my precious daughter and companion. Please, do not get upset if I, an old man, weep as you go home to the Lord. I will miss you so much. I see the angels are slowly getting ready to take you to Heaven. Please give my love to Tillie, Anita, Gail, Dora, Joseph, and a new unborn spirit named Logan—whose mother is a dear friend. I am certain you will like him. Please also give my love to departed friends and family. Darling, thanks for giving me a hug and a kiss. I love you forever little Pilgrim, and I look forward to seeing you again, and being with you someday. Thank you wonderful angels for coming to take my beautiful daughter home to Heaven. Goodbye my darling Pilgrim.

Go with God.

Dad

CONCLUSION

I just said goodbye to Pilgrim. It was so very difficult to do. My heart breaks thinking of her and the beautiful angels who took her home. Yet, I know my darling daughter is back in Heaven making many new friends, and renewing old friendships, such as with Jesus. I am certain they will all have a great deal to talk about; I miss her so much. Yet, to reminisce, back in 1963, when Pilgrim was cruelly and traumatically aborted on a hospital gurney either in Southern California or in Mexico, our Heavenly Father tearfully sent two of His fastest and most powerful angels to quickly bring her home to Heaven. He wiped her tears away, cradled her in His bosom, as she cried, while comforting her with His own tears. The Lord must have spent a great deal of His time during the four decades since Pilgrim's death comforting millions—or maybe billions—of other aborted babies.

I had a wonderful time taking Pilgrim with me through forty-plus years of living. As I mentioned earlier, the Lord decided to put Pilgrim's spirit back on earth to take an odyssey with me through life. I did not enjoy having to relate to my daughter the dynamics of her conception and eventual abortion. It, however, was essential that I shared with her the thoughtless behavior, irrational attitudes and lifestyles of her two biological parents, and how their tragic behavior factored in to her death. Yet, in turn, Pilgrim was able to love us and forgive us.

Otherwise, to not reveal the symbiotic behavior of two selfish, immature young adults would have been an emotional, and spiritual injustice. Painful as it was, it had to be done if the evil of the abortion was ever to be excised.

I wrote these letters to Pilgrim to acknowledge, humanize, and memorialize her. No one else gave credence to her. She deserved life; instead, she was brutally killed. As I said in an earlier letter, I was her only advocate. Tragically, the advocacy was unsuccessful, and Pilgrim died. I also wrote this missive to bring to the attention of the reader how the abortion of my child affected me—her father. Fathers of aborted babies have been looked upon as being insignificant, and thus, not worthy of any consideration as a person or as one of the parents of an aborted baby. That assessment is so very inaccurate. We fathers are worthy of fatherhood, and all the emotions that go with it. We warrant being loved no less than our aborted infants, or the mothers who aborted our children. The manuscript also examined my pain as Pilgrim's father, and my efforts to transcend the horror associated with the loss of my daughter, and the ever-present terror that something tragic could have happened to Willow during the abortion.

The text united Pilgrim and I as we spent forty years sharing life with one another. I gave Pilgrim a hypothetical, but realistic, chronological life—because I believed she deserved one. Subsequently, she and I became as comfortable with one another as a pair of old shoes. I had fun throwing in bits of history that Pilgrim might very well have witnessed had she lived, and I personalized our odyssey by taking her with me all over the country, where we both met wonderful people, shared unique experiences, had blessed opportunities to get a wonderful and enriching education, and fantastic career moves.

The greatest event enjoyed by Pilgrim and I was the birth of her brother Mark—who she adored. Pilgrim also lovingly comforted me when dear friends and loved ones died, and when I failed at relationships—particularly marriages.

Pilgrim and I had to deal with the saga of Tillie, my beautiful, but troubled mother, who as a very young woman was beaten and sexually assaulted, and from this rape, I was born. I shared with Pilgrim the extended tragic circumstances of Tillie's and my life. Pilgrim also became privy to my reliance on the Lord. It was during the time that I spent with Pilgrim and Mark that I realized how important children are. Yet, as Pilgrim and I moved through the four decades that we were together, I noticed that she spent more time looking toward Heaven. I knew Pilgrim wanted to go home, and that it would not be very long until the Lord summoned her home. I tried not to be selfish with the gift that our Heavenly Father had given me. Every so often, I kept thinking that perhaps the Lord would give her an extension here on earth. I knew, however, that my wishes could not, and should not, counter the Lord's will. I finally resigned myself to the fact that someday Pilgrim would be going home.

Remember, as I described the two beautiful young angels who came to take my lovely daughter home? To see these heavenly beings was enthralling. It was the most touching moment that one could have imagined. Pilgrim looked lovingly at me, and mouthed, "I love you, Dad" and blew me a kiss, as she slipped her hands into those of the two angels, smiled once more at me, and then in a flash was gone. What a wonderful experience to watch Pilgrim fly home.

Pilgrim's return to Heaven indicated how much I had come to rely on her as part of my life. I am now able to reflect on the love of our Father in Heaven who though seeing an innocent baby girl aborted many years ago, lovingly gave her grieving human father his baby daughter's spirit as his companion and guide through life. Pilgrim and Mark were two of the most significant examples of the Lord's endless and unconditional love.

I wrote this book as a tribute to Pilgrim; therefore, I have chosen to end the final two paragraphs of this book by paying tribute to my daughter. I do it by remembering the beauty of her spirit as she gloriously overcame the horror of abortion four decades ago, and was triumphantly taken to Heaven by powerful, yet gentle angels. I also recall our love for one another as father and daughter. Pilgrim—her birth name—will be forever enshrined in the Halls of Heaven, and in the Book of Life, and within my heart and soul as well. As of the summer of 2005, Pilgrim will also have her name put on a plaque at the National Memorial for the Unborn in Chattanooga, Tennessee, which can be visited by those parents honoring the memories of their unborn babies. I plan to visit Pilgrim at the memorial. I hope other post-abortive parents will visit their children who are there also.

I also honor Pilgrim by thanking our Heavenly Father for granting me the privilege of being her father. Lord, Your love for Pilgrim showed me that eternal love triumphs over death; good transcends evil; and forgiveness overcomes measured hatred. Those who have abortions kill only the baby's body. They cannot kill its spirit. Therefore, Willow's and my daughter will always live—with our Lord in Heaven—and for that I am so thankful. She will always live with me as well. Dearest Father in Heaven I thank you for allowing me to share my story.